BAGPIPE BROTHERS

KERRY SHERIDAN

BAGPIPE BROTHERS

THE FDNY BAND'S

TRUE STORY

OF TRAGEDY, MOURNING,

AND RECOVERY

Rutgers University Press
New Brunswick, New Jersey, and London

Library of Congress Cataloging-in-Publication Data

Sheridan, Kerry, 1973–
Bagpipe brothers : the FDNY Band's true story of tragedy, mourning, and recovery / Kerry Sheridan.
p. cm.
Includes bibliographical references
ISBN 0–8135–3396–1 (hardcover : alk. paper)
1. FDNY Pipes & Drums. 2. Fire Fighters—New York (State)—New York. 3. Bagpipers—New York (State)—New York. 4. September 11 Terrorist Attacks, 2001. I. Title.
ML421.F39S54 2004
788.4'9'0607471—dc21
2003014220

British Cataloging-in-Publication information for this book is available from the British Library.

Manufactured in the United States of America

For my brother

CONTENTS

Acknowledgments

In the early days after September 11, what fascinated me most about the Fire Department bagpipers and drummers was their ability to stand tall and march on, despite such unfathomable repetition. I watched them do it again and again, too many times to count. At those terrible moments, when another family came to despair the loss of yet another son, the band moved through the crowd and, in the subtlety of symbol, showed the families they could do it, too. I am deeply grateful to the firefighters who shared their lives with me during the dark period after September 11, so that others could know, and so that others would not forget, this chapter of our nation's history.

Endlessly modest and faithful to the group ethic, no firefighter in the band wanted to be singled out for this book, reluctant to make it appear that one man's story was more important or significant than another's. Many, many New York City firefighters worked daily at the World Trade Center site, and many band members experienced similar emotions during the span of funerals. I chose to tell the story of many through the lens of a few. But it is important to remember that this was an ordeal they all went through together, and though many men are not named in this book, all of their experiences invaluably contributed to the narrative.

This project began as a day story that I reported while at the Columbia University Graduate School of Journalism. I owe an immense debt of gratitude to professor and author Samuel G. Freedman, who encouraged me to keep following the story in its early stages, who nurtured the idea from its inception through to the book, and who continues to be an unparalleled mentor, editor, supporter, and teacher. Special thanks to my editor, Marlie Wasserman, and equally to my agent, Heather Schroder, both of whom believed in this story when it seemed no one else in the publishing world did. This book would not be what it is without the careful dedication of my wonderful copy editor, India Cooper.

Thanks to my parents, Chuck and Cheri, my brother, Matt, Alan and the many friends who listened to me tell stories of men they didn't know for months on end. Much to my relief, they continue to be my friends and supporters.

Authors Anne Nelson and Dennis Smith, who have both written in depth about the Fire Department, provided sagacity and insight on the subject matter. I am also grateful for the support and encouragement of Elizabeth L. Dribben and John Dinges.

Spiritually, the Rev. Everett Wabst provided more sustenance than can ever be measured during the months after September 11, not only to hundreds of those in the Fire Department family but also to me. Father Brian Jordan, Father John Delendick, and Father Christopher Keenan also brought light and understanding to many people, both before and after September 11.

I thank all the brave men at Rescue 4, especially Liam Flaherty, Billy Murphy, Eddie Zeilman, Richie Schmidt, Jim Schumeyer, Lt. Tim Kelly, and Capt. Paul Heglund, who opened their lives and journal to me, allowed me to sit at their kitchen table and fed me on many a night, let me ride with them in the firetruck, and took me to what turned out to be my first fire. I also thank Lt. John Atwell and the men at Engine 219 and Ladder 105, who also welcomed me in their kitchen and shared their stories of Vinny Brunton.

I am immensely grateful to all the band members. They have endeared themselves to me forever. All their names are too numerous to include here, but I do want to mention Mike Brunton, Tommy Brunton, Teddy Carstensen, Jack Clarke, Gerard Coughlin, Billy Crowley, Tom Dooley, Bill Duffy Sr., Joe Duggan, Kevin Fahey, Charlie Fitzpatrick, Tom Fitzpatrick, Tom Foy, Ed Geraghty, Tom Gerondel, Jimmy Ginty, Kevin Grace, Tim Grant, Tommy Killian, Bobby King, John McCarthy, Frank McCutchen, Jim McEnaney, Danny McEnroe, Tom McEnroe Sr., Tom McEnroe Jr., Jimmy McHugh, Ed McLoughlin, Joe Murphy, John O'Hagan, Kevin O'Hagan, Jimmy O'Neill, Frank O'Rourke, Larry Reilly, Jim Schumeyer, Pete Sheridan, Kenny Sullivan, Mike Tully, Chris "Kippy" Walsh, and Bob Wright for their contributions to this book. Also, thanks to John Daly and Pete Hedderman from the Dublin Fire Brigade, Jimmy Miller, John Welch the Cork fireman, "Belfast Joe" Connolly, and the musicians in carpenters' Local 608.

The women who shared their experiences for this book brought a great richness to the story that could not have been achieved without them. Thanks to Kathy Brunton, Maryann DeLuise, Karen Jelinek, Maureen Flaherty, Denise Fowler, Jeannie Moore, and Mary Walsh.

Others in the Fire Department who helped with this book include

Gerry O'Donnell, Ron Spadafora, Jack Corcoran, Steve Rasweiler, Jerry Silcox, Michael Loughran, Billy Burke, John Leimeister, and Bill Waring; from the Fire Department Mand Library, Jack Lerch, Dan May, and Fred Melahn Jr.; and from the ceremonial unit, John Burns, Walter Dreyer, and Jimmy Sorokac. Special thanks to Gearóid O hAllmhuráin, Terry Moylan, Pat O'Gorman, Andrew Lenz, and Joe Brady Jr., who helped in consultation on Irish music and bagpiping.

BAGPIPE BROTHERS

PROLOGUE

TOMMY turned his back on the devastation and walked away. After what he'd seen that day, he was done. No more digging, no more stooping to collect pieces of torn flesh and bone, no more tucking away the bits of gore into flimsy plastic bags. His boots crunched over the unstable shards of steel and rubble, which jabbed back at his soles. The words his friend had spoken to him made this walk possible. After this, he'd never go back.

Standing near the trunk of his car, he elbowed out of his dusty bunker jacket and peeled off his thick pants. The dark, unwieldy material reeked of mildew and rot, the sharp smells of death and fire and chemicals. He pushed the gear into the open trunk and shut the door.

The next morning, or maybe it was the morning after that, Tommy rose with the sun. Hours blended across barriers of day and night, making some recollections, some days, fuzzier than others. He reached into his closet and pulled out his white short-sleeved dress shirt—a pale blue square patch on one arm, anchored by a Maltese cross and shamrock, and a Fire Department shield on the other. His kilt, in green, indigo, and black tartan. A two-foot-long swatch of horsehair and a belt. His green socks, spats, and black shoes. A beret.

One of his friends had been found: a fellow Fire Department lieutenant named Timmy Stackpole. He'd lived in the same neighborhood, so close that Tommy could look out his kitchen window and see Timmy's backyard. Today, they would bury Timmy's remains.

He drove to church, twelve blocks away, and found a parking space. He pulled his case from his car, opened it, and looked down at the instrument inside. Three dark wood pipes lay folded over a green corduroy bag. A braided kelly green rope linked the pipes together. On one hung an American flag.

Tommy picked up the lifeless bag, reinforced on its interior by several bonelike columns leading to a thin box at the back. He pushed the tubular chanter into a stock at the bottom of the pipe bag, then twisted the six-inch-long bass drone onto the top.

He wrapped his left hand around the front curve of the bag, tucked his elbow around the outside of the fabric, and held the lower edge of the blowpipe for stability. Reaching his arm out slightly, he positioned the instrument to his front, a couple of inches away from his stomach.

His eyelids dropped, and he focused on a point unseen. He filled his chest with air and blew into the mouthpiece, one, two, three times, until the bag puffed like an oblong balloon. With his right palm, he struck the inner side of the bag and pushed it backward, under his elbow and against his ribs. In response to the punch, the pipes cried out: a short wail, then a dismaying sustained moan. His weathered fingers dropped to the chanter. And he began to play.

INTRODUCTION

A Brief History of Bagpiping and the Irish Traditions of the New York City Fire Department

IN the winter of 1962, a group of Irish-American firefighters traded their Monday nights in the tavern for weekly practice sessions in the basement of a South Bronx church, and soon an age-old tradition of bagpiping was reborn in New York City.

The seventeen firefighters who formed the original band were young men, mostly in their late twenties and early thirties. The majority of them worked in the South Bronx, at the busiest firehouses in New York City. All had parents or grandparents who had been born in Ireland, so learning how to play Irish music carried a tangible appeal for them. And they were all members of the Fire Department Emerald Society, essentially a goodwill group of Irish-American men, created in 1956 in the name of upstanding citizenship and knowledge of Irish culture. An Emerald Society branch in the New York City Police Department had begun three years earlier, and it wasn't long before there were Emerald Societies in many civil service units, including the Board of Education, the Transit Authority, and the sanitation and correction departments.

The Emerald Society of the New York City Police Department established its own bagpipe band in 1960. The NYPD band even marched in the New York City St. Patrick's Day parade in 1961. Still, it wasn't until the following autumn that the then secretary and treasurer of the FDNY Emerald Society sent out a meeting notice that read in part, "Why haven't the Fire Emeralds started their own bagpipe band?" Professional envy began to seep through the ranks. The policemen had beaten the firemen to a great concept. And after all, who was more Irish? The firemen or the policemen? The firemen were sure they were, so at the next meeting of the Emerald Society Jimmy Ginty stood up and made a motion to start the band, which was promptly seconded by Pete Sheridan.

After seeing the notice, about fifty-five firefighters showed interest. Besides the more temporal desire to show up the cops, each man who joined in the beginning had his own reasons. Although the American-born firefighters considered themselves U.S. citizens first and Irish second, they were stubborn in their commitment to be distinct and, as a group, distinctive. To have a group identity in which they all shared a skill and could perform served to solidify their bond as Irish-Americans and elevate them as people who studied, appreciated, and preserved their heritage. Now, these American-born Irish would be playing tunes they'd heard their parents sing. Forming the band was an act of patriotism as Americans of Irish descent. Many of the men also had military backgrounds. Some had seen the bagpipers in the Cary Grant film *Gunga Din,* marching the British troops into battle in India. There was a glamour associated with the instrument, and a connotation of war and honor that went with it. The thickness of the instruments' wail lent an aura of importance to ceremony that words could not convey. There was one problem, though. No one in the Emerald Society knew how to play the bagpipes.

Bagpipes are reed instruments, much like an oboe or a clarinet, in which air pressure pushes through the reed to produce sound. But instead of a single outlet like a horn, bagpipes utilize four holes to provide the venues for sound to emerge—the high-pitched chanter, one bass drone, and two tenor drones. The piper puffs into a blowpipe to fill the bag and then squeezes the bag under one arm to produce constant air pressure through the chanter and drones. By alternating between the "blow" into the blowpipe and the "push" of the elbow against the bag, the piper can take breaths without the music doing the same. Using fingers to cover the selected holes on the chanter, the bagpiper produces the melody. The bagpipe scale has only nine notes, from A to A with an extra G below the octave, and unlike on a piano, the intervals are not evenly spaced. The sound of notes that are slightly off what our ears perceive as the regular scale accounts for the unnerving aspect of listening to the bagpipes; they give the ear a sense that something is not quite right, yet produce enchanting layers of music at the same time. On its own, the chanter can sound piercing, like a squawking bird, but with the hum of the drones behind it, the music becomes complex and textured.

The firefighters found a few musicians who volunteered to teach them to play; one was from the NYPD band, and two were from Northern Ireland–based pipe bands.[1] The men had to first learn how to blow and finger the notes on a practice chanter, with no bag attached, which when played, sounds akin to a kazoo.

The first three tunes they learned were "Minstrel Boy," "Let Erin Remember," and "The 100 Pipers." Thomas Moore wrote "Minstrel Boy" in 1808; a basic 4/4 march, it has a rolling melody and a patriotic Irish theme. The lyrics tell of a musician-soldier who goes to war to avenge his father's death, carrying his father's sword and a "wild harp." Alone, he fights for freedom in a world that had betrayed him and his cause. When he is captured, he rips his harp strings so that his music would not be soiled by slavery. He dies, but the music lives on as a beacon of freedom for those who fight in his name.

No pipers ever use sheet music when performing. They must memorize every tune. Not all the firefighters knew the words to the tunes, but for the ones who did, the verbal familiarity proved some help in memorizing the fingering. Their instructors emphasized precision and discipline, especially in the grace notes, which are embellishments included to vary and add artfulness to the music. Only a uniform sound from each bagpiper could produce the buzzing, powerful effect of a solid outfit.

Once they were able to commit about ten tunes to memory on the chanter, they added the bagpipes. The instruments arrived from Scotland in July. Beads of sweat bulged from foreheads as the men puffed to fill the airbag, then brows would furrow in concentration as they tried to establish a rhythm of blowing into the pipes and pressing on the bag from the elbow to the armpit when they needed to inhale. Blow, push, blow, push. Finally, the pipers were ready to start learning to march. But walking and piping at the same time was harder than it looked. The first few times, they knocked into each other, bumped elbows, stepped off on the right instead of the left, and forgot the notes. So they'd start again. The instructor would call, "Minstrel Boy!

By the center! Quick! March!" The drummers would stand at the back and deliver two steady drum rolls. The pipers would blow furiously into the pipes and raise the bag in front, then each would strike up the pipes by punching his bag and tucking it under one arm. The low hum of the drones would begin, and with the first note on the pipes, they'd step off on the left foot. A couple of steps and they'd stumble over each other again. The art of marching in a solid formation would take some time to perfect.

The firefighters practiced in their spare time, which was rare. Sometimes they'd seek out an empty nook in the firehouse, or sit in the basement and work on the tunes, trying not to squeak or mess up halfway through by hitting the wrong notes. Other guys in the firehouse covered their ears and moaned. The pipes, played by an amateur, could sound like a gang of sick cats. The firefighters threw firecrackers and trash barrels at the novices to try to get them to stop. But for Jimmy Ginty and the sixteen others who eventually made it through the training to become the original members of the band, the idea meant too much for them to give up.[2]

Contrary to the widely held notion that bagpiping originated in Ireland or Scotland, the instrument's history is not so recently traced. According to some experts, trying to identify the exact origin of the bagpipes is like trying to determine where and how the concept of drumming began. Various sorts of hornpipes likely existed long before humans ever left behind a written history. Relics of shawms and hornpipes have been discovered in Egyptian tombs, and there is mention of an emperor playing the bagpipes in ancient Rome.[3] Most historians on the subject acknowledge that no nationality can claim initial ownership of the pipes. Anywhere that animals like goats, deer, cattle, or sheep roamed, where their skins could be used as a bag and their bones and horns carved into pipes on which to blow, people could have been, and probably were, playing some form of the bagpipes.

A violent intersection between Christian and Muslim history resulted in the bagpipes' arrival in Ireland, Scotland, and England nearly a thousand years ago, during the Christian Crusades. The Crusades began, at least symbolically, in the name of justice for the Holy Sepulcher, the sacred burial site of Jesus Christ, which was attacked by a Muslim conqueror in 1010. Christians from across Europe answered the call to war, to reclaim the territory of the Holy Land and rebuild the church that had been destroyed.

The Christian Crusaders grouped all enemy Arabs and Muslims under one term, Saracens, which included any hostile Islamic group, regardless of the intricacies of their faith. When the Crusaders reached the Holy Land, they encountered a weapon for which they were entirely unprepared. Flowing in some areas beneath the ground was a substance called naphtha, a colorless liquid similar to kerosene. The Saracens threw glass bombs containing the fluid at their Crusader enemies and tossed burning branches over the city walls, igniting the Christian Europeans in searing flames.

Another surprise for the Crusaders was the Saracens' music. Western European military units used musicians in battle prior to the Crusades, though they played mostly just trumpets and horns. Military bands lent greater significance to each function of war—marching into battle, rallying group spirit, burying the casualties, and celebrating the victories. The Muslim armies used a wider array of musical instruments, including the reedpipe, shawm, kettledrum, cymbals, and bells.[4] The Saracen musical units rallied their fighters to action with sounds that the Europeans scarcely recognized. The bands played on while the fighting progressed. The sound of silence was an undeniable signal that the battle had been lost. The English called these military musicians "minstrels,"[5] and the term came to describe men who played instruments a short distance from the battlefield; their instruments' cries urged violence and death and also championed victory.

Early firefighters also played an integral role in the war. A faction of warriors working in the Order of the Hospital of St. John of Jerusalem, known as Knights Hospitalers (also often called the Knights of St. John, or the Knights of the White Cross) were both fighters and healers. As members of a military and religious order, some fought for control of the city, some ministered in faith, and some bandaged and cared for the burned warriors. They distinguished themselves by the white cross with the widened ends that they wore over their dark robes, which became known as the Maltese Cross, since many of these knights later inhabited the island of Malta. In essence, the Knights Hospitalers were history's first group of warriors, clergy, firefighters, and paramedics, all in one.

In modern times, the American fire service adopted the Maltese Cross as its own identifying emblem. Today, each firefighter across the nation wears the cross on the badge, helmet, and shoulder patch. Relic of a thousand-year-old battle for religion and territory, a battle fought against Islam, and fought with fire, it symbolizes courage, rescue, and healing.[6]

Historians have found early mentions of the bagpipes in Europe in the eleventh and twelfth centuries, presumably after the Crusaders brought the instruments, or at least the idea of how to make them, back with them when returning home. One of the earliest is discovered in an Anglo Saxon riddle; another is a gravestone in Northumberland, which bore a rough carving of a piper, estimated to date from A.D. 1200.[7] Bagpipers are mentioned in two Irish poems dating to the twelfth century, one of which, "Carman," describes bagpipers among other musicians playing at a ritual harvest festival gathering that took place in 1079, near what would now be called the village of Lieghlinbridge, County Carlow. The poet first describes the upper-class entertainers.

> Is iat a ada olla
> Stuic, cruitti, cuirn chróes-tholla,
> Cúisig, timpaig, cen tríamna,
> Filid, ocus fáen-chlíara.
>
> These are the Fair's great privileges:
> Trumpets, harps, hollow-throated horns,
> Pipers, timpanists unwearied,
> Poets, and meek musicians.

Historian Sean Donnelly notes that the pipers in this first segment could not have been bagpipers (due to the word *cuisig*) and more likely were whistle or flute players. The poet goes on to illustrate the lower folk, some of whom were playing bagpipes. The passage indicates that bagpipes had quickly become an instrument of the common people.[8]

> Pípai, fidli, fir cengail,
> Cnámhfir and cuislennaig,
> Sluag étig engach égair,
> Béccaig ocus búirdaig.

> Bagpipers, fiddles, trick-of-the-loop men,
> Dice players, and flute players,
> A crowd hideous, noisy, and profane,
> Shriekers and shouters.

Another reference to a bagpiper in Ireland comes from the story of Saint Flannan, the patron saint of Killaloe in County Clare, which is believed to have been written between 1163 and 1167 by a foreign-born monk. He describes the funeral of a king buried "with keening and the sound of trumpets and pipes according to the custom and example of kings of the West."

Many European and British sources mention the instrument. In Chaucer's *Canterbury Tales* (c. 1386), the Miller is a bagpiper who leads the others out of town to the tune of his pipes. The skirl of pipes apparently proved suitable entertainment for kings, and early notes of payments in court records give proof of pipers in the 1400s and 1500s. Between the years of 1200 and 1600, little was written on piping in Ireland, during a time when most of the literature came from bardic poets, who specialized in a strictly stylized form of meter that often ignored military innovations and selectively mentioned only certain elements of contemporary life, such as favoring wine while excluding whiskey. The Statutes of Kilkenny, enacted in 1367 by King Edward III, suppressed use of the Irish language and also prohibited bagpiping by the "Irish enemies."

> It is agreed and forbidden, that any Irish agents, that is to say, pipers, story-tellers, bablers, rimers, mowers, nor any other Irish agent shall come amongst the English, and that no English shall receive or make gift to such; and that shall do so, and be attainted, shall be taken, and imprisoned, as well the Irish agents as the English who receive or give them any thing, and after that they shall make fine at the king's will; and the instruments of their agency shall forfeit to our lord the king.

Still, bagpipers continued to play. What we know of piping in the period points to the instrument's increasing use in Ireland and Gaelic Scotland for either war or funereal purposes, according to historian and author Roderick Cannon.

> In most places, the piper traditionally fulfills one (or both) of two roles: he is the village or town piper, a local "character," in evidence mainly at fairs and weddings, almost a beggar, drunk and disorderly by reputation

> if not in fact; or he is a shepherd, swineherd or goatherd who spends most of his time in the open air and uses his bagpipe not only for amusement but to call in his animals and lead them from place to place. In Gaelic Scotland and Ireland, however, we hear of the bagpipe being used as the incitement to battle, and for lamenting the dead. No doubt there were village and pastoral pipers in the Gaelic lands as elsewhere, but the contrast [in the sixteenth century] between bagpiping in Scotland and Ireland, and the rest of the world, is clear.[9]

Many of the earliest New York City firefighters were Irish immigrants who left their home country in order to flee the Great Hunger that gripped Ireland from 1845 to 1849. About two million Irish came to North America between 1845 and 1860, especially to cities like Boston and New York.[10] The early Irish who emigrated to the United States were largely regarded as scoundrels and thieves, were blamed for outbreaks of pestilence, played a significant role in the destructive 1863 draft riots in New York, and were rejected by the city's majority Protestant population. Even into the early twentieth century, those Irish who searched for work were often turned back by signs which shop owners or employers had posted: HELP WANTED. NO IRISH NEED APPLY. Like all of America's immigrants through the ages, the Irish made an indelible imprint on the fabric of this nation. But the Irish culture, molded by its new surroundings, retained identifiers from its history. One undercurrent of Irish cultural memory came from an unusual form of music, one that encapsulated the sounds of rebellion and defeat, of living and dying, of mourning and celebration. This sound echoed through the Irish consciousness and told the story of the people in a way that no words could. The Irish could not abandon this history, so they brought it with them—a love for the sound of the bagpipes.

Volunteer firefighters made up most of the force in New York City through the first half of the 1800s. Toward the end of the 1840s, around two thousand volunteers worked in the city, scattered among about eighty companies.[11] The Irish continued to flock to firefighting when the paid Fire Department was instituted in 1865, and the firefighters could collect a $700-a-year paycheck.[12]

Prior to the outbreak of the Civil War in 1861, some of the small factions of volunteer companies had formed their own musical groups.[13] Once the war began, two militias of courageous repute were the Fire

Zouaves, a group was drawn largely from New York firefighter volunteers, and the 69th New York Irish Brigade, also known as the "Fighting 69th." Both divisions fought side by side against the Confederates. Both had their own musicians. While the 69th was distinct from the Fenian militias that were springing up in the name of liberating Ireland from English rule, many of the members shared the same political stance. In 1860, the members of the 69th boycotted a high-profile parade for Edward, Prince of Wales. The 69th included at least one bagpiper, through he is mentioned in documents only once—playing his instrument around a campfire, which suggests the instrument's involvement may have been limited to entertainment at the war camps, not rallying on the battlefield.[14]

The firefighters' small volunteer bands dissolved once the department shifted to a paying structure in 1865, and there was no organized musical unit in the New York fire service until an official brass band started up in 1913. A revolving door of directors handled leadership of the band until 1927; many of them were politically connected, skilled classical musicians, paid by the city. In 1927, George Briegel, a trained trombonist and violinist and a close friend of New York City mayor Fiorello La Guardia's, was appointed to lead the band. Under his direction the band recorded a number of original marching tunes, including the "Fire Call March" and "Fire Department Legionnaires." Tubas, trombones, drums, and reed instruments were played by firefighter musicians at benefits, dances, and parades at the height of the big-band era. The Fire Department band lasted until 1958, when budget cuts forced it out of existence.[15]

In 1924, Congress passed quota limitations on the number of immigrants from each country allowed per year. Though the Irish were among the least affected by this development, the pattern of emigration still slowed significantly. During the last decade of the nineteenth century and the first decade of the twentieth, more than 330,000 Irish emigrated annually.[16] Just over ten thousand Irish came between 1931 and 1940, and almost twenty thousand came the following decade. Fewer Irish emigrating to the United States meant fewer native sources of Irish traditional music. The old Irish dance halls that had flourished prior to World War I were no more.[17] Irish traditional music—which incorporates jigs, reels, slow ballads, and melodies that range within two octaves, as well as a folk tradition of storytelling and passing bits from one person to the next—began to fade. Neighborhoods filled with Irish-born parents raising children with American accents. As the youth grew and the foreigners stopped coming in great numbers, a native Irish element that had been a driving force in New York's ethnic makeup began to be diluted. "Irish-American" became the term to define the new generation, those who were from Ireland but raised in America. Like most immigrants of the time period, rather than underscore their differences, they strove to assimilate into American society.

Then, in the late 1950s, Tommy Makem and the Clancy Brothers incited a revival in Irish music. The musicians took traditional Irish ballads, once sung as solos or a cappella, and traded the vocal melody back and forth with fiddles and whistles and Uillean pipes, an Irish form of the bagpipes. They also wrote original songs with thriving, toe-tapping beats and sang of fair ladies, hard laboring, drinking, and sports. Rolling stories, sung with authentic Irish brogues, were carried by an individual singer, with intervals of a group singing repeated choruses. Dozens became widespread hits, like "Four Green Fields," "Jug of Punch," "Wild Colonial Boy," and "The Bold Fenian Men," and the group eventually recorded fifty-five albums. The American public saw the group for the first time on the *Ed Sullivan Show* in 1961. Other Irish folk bands popular through the 1960s and 1970s included the Wolfe Tones, the Chieftains, and the Dubliners.

A rising desire among Irish-Americans to reacquaint themselves with Ireland began to seep into American music culture. In the mainstream, big bands and their distant, official airs had fallen starkly out of fashion. The seeds of a folk revival were planted, and the movement soon bloomed. Joan Baez, Bob Dylan, Simon and Garfunkel, and others played acoustic music and fashioned intricate storytelling through the music and lyrics. Melody and music became an art that one could do alone, or with a few instruments and a handful of friends. But the essence of folk music was that it came from the people, and the melodies provided the soundtrack for the influx of roots-consciousness that grew in many parts of American society through the 1960s and 1970s. Folk songs communicated slices of culture, feelings, and personal histories in ways no other form of music could. Beyond the knowledge that the sound of the bagpipes was the music of their own people, these modern impulses drove the firefighters in the Emerald Society Bagpipe Band.

The FDNY Bagpipe Band made its first appearance at Manhattan's City Center for an Emerald Society Dance in November 1962. Twelve bagpipers, three snare drummers, one tenor drummer, and one bass drummer stood onstage wearing their firefighters' navy blue uniforms and balmorals on their heads, and they nervously piped "Minstrel Boy" for a crowd that included Robert F. Kennedy.[18] The band marched in its first St. Patrick's Day parade in March of 1963—first through Yonkers for that town's parade, and the next week up Fifth Avenue for the New York City St. Patrick's Day parade.

The first drum major of the band was James Corcoran, whom most people called "Big Jim." He was a second-generation Irishman born in the South Bronx in 1934, to parents who'd emigrated to New York from County Kerry. Big Jim was a flamboyant marcher with a gray handlebar mustache and a grandiose way of puffing his chest out, extending his right arm, and planting his mace in the pavement at his side, as if New York City were the territory he'd staked out for himself alone. He'd been in the band since the beginning and led appearances on the *Ed Sullivan Show,* the Jerry Lewis telethon for muscular dystrophy, and the *Tonight Show* and at Madison Square Garden and Carnegie Hall. He steered the band out from 44th Street onto Fifth Avenue for the St. Patrick's Day parade in 1963, and after that he did the same for thirty-two straight years.

Over time, the band became more official and intricate in its operations. The members wrote up a constitution, outlining how responsibilities would be divided among officers, elected for one- or two-year terms. A chairman presided over the band but had no vote; other officers included a vice chairman, treasurer, secretary, pipe major, drum sergeant, and Emerald Society president. The pipe major was responsible for music selections and, according to the constitution, "has solute control of the Band on parade, functions, practices. His decision is final and is not to be questioned, especially in public." The band's first pipe major was an austere firefighter named Bill Duffy, whom the others admired because he could lead as easily as he could follow. The musical repertoire grew. In the winters, they practiced every Monday night, and they took the summers off to compete in Irish festivals of music, called "feis." They played at dinner dances and mayoral inaugurations, marched in parades and piped at summertime Scottish games.

The "Troubles" in Northern Ireland began to roil in 1968. Even though the belief was widely held among Irish Americans at the time that Northern Ireland should belong to the Irish Republic instead of being ruled by Britain, the band members tried their best to steer clear of expressing this or any other political stance in their performances.

One of the band's first instructors was a native of Northern Ireland, and he warned them early on that politics would not mix with their endeavors. The closest the band members got to expressing their personal views was banning from their repertoire a song called "It's a Long Way to Tipperary" during a high-profile hunger strike in Northern Ireland in 1981. The song is about an Irishman, "Paddy," who leaves Tipperary in Ireland to go and fight with the British in World War I. It was written by an Englishman who had never been to Ireland,[19] and although it became a famous war anthem, its meaning grew bitter when hunger striker Bobby Sands lay dying in his prison bed. Mostly, the bagpipers believed their presence as a group was enough to add strength to the Irish cause. They wore blue-collar attitudes, were pro-labor, favored traditional family structures in which the wife stayed home with the kids while the husband brought home the paycheck, and swung to the conservative right of the political spectrum. They tried not to get involved with controversial causes. As one band member put it, "You never know when you might be playing for the people you were just protesting against."[20]

Arson, riots, and false alarms ravaged New York City throughout what became known as the "war years" of the 1960s and '70s. The year the FDNY Emerald Society pipes and drums band formed, 1962, the department responded to 69,991 fires.[21] Eighteen firefighters were killed in the line of duty that year. The next deadliest year for the Fire Department came four years later. On October 17, 1966, eight firemen and four fire officers perished in a drugstore fire and building collapse on 23rd Street in Manhattan. Hundreds of off-duty firefighters showed up at the scene to help recover the firefighters' bodies from beneath the rubble. An estimated twenty thousand firefighters from across the country lined the streets for a somber procession four days later. Twelve coffins rode atop Fire Department pumpers driving down Fifth Avenue past St. Patrick's Cathedral. Ten of the coffins were draped in American flags, to honor those men who had served in the military. The other two were covered in Fire Department flags. The Power Memorial High School band led the march.[22]

Even once the pipe band was established, the Fire Department did not include it in ceremonies for line-of-duty deaths right away. After the brass band was eliminated, whenever firemen died in the line of duty, either a local high school band was recruited to march, or loudspeakers played somber recorded music, as a pumper escorted the coffin to the church. The idea of allowing a group of firemen the day off to play music at a fireman's funeral was too new, and most of the time, simply not feasible. The Bronx was burning almost daily. Firefighters were so busy, responding to multiple alarms on every tour, that extracurricular activity was not an option.

The first time the bagpipers played for a firefighter's death was in 1968, at the department's annual memorial service for all firefighters who'd been killed in the line of duty that year. On January 19, 1972, the Fire Department experienced its first casualty of the new year, when Lt. Joseph Connelly, a fifty-one-year-old father of four, collapsed of a heart attack while searching an industrial plant in Laurelton, Long Island, for evidence of fire.[23] Soon after, bass drummer Don Koehler contacted the Fire Department's ceremonial unit, which was charged with funeral arrangements, and told them that a dirge played by a selection of drummers would be more appropriate than the recorded music. At least that way, the fallen man would be escorted by some of his brothers in the department. Someone in the unit agreed. Five hundred off-duty firefighters lined the streets at 93rd Avenue and Springfield Boulevard in Queens Village and watched as the drummers marched the coffin of Lt. Connelly to the church doors on January 24, 1972.

As the years went on, when a fireman died, a few of the pipers began showing up to play at the funeral, but these appearances were occasional and did not involve the entire band. It would be another eight years before the entire pipes and drums band would play at a line-of-duty funeral. On June 27, 1980, twenty-seven-year-old firefighter Gerard Frisby of Ladder 28 and thirty-eight-year-old Lawrence Fitzpatrick of Rescue 3 were killed in an apartment house fire on 151st Street when a rope suspended by Fitzpatrick to rescue Frisby snapped, hurtling both men seven stories to their deaths.[24] On July 1, 1980, the band played at two funerals in the same day—Frisby's in the morning and Fitzpatrick's in the afternoon. After that, the entire band played whenever a firefighter died in the line of duty.

In all of the 1970s, an average of seven men died on the job each year. The next decade, that number dropped to two per year on average. Some years, there were no line-of-duty funerals at all. The most deadly year in recent memory was 1998, when six New York City firefighters were killed due to injuries sustained in three separate fires.[25] But by far, the band's funeral detail was eclipsed by a myriad of celebratory events—weddings, parades, fund-raisers, trips to Ireland and Scotland—and public performances.

Over the years, many men tried to get into the band and could not, because they lacked the commitment to learn the instrument. Those who wanted to join the band had to march with the color guard first, sometimes for up to two years, while they learned the bagpipes and demonstrated their commitment. Desire meant little if not backed up by honest work. And despite the growing numbers of men in the band, those who did not live up to the creed were abruptly exposed.

Among the tight-knit community of firemen, the pipe band was an even more insular group. Many of the members visited a tattoo artist in Westchester County named Big Joe to suffer through acquiring a special depiction of a blazing shamrock on one calf, with a script over and under that read FDNY BAGPIPE BAND. Then their commitment was forever inked on their skin. They took bus trips together, which grew to be notorious among the band for their rowdiness and overall bad behavior. They had certain phrases they used over and over, like "Shut up and listen," or "Hurry up and wait," which often seemed the modus operandi when the band had to arrive early at a function only to have to linger for an hour or more before starting to play. When time came to vote in new members, nearly everyone would raise a hand and call "Yea" in favor of the new guy, and a few would always shout, "Fuck him!" in playful opposition. Some used hand signals to communicate things they'd rather not say out loud, like, "Going for a drink later?" And a gesture to explain, "No, can't. I'm in trouble with the wife!"

What kept the peace within the group was each man's ability to harness his own showman's desire to be noticed and recognized. Boasting was simply not permitted. Braggers were chided and called "peacock," an appellation that not only implied a kinship to the bird with the wide expanse of colorful feathers but also reflected on the size of the subject's equipment.

The desire not to be shamed in this way was usually enough to halt a runaway ego. The men joined the band out of pride and then denied it outwardly once they were voted in as members. The men often said, "There's no rank in the band," and there wasn't. A piper who was a captain in the Fire Department had no higher status than a firefighter with just a couple of years on the job. Many if not all of the band members worked in the busiest firehouses in New York City. Everyone had a family lineage that originated in Ireland. There was no need for rank distinction in the band uniform; being permitted to wear it was distinction enough.

As long as in what they did and how they did it they reflected one another, the band remained a solid unit. As long as no one rose too high, no one needed to get hammered down. Ask anyone in the band why he'd joined and each one would give a similar response. "It was something I always wanted to do." They downplayed themselves and their status, which in turn gave them higher regard within the Fire Department. The band was an elite unit. The whole job knew it. Once everyone in the band followed the unspoken rules, their bond solidified. In this silence, respectful of things that needn't be said, there was an understanding of the truth.

Like the Maltese Cross they wore on their uniforms, the bagpipes came to symbolize a part of who they were. For more than forty years, they puffed their own breath into a relic from the past, an instrument that reminded them of their identity, and an activity that reaffirmed their bond to one another in good times and bad.

On March 17, 1995, Big Jim Corcoran strode through the cheers and applause for forty-two city blocks and finished the St. Patrick's Day parade, his thirty-second, as usual, at 86th Street. Then he went down into the subway, still wearing his fire-engine-red tunic and deep green kilt, sat down on a bench on the platform, and collapsed. His heart stopped beating in the late afternoon.

By the time Big Jim died, the band had played at several funerals for band members who'd died of natural causes, but no one in the band had ever been killed in the line of duty at a fire. Big Jim's death came the closest, since he'd died after the parade. Three days after Big Jim strode by St. Patrick's Cathedral for the final time, the streets of midtown Manhattan came to a halt for his hearse. A pumper from Ladder 19 led the way, and the pipers and drummers escorted his body toward the church, marching and playing the tune of "Will Ye No' Come Back Again," a Scottish lament.

> Bonnie Charlie's noo awa
> Safely o'er the friendly main
> Mony a heart will break in twa
> Should he ne'er come back again.
>
> Will ye no' come back again?
> Will ye no' come back again?
> Better lo'ed ye canna be
> Will ye no' come back again?

Big Jim's coffin was covered in an American flag and lifted in through the gilded doors of the majestic church. Father Mychal Judge, a Franciscan priest, waited in the foyer to say a prayer over the casket when it reached him, then lead it to the front by the altar. Even though he was technically a part-time Fire Department chaplain, he gave much more of his time to the job than his title required. He could often be seen at Fire Department functions wearing his brown habit and sandals, with his white hair parted neatly on one side. Several years before, when the band chairman asked if he would be the group's special chaplain, Father Judge said he was deeply honored and agreed. He maintained a close relationship with many of the members.

On the day of Big Jim's funeral, Father Judge stepped up to the podium in St. Patrick's Cathedral. He began his homily with a short reading from the first chapter of John, in which Jesus meets Nathanael, who will become one of his disciples. Father Judge's elfin voice echoed across the cathedral, and he explained the story with an aura of wonder in his words.

"When Jesus of Nazareth saw Nathanael coming toward him, He remarked, 'This is a real Israelite! There is no guile in him.'

"Nathanael asked, 'How do you know me?'

"Jesus answered, 'Before Phillip called you, I saw you under the fig tree.'

" 'Rabbi!' said Nathanael. 'You are the Son of God! You are the king of Israel!'

"Jesus replied, 'Do you believe, just because I told you I saw you under the fig tree? You will see much greater things than that.'

"Then Jesus went on to tell him, 'I solemnly assure you. You shall see the sky open and the angels of God ascending and descending on the son of man.'

"The Gospel of the Lord," Father Judge said. He kissed the open book and set it aside. Then he climbed down and stood to face the mourners on the floor level of the church. He took on a conversational tone.

"Must have been a beautiful moment for Nathanael," he said. "Sitting under the fig tree, never realizing his life was about to change so radically."

He moved easily from left to right, and he massaged the words again.

"Behold the Israelite in whom there is no guile. A real, sincere, honest, no-frills man. That's a very nice story, a nice Bible story. The man in whom there is no guile."

Standing before several dozen pipers and drummers in red tunics, Father Judge then told of how he'd once met a piper in Scotland and had asked him to explain the magic of the tradition. The piper had told him there wasn't much to say. In America, the piper told him, bagpipers play in groups, while in Scotland they often roamed the Highlands alone. It had been said that warrior pipers wrapped themselves in the long fabric of their kilts to keep warm at night, and the reason they wore the high feather bonnets was to keep their heads warm, as well as to be noticed from afar when they were weary and traveling toward a village, hoping for shelter.

Then Father Judge recounted how, some years back, he'd been asked to become the chaplain of the Emerald Society pipes and drums band. "Wow!" he gasped, and grinned. "Maybe they'll give me one of those kilts and a high hat!" A chuckle rose from the pews in the church.

And, he continued, he'd met Big Jim one day. Jim had swaggered over to Father Judge and saluted. The priest saw Big Jim wink under the shield of his stiff hand. "Wow!" Father Judge whispered again, in awe of the memory. "Wouldn't it be great to see him strolling the Highlands of Scotland!

"What a way to live," Father Judge sighed. "What a way to die."

He turned to the band members, who sat close together in the front pews. "You, marching up Fifth Avenue. What pride you gave him. That his move and his word should be your move and your word. It was a great day. You've taken the best you had and given it back to the Lord. You're generous in that way, and kind."

He paused.

"Let me tell you what happened that day."

Father Judge now held the attention of the mourners as if they were young children waiting breathlessly for the end of the fable. For the moment, they'd entirely forgotten their grief. He told them the legend of their own.

"He made the turn onto 86th Street. He passed all of us. He gave us the wink and the salute. He went down to the subway station. What happened was, he kept on marching. Through the clouds. All of a sudden, he saw the Highlands. And up he went. And when he turned, he looked behind him and saw all those who had died on St. Patrick's Day had come to march with him. And the gates opened, and he walked up to the throne, still holding his baton. The Lord stood up and saw him, and said, 'Jim! You're here. I called you.'

"And then He said, 'Behold the New Yorker in whom there is no guile.'"

CHAPTER 1

IRISH FAIR

Because the pain was genuinely unanticipated, there was no residue of anxiety to alter my experience of it. Anxiety and anticipation, I was to learn, are the essential ingredients in suffering from pain, as opposed to feeling pain pure and simple.

—Lucy Grealy, *Autobiography of a Face*

On the morning of September 8, 2001, the twenty-first annual Great Irish Fair opened its gates in Coney Island, Brooklyn. Under a sweltering sky and a blanket of impenetrable humidity, half a dozen giant beer tents sprawled across a dirt-and-grass field and, beckoning with their shelter and libation, soon proved to be the anchors of the event. Old ladies sold Irish brown bread from little booths. Craft vendors displayed dolls in green dresses and pint glasses with harps on them. Dozens of portable toilets formed an ample row right down the center of the fenced-in terrain. The outdoor festival took up less space than a football field, but it was touted by organizers as "the largest in the world." A celebration of high-minded Irish culture it certainly was not. But the fair did provide a suitable late-summer excuse to drink lager and stout all day, and for this reason the Catholic Charities always collected plenty in the way of ten-dollar entry donations at the gate.

This year, the event was dedicated to three New York City firefighters who had been killed barely three months earlier, in a fire that erupted on Father's Day in Astoria, Queens. Two firefighters from the Queens-based company of Rescue 4, Brian Fahey and Harry Ford, had died, as had firefighter John Downing, who was from the nearby company Ladder 163. They, along with hundreds of other firefighters, had responded to a five-alarm blaze in a hardware store that turned fatal when chemicals in the basement caused an explosion that trapped Fahey under a stairwell and buried Ford in a pile of rubble on the sidewalk. Their deaths left the department reeling. Ford was a twenty-seven-year veteran of the Fire Department and father of two, legendary among firefighters as much for his acts of daring as for his wry views on life. Like Ford, Fahey was a seasoned firefighter, with fourteen years on the job. He left behind a wife and three boys.

While that aspect of the Irish Fair would certainly be solemn for the FDNY, another would be celebratory. The Irishman of the Year Award would be going to a popular lieutenant, a Brooklyn fellow named Timmy Stackpole, who'd recently come back on the job after suffering fourth- and fifth-degree burns over 30 percent of his body when a floor collapsed during a fire in East New York in June 1998. One firefighter was killed in that blaze, and another succumbed after a twenty-nine-day battle in the burn unit. Five other men had been injured in the fire.

Even at events that weren't otherwise significant, the bagpipers arrived and, by way of the wrenching skirl of their pipes, made them so. The band could magnify the elation of a joyful moment and twist tears from the most stoic in times of mourning. And so today, to commemorate both the men who'd died and the men who'd lived, a contingent of about thirty Fire Department bagpipers would be there, puffing air into their pipes and playing Irish tunes to honor their triumphant brother firemen.

Liam Flaherty arrived early to set up a table near one of the beer tents, where he and a few other firefighters from Rescue 4 would be selling T-shirts bearing the names of the three fallen firefighters in order to raise money for their widows and children. Liam was a firefighter in Rescue 4 and the ceremonial leader of the FDNY Emerald Society bagpipe band. Standing six-foot-five, Liam rose several inches taller than most of the band members. At thirty-six, his milky skin remained soft even after years of laboring as a carpenter and countless plunges into sooty, smoky fires. His boyish face, with its azure eyes and reddish cheeks, was topped by a full head of curly black hair. As drum major, he led the band through every parade, every wedding, every funeral. He stood in front, while the rest of the band followed ten feet behind, and his uniform was distinguished by his green and gold sash, the ornate white stitching on his collar, and the long metal staff he carried, known as the mace. Even though the drum major was not part of the band's leadership committee, Liam was the one who shook hands with the governor and the mayor and other big-name politicians at city events. Of all the city's eleven thousand or so firefighters, Liam was the one with the front-row seat. He was in the public eye. And he savored the celebrity.

Liam took the navy blue T-shirts out of boxes and laid them on the table. On the front right chest of each shirt was a collection of symbols forming a crest, which had been designed by another member of the pipe band, a Brooklyn firefighter named Tommy Brunton. He'd set the names Ford, Downing, and Fahey in Gothic script arcing across the top, and along the bottom were the words "Father's Day Fire." In the center sat the FDNY's gray Maltese Cross with a shamrock in the middle. Three small helmets bearing the men's company numbers formed a triangle around the cross. Two long halligan tools, which firefighters use in combination with an ax for forcible entry, were anchored by a gold harp at the bottom. On the back of the shirt was a cartoon that had appeared in *Newsday* a short time after the men had died. On it, three firefighters were approaching the gates of heaven. Harry Ford was depicted with his arm around Brian Fahey's shoulder, as John Downing stood in front. A speech bubble leading to Ford read, "We're safe now, guys . . . that's not smoke, it's clouds."

Soon Bronko Pearsall, Liam's best friend of eleven years and a fellow member of Rescue 4, arrived at the table and began helping Liam set up. Bronko played snare drum in the band and was cocaptain of the Fire Department football team. Today he wore the band members' summer uniform—white short-sleeved shirt, which strained against his enormous biceps, knee-high green socks, and green-and-blue tartan kilt. Perhaps no one in the band was prouder of his kilt than Bronko, and his kilt was one of the biggest, since it had to wrap comfortably around his forty-two-inch (sometimes forty-four-inch) waist. When he walked, it swished in the wind and flapped against the back of his thick knees. People took a step back and looked up at him when he was wearing it, as if watching a Hollywood star pass. Without that kilt, Bronko often deadpanned, he'd have been just another fat man at the bar.

Bronko's real name was Durrell, but no one ever called him that. When he'd experienced a sudden teenage growth spurt, his mother began calling him Bronko, after the 1930s football legend Bronko Nagurski. Like Liam, he was a hulking physical presence with a personality to match. At six-foot-two, he was built like a barrel with olive skin and charcoal-black eyebrows that he could twist into a fierce furl.

A few years earlier, a new piper named Jimmy O'Neill had been warming up with the band near Fifth Avenue in nervous expectation of his first St. Patrick's Day parade marching with the group. There were close to seventy men in the band, so it took the new guys a while to get to know everyone. O'Neill was big and burly but shy. He kept to himself. He wouldn't have strutted over to all the men and shaken hands to introduce himself, never. O'Neill figured he'd meet who he was going to meet. He had a few friends in the band already, and he didn't want to make a bad impression by being overly outgoing. While O'Neill stood warming up his pipes, looking around at the pre-parade commotion going on all around him, he suddenly felt a slight draft at the back of his legs. Bronko had snuck up behind him and extended a narrow drumstick to investigate whether the new guy was following the tradition of "going regimental" or was wearing underwear beneath his kilt. O'Neill whirled around, but it was too late. He was wearing shorts! Bright red boxers, no less! To match his red tunic! Hooting and hollering, Bronko and a couple of other drummers grabbed at O'Neill's waistband and tore the boxers right off him.

Bronko helped Liam set up the table, and by around 11:00 A.M. most of the band had arrived at the fair.

Father Mychal Judge began saying mass inside a tent at one end of the field. While a hundred or so people crowded into the tent to pray, most of the pipers hung around in the parking lot, tuning their instruments and gossiping as they always did. As the mass was about to finish, around noon, the FDNY band lined up near the tent. Liam called out the order to march, and the band followed him. They wove a winding path around the tents and past the vendors. The pipers blew heartily at their instruments and a myriad of charming, proud-sounding notes filled the air. At the back, Bronko and the other drummers chipped and rolled on their white snare drum heads. The band marched around and around, playing a selection of Irish tunes, then arrived in front of the main stage, where the awards ceremony would begin.

The Fire Department band assembled in formation in front of the stage along one side, and the Police Department band stood on the other side. A white-haired emcee, who'd formerly been a top man at the New York division of the Ancient Order of Hibernians, took the microphone and began to banter. Some guys in the band called him a "peacock," because he was a showoff who loved the spotlight a little too much. He could talk and talk, and today, true to form, he did. He had plenty of awards to give out, and it seemed that he prefaced his speech before every one with "Let me tell you a little story about this one . . ." The Chief Brehon Award, for an outstanding citizen of Irish heritage. The Paul O'Dwyer Memorial Award, for a great humanitarian in the community. The Irish Bard Award, for a distinguished Irish writer. Each awardee then stepped to the stage and took the mike to embark on a recitation of his own.

The sun beat down on the pipers. Tommy, who had designed the logo for the Father's Day shirts, stood grimacing in the lineup as sweat poured down the sides of his face, moistening his gray temples until they appeared a slick black. "Sshhut up," he began muttering to himself, repeating and lengthening the *sh* and marking the hard *t.* The words had a soothing effect. Liam stood stiff and motionless at the far side of the formation, looking skyward, holding his mace upright. His shirt had begun to stick to him.

The ceremony dragged on for an hour, with the main awards yet to be distributed. The summer heat was overwhelming. One of the men in the color guard began to sway, and he escaped for some shade and a chair. By the end of it, Tommy was glaring up at the stage and swearing right out loud. "Shut the fuck up." He didn't care anymore who heard him.

The first deputy police commissioner, Joseph Dunne, stepped to the stage to receive the Round Tower Award, which, the emcee explained, was given to an outstanding figure in the community who personified the principles of the fair—"a family festival celebrating an honored culture and helping to improve the quality of life for those less fortunate than ourselves." Then, finally, the Irishman of the Year Award was given to Fire Lieutenant Timmy Stackpole. A collective sigh rose from the pipers. They all loved Timmy, but they knew that Timmy loved to talk. Today, though, he didn't. He could see his men were suffering in the heat. He voiced a quick thank-you and stepped down.

At last, it was over. Liam wasted no time in turning on his heel and growling, "Band dismissed!" No sooner had he said the words than most of the men disappeared into the closest beer tent. Inside the larger tents, Irish folk musicians, their instruments hooked up to mammoth speakers, plunked out tunes from atop plywood stages as the lines for the nearby taps grew longer and louder. Back at the shirt table, Bronko and Liam drank Budweiser out of tall thirty-two-ounce Styrofoam containers called hats, which kept the amber liquid cool despite the increasing heat of the day. As the afternoon went on, they sold hundreds of shirts. Liam and Bronko schmoozed with a reporter from a local TV channel who promised to publicize the shirts on a morning broadcast later in the week.

Timmy Stackpole stopped by the booth for a chat. Liam, like most men in the Fire Department, held Timmy in high regard. He loved the Fire Department as much as Liam did, and he'd come back from an injury that doctors had predicted was career-ending. The two had a tradition of meeting in the Buckley's tent every year for a beer. Now, because of Timmy's injury, it had been three years since they'd had the chance. When Timmy stepped away, he offered the invitation, and Liam agreed to meet him there later.

The day sped by, and before Liam knew it, it was nearly 4:00 P.M. Liam never got the chance to meet Timmy, as they'd planned. The band members started to disappear one by one. Many would be going to play at the wedding of a fellow piper that evening, and most wanted to get home for a shower first. Liam and Bronko left the shirt-selling to the other guys and got ready to leave. The beer buzz left their heads a little lighter. Suddenly, it was the end of an enjoyable afternoon.

As they walked to the parking lot, Bronko asked, "Are you wearing your kilt tonight?"

Liam was hot, and the wool of the kilt was prickly against his damp legs. All he could think about at that moment was getting out of his kilt and starting the air-conditioning going in his car. The band members would be bringing their kilts to change into at the reception, but Bronko wanted to wear his all night, and he didn't want to be the only one. So would Liam wear his, too?

Liam called Bronko a sissy. Asking if they could wear matching outfits to the same party? Come on. Bronko persisted, and Liam shrugged and said all right, yeah, he probably would wear his kilt. Bronko climbed into his Blazer and took off for his house in Long Island. Liam headed back to his apartment in Brooklyn.

Liam and Bronko spent a lot of their free time together. Liam had gotten Bronko to join the pipes and drums band soon after he did. Liam also had recommended Bronko to the brass at Rescue 4 and helped him get on the job there in 1999. Liam had a quiet side, but Bronko could always draw him out. They shared the same perverse sense of humor, the same love for the comedy cartoon *The Simpsons* and the MTV stunt show *Jackass,* the same appreciation of their Irish heritage, and the same joy in prodding each other to hysterics by recounting their drunken escapades of the night before. When they were around each other, they were rarely serious. After a few drinks in a bar or at an outdoor festival, they often made themselves into a human trampoline. Facing each other, they'd extend their arms, grab each other's elbows, and entice a willing female to lie on her back across their arms. Then they'd toss her up in the air and catch her, over and over, until she was giggling so much she could barely breathe.

Bronko was deeply proud of the Irish half of his heritage, but he looked so Italian that his friends teased him relentlessly, calling him a "*Sopranos* reject" or sometimes, because of his sallow skin, an "Arabian sheik." Bronko was a performer. He was a member of the Screen Actors Guild and once portrayed a Jets player in a Tostitos commercial. His friends also poked fun at his fluctuating weight, which ranged from 230 to nearly 300 pounds. A circular wooden backboard of a giant Christmas wreath hung on the kitchen wall in Rescue 4, painted in blue with the words "Bronko-Meter 300." The guys would drop it over Bronko's head and let it fall at his midsection to see how heavy he'd grown, an exercise that always brought gales of laughter from the other men in the firehouse. Picking on Bronko was like playing with a big lion. Liam, especially, would tease Bronko until he reached the breaking point. They came close to a real fight only once, after a long night of drinking, when Liam was messing around with Bronko, grabbing at his back and squeezing until Bronko yelped in pain. Bronko threw punches at Liam, and they tangled and wrestled for a few minutes. The fight was over as soon as it had started. Any remnants of ill will were forgotten the next morning.

Bronko and Liam used their vacations to take trips with a crew of their bachelor friends. They would visit a different city every year—Prague, New Orleans, Munich—where they would go to bars, have some laughs, and chase women. Bronko, the documentarian of the group, took hundreds of pictures during their various excursions over the years. Because of his bulky frame, he drew attention wherever he went, especially in Europe, where the people seemed much smaller. And when Liam was with him, the two towering men with the loud voices turned heads. Once, in Munich, they joked with a waiter who'd remarked on their sturdy figures—Bronko would take one side of the menu, Liam would take the other half. On another occasion, when

Bronko and Liam sauntered into a pub in Galway and sidled up to the bar, the teenage barman, himself puny by comparison, gaped up at them. As he tossed beer mats on the bar, he said, by way of a placating opener, "Congratulations on your size."

Among all his friends, Bronko had the sharpest memory; in fact, it was near photographic. He was an expert at shouting out the correct answers to *Jeopardy.* He seemed able to remember everything, even when he was drunk—including every excruciating detail of the boys' foolish antics the night before. This made him an ideal second-in-command for Liam, whose friends knew him as the type who didn't let them get away with anything. Liam had a tendency to act as everyone else's conscience; he was critical of others who did not rise to his own standards, even in the smallest matters. Sometimes Liam's judgments were caustic, but most of the time they were taken in fun. After the boys went out for a night of drinking, Liam would tease and scold them about the various levels of their buffoonery the next day. He and Bronko could play off each other for hours.

But what Bronko liked most of all was singing Irish songs. He came close to being on key, even if he didn't have a spectacular voice, and he was a ham. When the boys in the band were out drinking, someone would start yelling the words to "Spancil Hill" or "Fields of Athenrye." "When New York Was Irish" was another of his favorites.

> I'll sing you a song of days long ago
> When the people from Galway and the County Mayo
> And all over Ireland came over to stay
> To take up a new life in Americay.
>
> They were ever so happy, they were ever so sad
> To grow old in a new world through good times and bad
> All the parties and weddings, the ceilis and wakes
> When New York was Irish, full of joys and heartbreaks.
>
> We worked on the subways, we ran the saloons
> We built all the bridges, we played all the tunes
> We put out the fires and controlled City Hall
> We started with nothing and wound up with it all.

Bronko sometimes started a song up himself, and if someone else started, he always joined in—and usually soon took over the lead, because he was the only one who infallibly remembered all the words and the order of the verses. Sometimes, if the guys were getting the song wrong, Bronko would cut them off and make them start over. His personal favorite was "The Wild Rover." He loved the song so much, he introduced to the FDNY team the tradition of singing it after football games.

> I've been a wild rover for many a year
> And I spent all my money on whiskey and beer
> And now I'm returning with gold in great store
> And I never will play the wild rover no more.
>
> And it's no nay never
> No nay never no more
> Will I play the wild rover
> No never no more.

In the early 1990s, around the time Bronko and Liam joined the band, a number of their friends also became new members. There was Chris Walsh, an outgoing firefighter who worked in Harlem and whose parents, like Liam's, had been born in Ireland. Chris went by the nickname "Kippy," a playful sobriquet he'd gleaned from a brother whose childhood way of pronouncing "Christopher" came out "Kippupper." He stood six-foot-three and years before had worked with Liam as a bouncer at an Irish pub in Woodside, Queens, near the neighborhood where Kippy grew up. Another member of the crew was Tim Grant, a sandy-haired firefighter with a dry wit who worked in the Bronx and had become friends with Bronko in the probationary class where they were learning to become firefighters. At almost every function, this clique of guys, with big personalities and loud laughs, hung together.

One of them, Gene Fraher, an impish firefighter who was often the center of attention himself, anointed the group with the name "Tumac." They'd punch their chests and growl "Tumac," as if it were a secret signal. The name didn't really mean anything—it came from a rugby chant—but Fraher said it was intended to make the other band members have to inquire about the meaning, and thereby make them jealous that they weren't a part of it. Fraher hosted a pool party every year, and the Tumac gang all went. When there was a band bus trip, they all sat together, slugged down cans of beer and hollered out Irish songs. Fraher made up a number of songs of his own, with satirical lyrics about fires and firemen, which he sang to familiar tunes. One of Fraher's inventions became a classic among the pipers—a song called "Fireman Fraher." The verses exposed a skittish fireman who found every possible excuse not to go into a burning building.

> Fireman Fraher had one thought in mind,
> In a fire don't ever get involved.
> And between you and me, as the tenants would flee,
> To this fact he was truly resolved!
>
> Oh the Rescue is fancy, but the work's hard and chancy,
> And the engine men haul in the hose.
> While the truckies are reeling from pulling the ceiling,
> And the smoke just got worse as it rose . . .
>
> So don't go into the building, Gene,
> I heard the engine men holler.
> Genie dear, won't you stay out here,
> The fire has spread through the parlor!
>
> And don't go into the kitchen, son,
> It's safer out here don't you know.
> So fireman Fraher, with his clipboard and cap,
> In the street he stayed safely below!

In all, there were more than a dozen of these new members, most in their thirties and forties. When they came into the band, many of the original members had begun to retire, and the band risked growing stodgy and boring. The old-timers sometimes begrudged the new circles that had arisen but admitted among themselves that this new crew brought back a much-needed spark.

Kippy was married to a Woodside girl named Mary, and one night at a barbecue he'd introduced Tim to his wife's best friend, Tara. A couple of years later, Tim and Tara were married. As time went on, Bronko and Liam stuck together as the only two remaining bachelors in their circle of friends. Liam, who feared little in life except what he called "getting pinned down by a girl," continued navigating an on-again, off-again relationship with a woman he'd met in a club four years earlier. Together, Bronko and Liam frequented the Manhattan bar circuit, went to "Nurses Night" at the Brooklyn pubs, and swore they'd never settle down. Bronko was thirty-four, and he never seemed to date anyone through what his friends teasingly called "the cycle of holidays." When another of his short-lived relationships would come to an end, his buddies would ask what happened. Bronko would answer, "Ahhh, it was too much pressure" or "I don't have the time, I'm too busy." They'd accuse him of just being too cheap to buy her a Christmas present or a Valentine's gift. He'd turn away, troubled, and rub his forehead with his thick fingers. When they bent around for a peek at his face, they'd see he was hiding a grin.

Lately, though, Bronko and Liam's bachelor bond was growing precarious. That summer, Liam had begun to notice that if he asked Bronko to go somewhere or do something, Bronko didn't always say yes the way he used to. Now and then, Bronko responded with "Nah, I can't make it," and he wouldn't always say why.

Bronko was getting serious with Karen, a tall, willowy blond from Long Island, whom he'd met just over a year before. Karen and Bronko had grown up in nearby towns on Long Island, traveled in the same circles, and shared many mutual friends, but for years Karen never met the boisterous fireman everyone was always talking about. "Oh, you just missed him," people would often say to her. Then came the Fourth of July 1998. The band had played at a parade earlier in the day, and Bronko, still wearing his kilt, stopped in at a party where she was. They shook hands and smiled at each other, then talked for hours. He was an excellent conversationalist and knew a little bit about a lot of things. They began dating in March, often going to parties, out for dinner, or to a baseball game.

When they started going out together, Karen told Bronko she thought they should take it slow. They knew so many of the same people, it would be a shame if they went too fast and things didn't work out. Bronko agreed. Then he called her the next day, and the next day, and every day after that. Karen knew this was the guy she was going to marry. In early 2001, he began studying for the lieutenant's exam, which required a lot of his time. "Let's get engaged," Karen would say. "After the exam is over," he'd tell her, and Karen would laugh. "Okay, but as soon as it's over, I'm gonna come knocking on your door!" He was scheduled to take the test in October.

Liam was just thirty-one when the band's first drum major, Big Jim, died. He'd been inducted into the band only a few years earlier. He didn't come from a firefighting family. His father, Billy, was a carpenter, born in County Galway, Ireland. Liam had learned his father's trade as a teenager and later worked alongside him as a member of Local 608 for several years while he attended college. Although he was a bright student, Liam gave up college before graduating. He was making good money as a carpenter, but the hours were long and tended to interfere with his studies. John Fowler, a childhood friend and his brother-in-law, had become a firefighter, and John often talked up the job. Being a firefighter offered a lifestyle that laboring could not match—the camaraderie of the brothers, constant pranks in the firehouse, a job with lifelong benefits and a guaranteed pension after twenty years.

Liam trained hard for the physical half of the fire exam, which was rigorous. Candidates were timed on a series of tasks: hauling up several flights of stairs a 2.5-gallon fire extinguisher, a rolled-up hose, a six-foot-long ceiling hook, a roof saw, and other firefighting equipment, which ranged in weight from five to forty pounds; raising a twenty-foot aluminum ladder to a building window; hoisting fifty feet of hose up several stories; using a ceiling hook to pull down a ceiling; and swinging a simulated ax or hammer at a door until it broke open. They also had to perform a search in a dark, tunnel-like maze and drag a weighted dummy through a thirty-foot-long zigzag course. When he was at a work site, Liam would run up and down the stairs carrying sandbags to get accustomed to the extra weight that firemen carried in gear and breathing apparatus. He took the police officers' exam and the fire exam and passed both with high marks. Eventually, when he was twenty-five, a spot for him opened at the Fire Academy.

Liam discovered that firefighting was a lot like carpentry, but in reverse. Instead of putting up buildings and creating rooms for people to live or work in, firemen knocked through ceilings to ventilate fires and searched hallways and hidden nooks to get people out. There was plenty of downtime in the firehouse, but the moment always came when the alarm sounded and the men sprang to their feet and raced for the rig. They could detect the slightest gravity or urgency in the voice of the dispatcher and know whether the alarm was a serious one. Being inside the giant solid truck, with the siren blaring and the angry horn rampaging as they roared across the neighborhood, felt oddly secure. They were insulated in hundreds of pounds of steel. Cars pulled aside and stopped for them. People paused on sidewalks to gape. Out the square windows, shielding the sky from view, the world passed by in neatly framed boxes —trees, cars, brick houses, bodegas, drugstores, gangs of kids. As the rig barreled closer to the scene, Liam would force himself to breathe slower and slower, swallowing more often, repeating a mantra or a song in his head. Then, sometimes, the waft of burn would tease ever so gently at his nose. In moments, seconds even, they'd jump out of the truck. This was what he loved: the cold fear of not knowing what lay ahead, of trying to get a handle on chaos, fighting to control what could not be controlled.

Liam gradually built a reputation in the department and worked his way up to a busy ladder company in the Bronx. The senior firefighters liked him immediately. Liam could follow orders. He knew when to shut up and listen. He also knew how to take charge of a risky situation. Plus, he was a buff; he learned everything he could about fighting fires and had a certain glint in his eye that revealed his enthusiasm for the job.

So it wasn't long after Big Jim died that Gene Fraher took Liam aside and told him he thought he should run for the position. Liam declined. Several veteran members of the band had put their names into the running, and some members were rumbling that the post should go to a guy with seniority; Liam tended to agree. Still, the seed of the idea was planted, and Liam began to consider it. Later that spring, Father Judge approached Liam at a plaque dedication ceremony and told him he would be great as the new drum major. Soon after, Liam called a former instructor for the band, Joe Brady Jr., and arranged a practice session.

Brady demonstrated the way a drum major marches and the moves he makes with his mace: the "walk," which has to demonstrate discipline and the deportment of a leader; the "trail," when a drum major suspends the mace parallel to the ground with both hands to signal the approaching end of a march; "pumping the mace," moving it up and down with a bent elbow during the march; and finally the flourishing moves, which include twirling and spinning the long staff like a flashy baton. Liam copied the movements, and Brady critiqued him.

Liam didn't go around talking about wanting to be drum major, but as word that he was going to run began to spread, Tim Grant began to lobby on his friend's behalf. He rattled off a list of reasons why Liam should win to anyone who would listen. Liam was a skilled musician with a good ear. He had a booming voice and could command attention. He looked the part. He was young enough to remain drum major for years and build up recognition in the post, the way Big Jim had. The chairman kept records of the men's attendance through a point system (for every appearance that a member turned out for, he would receive three points, and overnight trips earned nine), and Liam had more points than anyone else. Most important, Tim said, Liam was the "most Irish," since both his parents had been born in Ireland.

Tryouts took place one autumn night on the second floor of the Elks Lodge on Queens Boulevard, where the band practiced. Everyone in the band showed up. Most filed into seats in the dimly lit balcony, from which dusty stained-glass signs reading "Brotherly Love" and "Fidelity" hung above the open floor. Several pipers and drummers remained below to form a miniature band for the tryouts. One by one, the candidates for drum major auditioned by marching in front of the pipers, calling out orders and signaling with the mace. When Liam began to march, his voice echoed off the walls. He strode stiffly, with an official air, his head tall, shoulders back, his muscular arm curling the mace up and down with strength and rhythm. He twirled the mace behind his back like a baton, and the men above whistled in approval. When the tune finished, he raised the mace straight up in the air and jerked his wrist right-left, right-left, then let the staff slide seamlessly down into his hand. A cacophony of cheers and shouts filled the room. Some spectators pretending to be judges held up signs reading "10." No one could come close to Liam's performance. Within seconds, the poor firefighter who had to follow him was assaulted by hecklers with calls of "Dead man walking!"

When the ballots were mailed in and counted, they showed a significant majority in support of Liam. He was the one man the others could follow.

The next St. Patrick's Day, the band marched up Fifth Avenue without a drum major, to honor Big Jim. After the ceremony, the band gathered at the 69th Regiment Armory, where Mayor Rudolph Giuliani and Jim's widow, Elaine, handed Liam the silver-and-gold mace, which now had Jim Corcoran's name engraved on it.

The task before Liam required a dexterous balance of leading and following. Almost every man who joined the pipe band did so as much for the recognition as because of the desire to reinforce his Irish identity. Every one of them wanted to stand out. Now Liam would stand out more than any of the others, but he couldn't—and didn't—appear to be pleased by the attention.

Karen arrived at Bronko's house in Hempstead, Long Island, around 5:00 P.M., soon after he'd returned from the Irish fair. Bronko told her he would just take a quick shower and they'd be on their way. Karen looked stunning, outfitted in a silky silver dress with spaghetti straps. He asked her what he should wear. His kilt or his suit? No, he was sure Liam was going to wear his kilt. He'd asked him, and Liam had said yes. So he'd wear his, too. Karen just laughed at him. He and Liam did everything together. They had all kinds of inside jokes, little competitions, pretend insults that they'd throw at each other. She barely knew Liam, since he and Bronko usually hung out together without her, but she found it amusing how close the two were, and how boyish. She lingered in Bronko's living room, watching TV, waiting for him to get dressed. Bronko always seemed to take forever getting ready. Karen would have to tell him things started an hour in advance of when they really began, just so they could get there on time. But she didn't mind. His house was an entertaining place to be, in a bachelor-pad sort of way. An enormous moose head loomed over the living room; a giant maroon couch monopolized the floor. The sofa looked to have been built in the 1950s. The cushions were so large that if you sat all the way back on it, your feet wouldn't touch the ground.

The wedding reception was held in the Mannursing Island Club, overlooking Long Island Sound. White columns framed the entrance, and lush plants hung from the open windows that reached from ceiling to floor. A breeze, cooled by the coastal currents, blew through.

Upstairs, the bar was packed. Almost immediately Bronko and Karen ran into the groom, a young firefighter and bagpiper named Danny McEnroe. They offered their congratulations to him. As usual, Bronko knew plenty of people, and he made the rounds, chatting and joking. Karen knew a couple of people, too. Bronko introduced her to his friend Tim Grant, and Tim talked with her while Bronko went to the bar.

Tim was the band's pipe major, and had been for almost two years. The pipe major, second only to the band chairman in the leadership hierarchy, was in charge of choosing all music, running band practices, and tuning members' instruments before performances. Usually, the pipe major marched in the front line of the pipers' formation, on the band's far right side as they faced forward. He appointed a series of men below him, called pipe sergeants, to assist with the more onerous duties like tuning—going around to each piper and holding a tuning instrument at the tips of the drones to make sure they all matched the same pitch. While appearances led most to believe that Liam was the leader of the band, since he called the tunes and marched in front, Tim was actually the one who controlled the musicians and quietly told Liam which tunes to shout.

When Tim was a young boy, his father had taken him every year to watch the Manhattan St. Patrick's Day parade. Tim would hang on the edge of the police barricades and gaze at the various bagpipe bands as they marched past, skirling majestic-sounding music. Tim's father's parents had been born in Ireland, so when Tim was growing up, Irish folk songs were played frequently at his house. As a teenager, Tim bought the FDNY bagpipe band's record album. Sometimes, as the record spun on his turntable, he studied the photo on the front, which showed the twenty-seven smiling members of the band posing in full red uniform before a backdrop of the daytime New York City skyline featuring the Twin Towers. On the back was a black-and-white shot of two firefighters climbing a ladder into a smoldering building, with an inset photograph of the band members wearing their firefighting gear.

Tim thought he might join the Marines after high school but decided that what he really wanted to do was become a firefighter. He took the test in 1987, when he was twenty years old. He scored high, but five thousand or more firefighters made it onto the list that year, and so he had to wait. In the meantime, he went to college at SUNY Cortland and obtained a business degree. But the fire department, and the bagpipe band, stayed on his mind. One day he doodled a drawing of a leprechaun playing the bagpipes, which he thought he might have tattooed on his leg, but he never went through with it.

Tim had met and befriended Bronko in July 1993, when they were both in the same class in probie school at the Fire Academy. The next summer, Tim saw the FDNY bagpipe band play at the Fire Department's Medal Day ceremonies. He admired the way the drum major, then Big Jim, held his chest and head high and the way he commanded the rest of the band. When the pipers began to play, loud and triumphant, the hairs stood up on the back of Tim's neck. Seeing them for the first time as a firefighter, he suddenly felt compelled to join them. When the event was over, he found Bronko, who was by then already a snare drummer in the band, and asked how he could get in.

Bronko introduced Tim to pipe major Tom McEnroe, a beefy firefighter with low-lidded, pale eyes and strawberry blond hair. The band was not giving any classes at the time, McEnroe explained in his usual all-business manner, but when Tim pressed he agreed to give him the sheet music so he could learn on his own. Like most of the firefighters in the band, Tim had never seriously played an instrument before. He bought a practice chanter in August and hired a private instructor. Tim picked up the tunes quickly. Many of them were already in his head, from listening to the Irish records his father had played.

That October, Tim began attending band practices and stood in the circle with the others, playing his bagpipes. One night, the band's founder, Jimmy Ginty, told them that a longtime member of the band was gravely ill. "Let's all take a knee and say a Hail Mary for our brother Don," he said. The forty-five firefighters in the room, dressed in sweatshirts and blue jeans, knelt together and murmured the familiar prayer. The demonstration of shared faith and brotherhood Tim witnessed that night struck him deeply.

In January 1995, less than six months after he'd started playing, Tim sat for an audition. He passed easily and was soon voted into the band, even though he wasn't part of a new class of pipers and hadn't served the traditional apprenticeship of marching with the color guard.

Marching in his first St. Patrick's Day parade that year was an event Tim regarded as one of the highlights in his life. Before the parade, his father gave him a crock of Tullamore Dew Irish whiskey, since the tradition among first-time pipers was to bring a bottle of whiskey to share with the rest of the band after the parade. Tim tucked it away at the gym where the pipers warmed up, then followed the other band members to 44th Street, where they tuned again. In the buzzing commotion, Tim focused on tuning his bagpipes so the instrument would sound its very best. Finally, the moment came. Tim fell into his spot in the formation, and Big Jim led the band out onto the street.

As soon as the pipers marched onto Fifth Avenue, the cheering rose to a near-deafening level. To Tim, standing in the midst of the shouting crowd was like being in Yankee Stadium after the home team had just won. He was so energized by the thousands of people who crowded the edges of the street to applaud and point, he nearly forgot about how he was piping. As the parade carried on, he grew winded and sweaty from marching and blowing, but the cheering pushed him forward.

What began as a jubilant cavalcade ended in melancholy. When Tim walked into the Armory for the band's post-parade celebration, someone told him that Big Jim had suffered a heart attack. Instead of using his crock of whiskey to toast his own entry into the band, he poured it for the others and they toasted Jim Corcoran.

Piping quickly became Tim's full-time hobby. He became a part of the Tumac clique, along with Kippy and Bronko and Liam. He launched a band Web site in 1997. In August that year, the band traveled to Ireland for a piping competition. During the trip, he arranged for the pipers and drummers to gather around his girlfriend, Tara, on the Cliffs of Moher. As the band played, he brought Tara to the center of the circle, got down on one knee, and proposed to her. Giggling with excitement and shock, Tara said yes. They married the next year.

After three consecutive terms as pipe major, or six years, Tom McEnroe decided it was time to step down. Even though Tim was one of the most recent additions to the band, he ran for the slot. With his energy and skill and the support of the younger block of pipers, he won the majority vote and was elected. He rose to the top fast, maybe too fast. He was only in his early thirties and was still "little Timmy Grant" to the veterans. Some saw him as callow, a showoff. Once, after Tim stood up during a band bus trip and gave a speech about his recent accomplishments—"I've started up a band Web site . . . I produced the band's first CD"—an observant new band member, Billy Murphy, rose and, as he was wont to do, began poking fun at various firefighters in the seats around him. When Billy came to Tim, he grandly mimicked his speech, emphasizing all the times he'd said "I." Billy's apt characterization stuck; band members still sometimes referred to Tim as "I," as in "What did 'I' have to say about it?" Even his best friends sometimes jokingly called him a "peacock." Tim didn't seem to mind.

Liam soon showed up at the reception. Bronko looked over at him and groaned. Liam was wearing a purple shirt, a patterned tie, and black cotton pants. "You screwed me!" Bronko shouted. At the last minute, Liam had decided he was too hot to wear the kilt. Karen laughed: "You're like a couple of women, I swear!" A TV set in the corner was showing a football game. Notre Dame's Fighting Irish, Bronko's favorite team, was playing. They were down 0–2 on the season. Bronko settled onto a bar stool near the set, lifted a glass of beer, and grinned for someone who paused before him with a flashing camera. He looked at Karen and smiled. Cocktail hour, he told her, was always the best time of the night.

Later, Karen and Bronko filled their plates from a buffet and sat down outside at a table with Liam and a few other guests and pipers from the band. When the music began, Karen jumped up and tried to drag Bronko onto the dance floor, but he refused. No, firemen don't dance. No, he'd rather talk to people. Not even for a slow song; he didn't like them much, either. So Karen danced with Liam's date, in the pulsing crowd at the center of the dance floor. The bride, Jeannie, spun by, still wearing her veil and long gloves. This night cemented the first moment of a halcyon life. A nurse marrying a fireman. Jeannie wished it would last forever. The boys hung out around the edges of the dance floor, drinking beers and shouting above the blaring music, making plans for their next trip. The lieutenant's exam was going to be held on October 26, and the usual crew wanted to take off right afterward for a celebration in New Orleans, another bachelors' weekend. They agreed on the date—November 2, 2001, it was.

Once night had fallen, forty or so members of the band lined up outside, preparing to march in the doors together and play a few tunes for the bride and groom. Liam stood at the front. He adjusted his tall black feather bonnet and grinned at Tim, who faced him from a few feet away, holding a small video camera. Tim had decided not to play that night. He brought out the camera to film the band instead, hoping to use the footage to create a promotional video for the band's Web site.

Behind Liam, the pipers began to skirl the tunes from a set called Irish III. First came "Twenty Men from Dublin Town," which the band played while outdoors. "Let Erin Remember" began as the pipers marched in.

> Let Erin remember the days of old
> Ere her faithless sons betrayed her
> When Malachy wore the collar of gold
> That he won from the proud invader
> When her kings with standards of green unfurled
> Led the Red Branch Knights to danger
> Ere the emerald gem of the Western World
> Was set in the crown of a stranger.

The brother and father of the groom, Tom McEnroe Sr. and Tom McEnroe Jr., led the pipers. They marched in two rows past Tim, who stood in the center, filming the men's faces. When the two bass drummers reached him, with their bulky drums at their chests, he had to step to the side to let them pass. The band reached the final bars of "Let Erin Remember" as the snare drummers came in. Tim zoomed in on Bronko, aiming his camera's light at his friend and following him as he strode by. Bronko had a way of subtly rolling his shoulders to the beat, swaying ever so slightly as he marched. His beret clung dignified over his close-cropped hair. The last tune of the set was "Dawning of the Day." The band formed a circle as they piped the notes to the song, played to a fast beat called a quick march.

> On Raglan Road on an autumn day,
> I saw her first and knew
> That her dark hair would weave a snare
> That I may one day rue.
> I saw the danger, yet I walked
> Along the enchanted way.
> And I said let grief be a falling leaf
> At the dawning of the day.

The pipers puffed heartily. A tenor drummer swung and swirled his white padded sticks in the air. The bass drummers swiped and pounded in unison, and the snare drummers drilled artfully on their drums. Most of the men wore black dinner jackets over white shirts, and, of course, everyone but Liam wore a kilt. Some of the men's bagpipes looked worn; ripped tassels and strings hung freely from the green corduroy bag covers. Every now and then, an odd squeak or squawk would escape from a piper whose instrument was out of tune or who hit a note half a beat later than the rest. But it was late in the evening, the drinks had been flowing freely, and none of the revelers seemed to notice. When the set was over, the crowd around them hollered and whistled; women screamed wildly in appreciation.

Liam stood at the center of the circle and hollered the call for the next set. "Shenandoah! America! Marine Corps! Ready! By the center, slow, march!" The band began to play again. Liam marched around the borders of the inner circle, swinging his mace and occasionally brushing accidentally against the chanter of a nearby piper. A few photographers elbowed into the circle, trying to negotiate the best shots. Karen stood in the crowd a few feet behind Bronko. She smiled, tucked her blond hair behind her ears, and clapped to the beat.

After the set, Liam reached for the bride's hand and pulled her into the center of the circle, and the groom followed. Danny's brother and father played a duet of "Amazing Grace" as the couple looked on. After one refrain, the whole band joined in. The bride and groom held each other, the smiles evaporating from their faces as the solemn notes sounded. When "Amazing Grace" finished, the band transitioned to an upbeat tune, "The Rakes of Mallow," a trilling, dancey reel they often played at weddings—only all the members didn't seem to know that was next, so just some played the first few notes until the rest caught up. The towheaded groom began to bob and looked down at his new bride. She whispered in his ear, her neck and shoulders stiff. She didn't want to dance to this. The groom stared blankly at her but obliged. He raised one hand to signal the band that one time through was enough, and they soon stopped. Liam called out the last tune, and the band began to follow him out the door. Tim aimed his camera at their backs. The guests clapped and cheered. As the sound of the pipes faded into the dark outdoors, the drummers' chopping lingered on, the stark skeleton of a tune that could no longer be heard.

CHAPTER

2

THE BRUNTON BROTHERS

Now plainly in the mirror of my soul
I read that I have looked my last on youth
And little more; for they are not made whole
That reach the age of Christ.

—Thomas Kinsella, "Mirror in February"

TOMMY Brunton's phone rang early in the evening on September 10. On the other end was his youngest brother, Vinny, calling to ask a favor. A friend's father had died. Tommy knew the man's son, Chip, who was from Engine 204, the company where Vinny had originally been assigned.

"Chip's looking for someone to play at his dad's funeral," said Vinny.

"Yeah, I can do that," said Tommy. "No problem."

For Vinny, anything. Tommy was the oldest in a family of four children, and he never said no to his baby brother. There were three Brunton brothers, Irish triplets they were called, all about a year apart in age. Tommy was forty-six, then Mike, forty-five, and Vinny, forty-three. The youngest in the family was their sister, Maryann, who had just turned forty. They'd grown up in Windsor Terrace, a close-knit, largely Irish Catholic enclave in Brooklyn.

The Brunton boys were a rambunctious trio aged five, four, and two when their parents first moved into the sturdy brown brick house on 16th Street in 1962. As the boys grew, their mother dressed them alike in blue Yankees caps and coats and bought them the same red plaid swimming trunks. They jostled each other on the way to Holy Name grammar school, played stickball in the street, and prodded sweet little Vinny into singing the jingle from a commercial—"Winston tastes good like a cigarette should!"—so they could all get a free piece of candy at the corner store.

The brothers continued to live at home after high school, working blue-collar jobs during the day, drinking at the neighborhood pubs at night. All three also worked bartending jobs. Vinny tended bar at the corner pub, Farrell's, and took a job as a security guard. Tommy worked loading furniture, which paid well, but it didn't include benefits and wasn't the kind of labor he fancied doing his whole life. When Tommy and Vinny were in their early twenties, they decided to become firefighters and enrolled at the Fire Academy together. Vinny always seemed to score higher on the tests than Tommy, but their competition was lighthearted. Mike had a good-paying job with United Parcel Service, but a few years later he, too, got on the job as a fireman.

Eventually Tommy and Mike became lieutenants in different engine companies in Brooklyn, and Vinny became a captain. Whenever a firefighter met Maryann for the first time and learned that her three brothers were firefighters, he'd inquire about their last name. She'd answer, "Brunton," and the firefighter would say, "Oh, Vinny!" It was always the same. Everybody seemed to know and respect Vinny.

Vinny had been an athlete in high school, a top player on the Holy Name basketball team even though he stood barely five-foot-eight. Now his reddish hair was beginning to thin at the crown, but he continued to jog almost every morning. He ran outdoors on the hottest summer days, when it was ninety-five degrees and chokingly humid, and on days when it rained. Even if he'd been out drinking late into the night, Vinny would rise early and head out the door for a tour around the neighborhood. He thrived on the basic thrills in his Brooklyn life—going to Yankees games with his friends and brothers, setting up tailgate grills and cracking open coolers full of beer before Giants football games, lying out in the summer sun to add color to his fair skin.

Tommy wasn't much taller than Vinny, but he exuded the tough attitude of a hardened scrapper, a guy who threw his share of punches in brawls as a kid and more often than not came out on top. Tommy wore his gray hair in a crew cut and was a two-pack-a-day smoker. He could be foul-mouthed and brash around men, but in the company of women he'd transform seamlessly into an utter gentleman who pulled out chairs, held doors, and mindfully adjusted "fuckin'" to "freakin'" and "breaking balls" to "busting chops." People enjoyed being around

Tommy. He was an entertainer. After a few beers, he often recounted dirty limericks and off-color stories that were so crude people couldn't help but giggle at them.

Tommy was also an artist, who quietly painted and designed logos in his free time at home or in the firehouse. An image of a group of pipers he'd drawn appeared on the back of the band's T-shirt.

He joined the pipe band in 1997, in one of the few endeavors of his life that did not involve the close circle of friends and family he had in Brooklyn. Being in the pipe band meant being a part of an elite group within the Fire Department. Like a catcher in a baseball game who is in on every play, the pipe band was front and center at every major event. The pipes were difficult to master and, to Tommy, somewhat eerie in their ability to move people to tears. He'd always loved the sounds they made, and he looked up to the men who played them. In his heavily Irish Catholic neighborhood, "stand-up guys" were the ones everyone respected. To Tommy, being in the band was a way to be one of them.

Mike, the middle brother, was the bull-headed one. He had a fiery temper and a stocky build, with wide shoulders, a round face, and a chin that seemed to lock down over his neck. Mike and Vinny looked the most alike of the three brothers—they resembled their father, while Tommy and Maryann both had their mother's narrow face and wide, soulful eyes—but their personalities couldn't have been more different. Vinny rarely got angry; he was gentle and had a wise way about him. Things just didn't bother him the way they did Mike. When Mike and Tommy bickered, Vinny would step in, tell them they were both being jerks, and calm them down. Friends who knew all three brothers often mistakenly took Vinny for the oldest.

The Bruntons' mother died in the mid-1970s, and their father in 1981. By that time, Vinny was living with his new wife, Kathy, and their baby in a cramped, one-bedroom apartment down the street. He and Kathy had known each other since they were in eighth grade. They grew up a few blocks from each other, ran in the same circles, and celebrated birthdays that were just a week apart. Kathy was a tomboy who played basketball and baseball with the boys at the park. She was seventeen when Vinny approached her one night in a pub, looking for a partner at the pool table. She picked up a pool cue, and that was it. In later years, Kathy wouldn't remember how well they played or if they even won that night. She'd like to think that they did.

Kathy was twenty when she found out she was pregnant. There was no time for a romantic proposal, no money for a lavish honeymoon. She and Vinny rushed to their parish priest, Father Gildea, and asked if he would marry them. "Could I still wear a white dress?" Kathy asked. The priest smiled sagely. "Of course you can," he told her. "You only get married once." They exchanged vows at a low-key service that April. Their first child, a daughter named Kelly, was born six months later.

Vinny worked overtime to pay the bills. Kathy quit her job to stay home with the baby. Money was tight. Mike was single, still living at home and making fourteen dollars an hour for UPS. He bought Vinny and Kathy a car and pressed his extra cash into their hands, though they never asked for it.

After the Bruntons' father died, Mike, the executor of his will, suggested that Vinny and Kathy move into the house and make it their own. Soon the three-bedroom home was crowded: Vinny, Kathy, baby Kelly, Mike, and Maryann all lived there together. Tommy had moved out and had a new baby of daughter of his own with his wife, Mary, but he often came around to be with the others. Kathy loved it. She cooked big breakfasts for everyone, trying her hand at being a mom to all. Friends and relatives streamed in and out of the door to dote on the new baby. No one ever knocked. There was never any need to. The house was alive and bustling again.

Vinny and Kathy had another baby, a son named Thomas, a couple of years later. Tommy and Mary had two more children. Mike married and moved into a family home with his wife, and they soon had three sons. When Maryann's wedding day arrived, Tommy walked her down the first third of the aisle, Mike waited near the edge of a pew to walk her down the second third, and Vinny took her the rest of the way.

As years passed, their children grew, but other than that things hardly changed. Vinny rose to the rank of captain in the Fire Department but still held on to his side job at Farrell's. His brothers and their families lived nearby. Everyone always gathered at the house for Monday night football, for Vinny's famously elaborate summertime barbecues in the backyard, for Christmas and Easter and birthdays and plenty of less-than-special occasions in between.

Tommy sometimes felt that he and Vinny lived parallel lives. They'd gone to probie school together, had their first and second children within months of each other, worked the same jobs as bartenders and firefighters. They saw each other so often, there was no need for lengthy phone conversations. And they definitely weren't the kind who said "I love you" to each other. But on the night of September 10, the oldest brother chatted with his youngest brother for a while longer than usual.

"So what, are you working tonight?" Tommy asked.

"Yeah, I'm doing the first half of a mutual with the other officer," Vinny answered, meaning he would work the night shift, from 6:00 P.M. to 9:00 A.M., plus the following day shift, 9:00 A.M. to 6:00 P.M. Another lieutenant, Bill Burke, was Vinny's "mutual partner" at the firehouse. They paired up to exchange shifts so they could each work twenty-four-hour tours, or what firefighters called "mutuals." Burke's son would be celebrating his birthday on September 11, so Vinny had agreed to cover Burke's 9:00 A.M. to 6:00 P.M. shift that day. In exchange, Burke would cover Vinny's Wednesday day tour so that Vinny could be at his bartending job at Farrell's by 4:00 P.M. "When do you have to go in?" Vinny asked.

"I'm going in Wednesday night," said Tommy.

"Yeah," said Vinny. "Same shit, different day."

"All right. Have a safe tour," said Tommy before adding, as he habitually did, "I'll see ya when I see ya."

With that, the brothers hung up the phone.

Vinny hustled upstairs and got ready for work. The summer heat lingered late into the evenings. He and Kathy had experienced a revival in their relationship over the past few months. They had been the first of all their friends to get married. Now, at age forty-three, they were feeling like they were eighteen again. They went out nearly every night, almost always to local bars. Their kids were grown, still living at home but largely on their own, independent of their parents. Watching some of their friends in their forties just starting to have babies made them feel more carefree than ever. They did whatever they wanted to do. "Are you ever gonna take me out to eat, Vinny?" Kathy would tease. "Or are we just going to have a nosh?" It was usually the latter, either a late-night fry in the kitchen or a plate of greasy pub food in the bar, but that was okay with her. When they didn't go out in the neighborhood, they took impromptu trips to Atlantic City, to the Jersey Shore, once even to an island in the Caribbean. Vinny had taken up golf. Kathy held two jobs, working at a local school and assisting in the chemotherapy center at the nearby hospital a few nights a week. In the summer, when school was out, she had plenty of free time. If Vinny was working a night in the firehouse and she was off, he'd sometimes call and ask if she was going out that night. "Not tonight, are you kidding?" she'd say. "Why not?" he'd answer. "If I was home, I'd be out."

Vinny had spent his entire career as a firefighter in Brooklyn, first at Engine 204, then at Ladder 131 in Red Hook, and later at Ladder 176 in Brownsville. Over the years, he'd been recognized for valor six times. He'd received two Class III medals, awarded to a firefighter who submits himself to unusual personal risk in order to save someone; two Class-A medals for individual acts of personal bravery; and two unit citations, which the department awards an entire company for its outstanding work in a perilous fire rescue. At an apartment blaze on Sackett Street, Vinny had climbed up a gooseneck ladder at the rear of the building in search of an elderly man, reportedly trapped on the floor above the fire. He found the man, threw him over his shoulder, and carried him to the window. Just as he was handing the man to another firefighter, who was waiting at the window on the ladder, the man told him his senile wife was still somewhere inside. Vinny rushed back in. Flames were now licking up through the floor. He crawled through all the rooms, searching, and finally found her near the front of the apartment, unconscious. He dragged her back to the rear window and lifted her to his hip, then put one leg over the windowsill, struggling to balance her weight with his, and climbed down the ladder. The dangerous negotiation ended safely, and both husband and wife were saved. Vinny received one of his medals for that rescue, and another for a fire at which he brought out two women—one of whom had cerebral palsy and was confined to a wheelchair—from a top floor.

Faced with danger, Vinny worked and thought fast. Having lived and fought fires in the same neighborhoods for so long, he knew all the one-way streets in his area of Brooklyn, so if his chauffeur was unsure of the quickest way, Vinny could point him in the right direction without hesitation. He knew where every hydrant was.

At fires, Vinny refused to raise his voice. Yelling was contagious, and a shouting captain could ignite a wave of fear in his men. Vinny stayed calm, and his men followed suit. Afterward, Vinny could take a firefighter aside and explain to him what he'd done wrong by outlining what he had done right, and pointing out how he could do it better at the next emergency. He never made someone feel ashamed for his mistakes. Most of the time, a man left bolstered after a chat with Vinny, even if the reason for the talk had been something negative.

Now Vinny was the captain at Ladder 105, a firehouse located in Prospect Heights near downtown Brooklyn, which many called the

West Point of the Fire Department. Some dubbed it "the Chief's Son's House," because head honchos in the Fire Department who had boys just getting on the job often maneuvered to get them assigned there. When the company wasn't out responding to alarms, seasoned veterans led daily drills with the younger firefighters. Throughout Ladder 105 and Engine 219, with which it shared quarters, firefighters held a deep respect for all kinds of traditions that went back decades. Even the smallest details showed the quality of the company; for instance, everybody put down cash for the day's meal immediately, so nobody had to track down someone who'd neglected to pay. Every aspect of the firehouse ran efficiently, which made it a prime place for new firefighters to learn how to act on the job.

Vinny was assigned there initially when he received his promotion to lieutenant in 1994. Soon after he arrived, he met John Atwell, a recently appointed lieutenant at Engine 219. As they sat together in a back room upstairs on their first tour together, each man immediately began trying to feel out the other, to see what his political connections were or find out how he'd managed to get an assignment at that house. "Who's your father?" Atwell asked. Vinny shrugged and replied, "My dad worked for the phone company. Who's yours?" Atwell answered, "He was the man on the back step of Forty-eight," implying that his father was a top man at another firehouse. Vinny paused. Atwell broke in with a laugh. "My dad was in sanitation, in the Forty-eighth District." Vinny smiled broadly. Both had gotten there by luck or by merit, or more likely by the right combination of both. The two men soon became close friends.

Atwell admired the way Vinny handled things. If an officer in 105 asked Vinny to cover for him or exchange shifts, Vinny rarely said no. Even if he couldn't do it, because it was a Wednesday night and he was working his usual shift behind the bar at Farrell's, or if he had bought tickets to a weekend Giants football game, Vinny would always call back to see if an arrangement had been made. If not, he would volunteer to change his own plans to accommodate the other man.

Vinny didn't brag about his medals, either. He knew that every success was a result of teamwork, and each firefighter on the scene played a crucial role in the outcome. Besides, firefighters did not measure valor by number of medals. They encountered dozens of situations each year, even hundreds, that might merit recognition but didn't receive it. A hero one day could be a total screwup the next, and if your head got too big, the kitchen table could be a very humbling place.

One year on St. Patrick's Day, Atwell was out at a bar with Vinny and two others from the company; all of them had won several medals in the Fire Department—all except Atwell, that is. They encountered a group of civilians who noticed the colored bars on the men's chests and asked what they meant. Vinny and the others modestly explained that they were department citations for acts of bravery and tried to change the subject. The people turned to Atwell and asked why didn't he have any. Atwell answered, "Oh, because I'm the cook." Vinny chimed in, without missing a beat, "And a fine cook he is."

When Vinny was promoted to captain in May 2000, Atwell threw him a Hawaiian-themed party for his last dinner at the firehouse. He decorated the kitchen with leis and make-believe palm trees, and some of the men donned grass skirts and coconut bras. After that, Vinny bounced around, covering vacant captain slots at various firehouses in the 14th Division in northern Queens. Vinny knew that such firehouse transfers upon promotion came with the territory. Everyone had to do it. He never complained about his new assignments. When firefighters from 105 ran into men who now worked under Vinny, and who invariably spoke highly of their new captain, the Brooklyn men responded enviously, "You stole him from us."

Around the same time Vinny was promoted, his close friend Ed Moriarty, who had been the captain of Ladder 105 while Vinny worked there as a lieutenant, received his own promotion to battalion chief. Before long, Moriarty became executive assistant to Deputy Commissioner William Feehan, leaving the captain's spot open at 105. Usually the Fire Department balked at assigning a new captain to a firehouse where he'd served as a lieutenant, preferring to send him to one where he didn't know the men as well and could start out fresh with his new authority. But Vinny never had a problem earning respect from the people who worked under him.

Suddenly, Vinny had an "in," a close friend who worked in Fire Department headquarters, who could put in a good word for Vinny and possibly influence the location of his assignment. In addition, Moriarty himself had been a lieutenant at 105 and returned there as captain after stints in other firehouses. One day, Moriarty approached Vinny and asked what he would think about the possibility of going back to 105. Vinny's eyes lit up. Moriarty told him he'd work on getting him an assignment back in the 11th Division, where 105 was located, so Vinny could at least go back once in a while to cover when the new captain was on vacation or ill. Moriarty succeeded: That fall, Vinny received his assignment to the 11th Division, and by February 2001 he was back at 105 as the house's new captain.

Atwell was grateful to see his old buddy back. They often arranged their schedules so they could work together.

One night when Atwell and Vinny were working, the firehouse was called to respond to a fire in a four-story brownstone building on Ashland Avenue. The fire had ripped through the first floor and was threatening to engulf the second. Atwell and his men in the engine brought a line in on the first floor and began hosing down the flames. They extinguished the fire, backed out of the building, and progressed up the exterior stairs to the second floor to make sure no heat or fire remained. Meanwhile, Atwell noticed that Vinny, who had been with him just a moment ago, had disappeared. Then a window broke on the fourth floor. There was Vinny, climbing out the window and into the tower ladder bucket. Atwell sighed in relief. "Where'd you go?" he asked Vinny when he reached the ground. Vinny explained there had been a report of people trapped above, and he had just gone up the interior stairs to investigate. As it turned out, there was no one up there. "I knew you had it under control!" Vinny said. Atwell responded, with a laugh, "Don't trust me like that again!"

Their leader had returned. Vinny the captain was identical to Vinny the lieutenant.

CHAPTER

3

SEPTEMBER 11

Heroism feels and never reasons and therefore is always right.

—Ralph Waldo Emerson, *Essays: First Series*, "Heroism"

EVERY firefighter wanted to be at "the Big One," and Kippy Walsh didn't think he was any different. For the past seven years, Kippy had worked in Ladder Company 23, a firehouse located on 139th Street and Amsterdam Avenue in Harlem. Twenty-three Truck, as the firefighters called it, was known as an A-company, a busy firehouse located in the heart of the ghetto. The twelve firefighters who worked there, six in the ladder company and six in Engine Company 80 on any given tour, were experts at fighting fires in multilevel tenement buildings. When Kippy first started working there in 1995, the firefighters got calls to respond to several fires on nearly every shift—real fires, not just false alarms. But over the past few years, the action had slowed. A Starbucks coffee shop had opened on the corner near the firehouse. The neighborhood was gradually becoming gentrified, and so were the fires. Instead of being called to raging blazes that overtook several floors of an apartment building, the firefighters found themselves answering more and more calls for gas leaks, cooking fires, and faulty fire alarms.

Kippy craved more action, but he was too comfortable where he was to ever imagine requesting a different assignment. He had several longtime friends there, and he was fiercely loyal to those in his circle. Before he became a firefighter, he'd worked in construction as a heavy equipment operator and taken a side job as a bouncer in an Irish pub. He spoke in a loud voice, drove a motorcycle, and read the end of books first so he'd know how they were going to come out before starting at the beginning. At over six feet, Kippy was one of the biggest men in the house; one of his best buddies there was one of the shortest, a guy named Jerry Silcox who barely topped five-foot six. He and Kippy had met in probie school and stayed friends through the years. Kippy stood up for Silcox when others picked on him because of his small stature, but he also didn't hesitate to tell Silcox to shut up when he thought it was called for.

Earlier in their careers, when they both worked in the same firehouse, an afternoon fire broke out in a multilevel tenement on 148th Street and Broadway. Silcox was the engine chauffeur that day, which meant he was driving the rig and would stay outside the fire near the truck and attach the hoses to the hydrant. Kippy was detailed from the ladder to the engine that day and had the backup position. His role was to run into the building and stay behind the nozzle man, stabilizing the hose while the nozzle man aimed the water at the fire.

As soon as the fire trucks arrived on the scene, the firefighters could see the thick flames licking out of the upper floors. People were hanging out of the windows. Kippy hurried up the stairs with the nozzle man, and together they knelt several feet from the wall of flame and positioned the hose. Suddenly, the snaking hose went slack. The pumps had lost pressure. No water came out.

The fire raged closer, and Kippy and the nozzle man had two choices. They could hold their position and wait for the water to return, or they could retreat. If they waited, the fire could get out of control and they could be overcome by the smoke. But if they gave up their position, they wouldn't make any headway against the flames and more lives could be lost, more property charred and burned. They chose the option that created more danger to themselves: they decided to wait. They crouched down low to duck the rushing smoke. Down on the street, Silcox scurried around the back of the engine, trying to figure out what had blocked the hose. In the building above, seconds passed like hours. The wall of flame rolled toward them, growing angrier and hotter.

Finally, the hose jolted and puffed taut. Water trickled, then surged from the nozzle. With the water pressure restored, the firefighters got control of the fire. Silcox gained a new level of respect for Kippy that afternoon, not because of any daring heroics but because of what he saw as his friend's courage and stability. Faced with peril, Kippy had maintained his position.

Now that there were fewer of those massive fires, all the men working in 23 Truck had to adjust. Every alert still had to be taken seriously. When the large fires happened, the men still had to be sharp. They didn't wish a big fire on anyone; no firefighter ever did. Still, they pined for adventure, and like firefighters across the city, those of 23 Truck often took their leave of each other by saying, "I'll see you at the Big One."

Since the first bombing in 1993, World Trade Center jokes and pranks had become common in the firehouse. Less than a year earlier, Kippy had been a party to one of them. Kippy had been sitting inside the house watch—the small booth where the computers and main phones are—as an alert came over the intercom speakers. The dispatcher's voice announced a 10–75 at Box 69, the preliminary code for a fire near the World Trade Center. Moments later, the voice called a 10–76, the code for a high-rise fire, sending an additional engine company, two ladder companies, Rescue 3, and the Field Communications, Hazardous Materials, Mask Service, and High-Rise units to bolster the six fire trucks and dozens of firefighters already at the scene.[1]

Mark, another firefighter in the house, paced around the kitchen. This must be the Big One. The terrorists who truck-bombed the towers in 1993 had hit them again. Holy shit. Would they get sent down there? Holy shit. He'd better call his wife. The other firefighters urged him on. They knew his wife worked for CBS, and they told him to call so she'd get the tip, besides just to tell her he was okay. When Mark got her on the line, she told him she hadn't heard of any bomb or fire at the World Trade Center, but she'd check it out and call him right back.

Kippy hunkered in the house watch, trying to stifle a laugh with one hand while he held the intercom handset hovering over a cassette player with the other. The tape he played was from the 1993 World Trade Center bombing. At one point, he'd been giggling so hard that he lost his hold on the button that transmitted the sound across the firehouse, but Mark had been so frazzled he hadn't even noticed. A few minutes later, when Mark hung up the phone after talking with his wife for the second time, he knew the culprit immediately. He ran straight for Kippy.

On the evening of September 10, Ladder 23 went out on minor, annoying alerts a few times during the night. Normally the kitchen would have been buzzing with activity by 7:30 A.M., but on September 11 most of the men, Kippy included, were still dozing at about ten minutes to nine, when the dispatcher's voice woke them. "A second alarm has been transmitted for Box 8085," the voice said, indicating a progressing fire in the World Trade Center.

Kippy didn't believe the alert. He would be off duty at 9:00 A.M., and he figured it was probably somebody messing around. But when Kippy came downstairs, he saw men gathered around the TV set in the house watch. This time, when he saw their stony faces, he knew it was real.

At 8:46 A.M. on September 11, Tommy Brunton sat at his kitchen table at home, reading the newspaper. At 8:48 A.M., his wife, Mary, told him she was going out to the deli for some milk. On the way out the door, she passed the television set, which was on in the living room.

"Oh, my God," she called out to Tommy. "A plane just crashed into the World Trade Center."

Tommy abandoned the newspaper and rushed in to see.

"Motherfuck!" he shouted.

Tommy knew the World Trade Center was about an acre wide on each side. The instant he saw the size of the hole in the north facade of the north tower, he could tell it had been a commercial jetliner.

"That was done on purpose," he said as he rushed back into the kitchen, toward the phone.

"Don't you think you're jumping to conclusions?" she called after him.

Tommy picked up the phone and furiously dialed Vinny's firehouse. On the other end, a firefighter picked up after a couple of rings.

"Is Vinny there?" Tommy asked.

"Turn on the TV!" someone up front called to the men gathered around the kitchen table in the back room of Rescue 4.

Bronko Pearsall was among them. The rescue officer on duty was Lt. Kevin Dowdell, and others from Rescue 4 were Pete Nelson, Terry Farrell, and Pete Brennan. Al Tarasiewicz from Rescue 5 was there, along with Bill Waring and John Leimeister, two firefighters from Engine 292. A pot of fresh coffee was brewing on the countertop. By 8:00 that morning, the shift of new firefighters had just begun to arrive for the scheduled 9:00 A.M. to 6:00 P.M. tour. Most were regular members of the firehouse; a few, like Tarasiewicz, were "details," men who worked at different companies and were assigned to cover an empty slot there for the day.

Firefighters always came to work early. Usually the crew that was about to be let off would gather at the kitchen table for an informal chat with the incoming group about what had happened on the previous shift. If there'd been a big fire, the guys who'd responded would recount all the inside details. If there'd been false alarms, they'd tell of those, too: How they'd been called out at 2:00 A.M. and wriggled into their skintight wetsuits to save a man who'd reportedly jumped into Flushing Bay, only to discover the call was a drunken prank. Or how many times over the night rescue had been called out to a fire way across the borough, only to be sent back because the nearby ladder and engine companies had it under control. Those chain-jerks happened all the time to a rescue company; they were the modern version of the false alarms that had plagued the department decades earlier. Although the rescue squads specialized in rope operations, car extrications, and other tricky rescues, sometimes the ladder guys could do the same work—and, in fact, did it all the time before the rescue companies were instituted in 1915. But rescue firefighters took special training in void searches—voids are spaces created when a structure collapses—and learning how to pull people from all kinds of delicate entrapments. They took pride in their advanced skills.

After a slow shift, the conversations hopped from the results of the Yankees or Mets game to the latest union gossip to the teasing of selected firefighters seated around the table. Three members of Rescue 4 were also members of the band, and Lt. Kevin Dowdell had two teenage sons, Patrick, nineteen, and James, seventeen, who played in pipes and drums bands at their high schools, so band matters or pipe music sometimes came into the conversation. Kevin even took up banging on a bass drum so he could march in St. Patrick's Day parades with his sons. A firefighter going off duty could get relieved as soon as his replacement arrived, if he had to be somewhere. But most of the time, whether there was big news or not, the men lingered until the voice came over the intercom to announce the official time of the shift change, either 0900 hours or 1800 hours, and only then got up to leave.

A friend of Bronko's named Michael Cawley was also at the table that morning. Michael was a member of Ladder 136 in Queens, but he had come in for the night tour on September 10 to cover for another firefighter in Engine 292, as he'd done a few times before. Michael's father was a fire buff who'd hoped to get into the Fire Department as a young man but couldn't because his eyesight was too poor. When Michael was little, his father had taken him around to firehouses near their house in Jackson Heights, and Michael played on the fire trucks and posed for photos with the firemen. The firefighters got to know little Michael so well that sometimes when they drove by in the rig they'd spot him with his dad on the sidewalk and yell out the window, "Hey, there's Michael Cawley!" And the little boy would wave back as they passed. He collected miniature fire trucks and pushed them around the floor, pretending they were speeding to imaginary fires. He once drew a picture of a fire truck in his composition book and wrote the number 292 on the rig. His parents couldn't figure out why he'd chosen that number, since his dad usually took him to a different company, Ladder 163 on 51st Street.

He'd graduated from a college in upstate New York with a political science degree, then signed up to take the fire exam. He trained for the physical portion by running up and down stairs carrying a knapsack full of sand. For three months before the test, Michael ate only pasta, bagels, and bananas and got his weight down to 200 pounds from his previous 230. The day after he took the written test, he prowled anxiously around his parents' house, lamenting to his mother over and over, "I think I only got a ninety-nine." As it turned out, he achieved a perfect score on both the physical and written portions of the test.

But there were hundreds of others who'd also achieved high scores, so while he waited to get an assignment, Michael continued to work a variety of jobs—bartending, pounding nails at construction sites, driving a truck delivering meat, even working as a security guard at a Victoria's Secret store. After Michael eventually became a firefighter, he called his father whenever he returned from a big job. Margaret, Michael's mother, wouldn't panic when the Cawleys' phone rang in the middle of the night. She knew it'd be Michael, calling to tell his dad about another fire.

Michael and Bronko were buddies from the FDNY football team. They'd worked the door at the same bar for a stretch and hung out together every year after the St. Patrick's Day parade. Upon meeting Margaret for the first time, Bronko told her that he was in the bagpipe band. Margaret stared at him and laughed. Surely he couldn't be serious, she thought. He just didn't look the part.

Michael knew Bronko was studying for the lieutenant's exam. He, too, wanted to move up in the Fire Department, but in a different way.

Lieutenants got paid more, but they also had to do more paperwork. Michael just wanted more action. When he filled in at Engine 292, he could be near the guys in rescue, and talk to them about the advanced training operations they did. He was serious about fire operations, but his joking manner fit in perfectly with the atmosphere of sick nonsense that pervaded the firehouse. He had some Irish heritage on his father's side, and although he hadn't told Bronko or Liam yet, he'd recently bought a set of bagpipes, which he'd stowed in his locker at his firehouse, awaiting the right moment to bring up to one of them that he'd like to get into the band.

Liam had been on duty for the day tour on September 10 and was relieved at 6:00 P.M. When the hour was announced over the intercom that night, he and Bronko left the kitchen conversation and went upstairs together to their lockers. Michael followed them up.

Rescue 4 had an opening for a new man. In Michael, Liam saw a reflection of himself. They came from similar backgrounds. Both were handy with tools. And Michael's drive and his desire to move up on the job mirrored his own. Liam told Michael, "You'd be a good guy to come over to Rescue 4." Bronko agreed, Michael would be perfect.

Rescue men usually got their assignments through a process of recommendation. Pedigree was a consideration—having worked in a busy house and having moved from an engine to a ladder company was key—but knowing others in rescue who wanted you in was equally important. Liam had been recommended by other men he knew in order to get into rescue, and once he had his assignment there, he and a friend named Mike Meyers had talked up Bronko to the senior men in the house until Bronko eventually got his assignment there in 1999. Rescue work was highly dangerous, but they covered each other's backs. Even while they were focused on saving a person in need, they always watched out for each other. The best kind of rescue firefighter was one who was in tune with the brothers. Adding men who were just like the ones already there helped the company run smoothly.

Since Liam was leaving for band practice, Bronko told him he would mention Michael to Lt. Kevin Dowdell, who was the officer on duty that night. Liam picked up his bagpipe case. Before he walked out the door, he got in one last jab at Bronko, who was staying on duty through the night and would be relieved at 9:00 A.M. the next day. "What are you doing working, you idiot?" Liam said to him. "Oh yeah, it must be Monday night. You're working."

Bronko rarely made it to band practice. He always seemed to have something else going on, or else, like that night, he'd scheduled himself to work.

"You're never where you're supposed to be," Liam said, in his brusque Brooklyn accent that refused to recognize the *r* sound at the end of words, flattening it to *ah.* Then he got into his car and drove away.

Later that night, the sound of wailing pipes could be heard in the darkening daylight as the band members rehearsed inside the fortress-like Elks Lodge on Queens Boulevard, about fifteen blocks from Rescue 4. A couple of hours into the practice, Liam stepped outside, pulled out his cell phone and dialed Bronko at the firehouse. Bronko told him he'd talked to Lieutenant Dowdell about recruiting Michael to Rescue 4, and he was all for it. Then Dowdell came on the line. "I love 'im," he said to Liam. Michael would schedule an official interview and get his paperwork started for the transfer assignment. Liam clipped his cell phone shut, satisfied.

Bronko did house watch duty overnight. House watch duty was considered the most undesirable post in the firehouse, especially the late watch, since the firefighter in that post had to remain relatively alert, answer the phone if it rang during the night, stay closed off from the rest of the firehouse, and grab what sleep he could in the least comfortable bed. But everyone had to do it now and then.

Rescue 4 was called out to a fire at 5:22 A.M., and Michael rose to cover the house watch for Bronko while he was away. Bronko and the firefighters returned and signed back in in the large book they kept in front, called the house watch journal, at 5:37 A.M. Their services had not been needed after all. Bronko came back to cover the house watch, relieving Michael.

The morning of September 11, at 8:00 A.M., fresh names were inked into the house watch journal, where every visitor, every new tour, just about every official activity that happened in the firehouse was noted. "Lt. Dowdell, COD, Farrell, COD," meaning that Kevin Dowdell and Terry Farrell were assigned to carry-on duty, working a twenty-four-hour tour from 6:00 P.M. the night before through to 6:00 P.M. that night. Below them, "Mahoney, R4, RFD, FF Brennan, FF Nelson R4 RFD," for Billy Mahoney, Pete Brennan, and Pete Nelson, the firefighters who were reporting for duty. At 8:47, a visitor entered the firehouse: a general contractor.

Moments later, John Gaine, an off-duty firefighter from Rescue 4, phoned the firehouse to see if the guys knew what was going on. Pete Brennan answered the call from the house watch.

"Are you watching the news?" Gaine asked. Brennan said no, then set down the phone to flick on the television.

Lt. Al Maurer, the engine officer on duty, led the contractor upstairs to discuss renovations in the office area and the possibility of adding a women's bathroom. He heard someone yell to turn on the television.

On the apparatus floor below, firefighters began scurrying around, gathering equipment, stepping into their bunker pants, yanking the suspender straps over their shoulders. They expected the alarm to come through any second. Though Rescue 4 was located in Queens, the company was often called to respond to serious high-rise fires in Manhattan.

Terry Farrell, who was assigned as Rescue 4's chauffeur and drove the rig during that tour, hurried up front to the house watch with John Leimeister. They stepped up into the elevated booth and looked up at the TV screen.

"This doesn't look good," Farrell said.

Finally, the alarm sounded from above. The computer screen began to flash, and a ticket shuttled out of the dot matrix printer. Rescue 4 was going. Leimeister said, "Be careful," to Farrell, his friend of ten years. "You be careful, too," Farrell answered as he climbed into the driver's seat of the enormous fire truck. "We'll see you down there."

In the back, near the kitchen, Michael Cawley asked Lt. Dowdell, "Think I could jump on?"

Bill Waring saw Cawley climb in the back door of Rescue 4's rig. The truck pulled away. It all happened so fast, Waring imagined that most of the guys in Rescue 4 must have climbed on the rig and been waiting to go before the official call ever came in.

The rig made a right turn out of the firehouse door, just as a firefighter who thought he was coming to relieve Cawley stepped out of his car. He lifted his hand in a wave and watched as the men drove away.

More alarms came over the intercom at the firehouse of Ladder 23 and Engine 80, as more fire companies were called to respond. Ladder 23 was not one of them. Engine 80 was a Certified First Responder with Defibrillation (CFR-D) unit, so the firefighters began packing boxes with all the medical equipment they could find—splints, bandages, rolls of gauze, ice packs. Their adrenaline surging, they expected they would be called soon.

In a moment of downtime, Kippy thought of his friend Liam. He'd often heard Liam telling stories of gutsy rescues and dangerous fire situations he'd been in, thinking nothing of the potential threats to himself, only of helping others. Kippy was certain Liam would be down there.

Liam Flaherty's phone had been ringing oddly that morning. A short ring, then nothing. When it rang again, he picked it up.

"Oh, thank God, you're not working," Liam's sister Maureen said. She was just a year younger than Liam. They looked alike—same round face, curly black hair, and big-boned frame—and they talked alike. They'd even invested in a business together, an optician's franchise in midtown Manhattan, which Maureen ran.

Liam didn't know what his sister meant by that. He'd awakened a few minutes before and was puttering around his small apartment, starting to get laundry together. He hadn't turned on the TV or radio; he rarely did in the mornings. His apartment in the Bay Ridge section of Brooklyn gave a clear view of the Twin Towers. Though no curtains blocked the sliding glass door that led to the balcony overlooking Manhattan, Liam had not looked outside.

"Liam, did you see that a plane hit the World Trade Center?" Maureen asked. "There was a plane crash."

He rushed to the window and saw a snaking plume of black smoke pouring from one of the towers. Liam thought of the hundreds, maybe thousands of people in offices above the impact zone who were likely to die. He told Maureen he was going to head over there.

Maureen burst into tears. She begged him to wait. She asked him to find out if their sister Denise's husband, John Fowler, was working. And she had just dropped off a friend at the airport. Maybe Liam could find out what flight number had crashed, so she could know that her friend was okay. Liam agreed to check, and they hung up. Liam rushed out the door.

"Nah, they left. They went out," answered the firefighter from Ladder 105 on the other end of the line.

Tommy's stomach dropped.

"Did they go to the Trade Center?" Tommy asked.

"Yeah, they went to the Trade Center."

"Did they get relocated there or did they get assigned to go to the building?"

A relocation meant Ladder 105 might have gone to fill in at a firehouse near the World Trade Center, where the company would sit in quarters and be held as backup. An assignment meant the firefighters would be responding to the scene of the fire.

"No, they transmitted a third alarm box from Brooklyn," the firefighter answered. The company was at the scene.

Ladder 105 was minutes away from midtown Manhattan, a short jaunt over the Brooklyn Bridge. Tommy thanked the firefighter and ran upstairs to get dressed.

At 9:03 A.M., Kippy watched, wide-eyed, as the second hijacked plane crashed into 2 World Trade Center. Many thought an explosion had occurred, triggered by bombs in the north tower. But minutes later, the news replayed the footage, and the firefighters saw the Boeing 767 tilt its wings and drill straight into the building. The purpose was undeniable. New York City was under attack.

Kippy's wife, Mary, was a veterinary technician, and that morning she'd been on her way to help pull a trapped dog out of a fence when she heard news of the attack. She called Kippy at the firehouse. He told her he was getting off duty and would be home soon.

Kippy hurried around with the others, filling boxes with supplies and pausing to check the TV every now and then. Smoke poured from the towers. Kippy saw people jumping from the top floors of both buildings.

Karen called her brother's cell phone all morning but couldn't get through. He worked at the New York Stock Exchange in lower Manhattan, near the towers. Finally he called her back. He asked about Bronko, had she heard from him? Karen said no, but Bronko worked in Queens. She thought firefighters in Rescue 4 stuck to fires within their borough, which they usually did. She couldn't see any reason why he would be down there. But she called him anyway, just in case, and left two messages on his cell phone. When she didn't hear back right away, she called Rescue 4, and someone on the phone told her he thought Bronko and Liam might be down there, but he wasn't sure. Then she started to panic.

Finally Ladder 23 got the call to go downtown, not to respond to the fires at the World Trade Center but to fill in at Engine 54 and Ladder 4 on 48th Street and Eighth Avenue. Ladder 4 had responded to the scene, and Ladder 23's truck was needed there to stand by as backup. At least they would be nearer to the site. The six firefighters on duty at Ladder 23 rushed onto the rig. As the truck's engine roared and it began to pull out of the garage door, the lieutenant called out to Kippy, who was technically off duty, standing in the house watch.

"Kippy, want to jump on?" he asked from the passenger's seat.

Kippy glanced inside the truck. Where would he sit? There were six seats—all were taken. And he didn't have a mask. There were six masks already in the truck, one for each man on duty. How effective could he be down there without a mask?

"You want to come?" the lieutenant called out again.

Kippy shook his head. "I'll catch up later," he said.

Liam sped through the side streets of Brooklyn. When he arrived at Union Street, several blocks from the Brooklyn Bridge, traffic snarled and came to a standstill. He jerked his head around, trying to figure out what to do. Would he park the car and run over the bridge? He looked up through his windshield at the burning towers. On the radio, the announcer was saying that a recall had been issued for all New York City firefighters. That meant every active firefighter who was not on duty was required to report to his or her firehouse. He looked out his side window and recognized a firefighter from Squad 252 in a car next to him. That firefighter told him he was going to go back to his firehouse. Liam decided to do the same. He maneuvered out of the traffic jam and made his way north to Queens. As he approached his firehouse, he reached his brother-in-law John on his cell phone. John was working, but his company did not go to the site.

Then the voice on the radio grew urgent. Liam heard a female reporter screaming, "Oh, my God!"

Kippy felt a stinging regret over the split-second decision he'd made. Maybe Engine 80 would get called down. Maybe he would go with them. But he still wouldn't have a mask. What would it matter, really? He should be there. But what if the engine company didn't get called down? His inner rage grew. He should have jumped on when he had the chance.

Then the men got word that Engine 59's spare rig was going to head downtown. (Engine 59, down the street from Ladder 23, is a part of the three firehouses that make up the local battalion—Ladder 30 and Engine 59, Ladder 28 and Engine 69, and Kippy's company, Ladder 23 and Engine 80.) The rig that was on its way had a spare set of tools and masks inside. The driver stopped at Engine 69 and picked up a few firefighters, then pulled into Ladder 23 to pick up the firehouse captain. Kippy and a couple of other firefighters started to climb onto the hosebed at the rear of the truck. The battalion chief told them to get off. He didn't want any guys hanging off the back of the truck, he said. They had to have their own equipment if they were going down. Kippy glared at the chief and yanked on the edge of his bucket jacket to demonstrate he was dressed, and he had his helmet on. But the chief shook his head and ordered them off. The coat wasn't good enough. They still had no masks or tools. Kippy jumped down and stormed into the kitchen. When the chief had turned his back, two other firefighters from Engine 80, Andy and Steve, piled on the hosebed anyway and caught a ride to the World Trade Center.

Kippy stood in the house watch and watched the towers burn on the screen. He could not reconcile himself to seeing it happen on television, not being down there to help.

Tommy picked up a firefighter in his neighborhood, whom he'd seen standing the street waiting for a bus to take him to Manhattan, and drove to his firehouse, Engine 310 in Flatbush, Brooklyn. Tommy gave the other man a set of his spare turnout gear. At the firehouse, everyone was rushing around, trying to coordinate a response team with the division. Suddenly, Tommy looked up and saw the television. The south tower was collapsing in a voluminous torrent of gray smoke.

Everyone froze. Not a word was spoken. Tommy felt sick to his stomach. "Jesus Christ," a firefighter uttered to no one in particular. "Do you have any idea how many guys we just lost?"

Everyone from Rescue 4 who hadn't been on duty that day seemed to arrive at the firehouse at the same time. All the men who'd been there when the first plane struck were now at the World Trade Center. To those who remained, waiting for an official order to report to the site was not an option. They snatched their tools and gear and went out onto the sidewalk, where they flagged down a passing city bus. The driver pulled up and told his passengers to get out, and fifteen or twenty firefighters climbed aboard. The bus driver immediately radioed his dispatcher and hollered that he was transporting the FDNY to the World Trade Center. He sped wildly down the streets, blaring his horn. The firefighters laughed at his moxie. "You want to be the next chauffeur for Rescue 4?" they joked.

Liam sat down in a seat near the front of the bus. He looked up and caught sight of a stiff-faced young probie standing in the aisle. He'd been selling shirts with them at the Irish fair just days before. This would be one of his first real fires. Liam wondered what must be going through the younger man's head. He told the probie to sit down next to him. "Relax, buddy," Liam said. "You're gonna see things you've never seen before in your life, a lot of stuff that nobody's seen before, so get your mind right." Liam told the probie what he told all the inexperienced firefighters he came in contact with. "When things are going bad, you should be getting calmer," he advised. "Panic is a bad thing. Fear is a counselor; don't let it be a jailer. All firefighters have fear. Acting in spite of it is what makes guys brave. All right?"

The probie nodded.

Maybe, with traffic being a horror show, people being evacuated, maybe Vinny's company got caught in a delay, Tommy thought to himself. But he knew Ladder 105 had responded early, too early for traffic to have held them back. Maybe they were in there and someone gave the call to evacuate.

Firefighters who'd reported late at Tommy's company, Engine 310, climbed into their cars and drove to the division quarters in Brownsville. They grabbed extra tools and commandeered a city bus. About a hundred men packed in, and they headed to Manhattan.

The closer the bus got to downtown Brooklyn, the more entangled the traffic became. Some men jumped out of the bus and ran ahead on foot, trying to tell drivers to pull aside so the bus could get through.

As the bus approached the Brooklyn Bridge, the second tower came down. From their vantage point, the firefighters on the bus couldn't yet see it. The news filtered in to men who had cell phones or radios with them.

Finally the bus came to a stop near City Hall. Tommy and the others climbed out into a massive dust cloud—particles of insulation, plasterboard, concrete, everything that had been pulverized when the towers fell. Tommy saw firefighters emerging from the smoke. Two men he knew came toward him, entirely encased in the gray debris. One's face was cut and bleeding; the other had a bloody nose. "Neil and Steve are dead," one man told him. They were good friends of Tommy's, firefighters in Engine 217 who'd owned a bar that Tommy and his brother Mike sometimes worked at on Staten Island. "How do you know?" Tommy asked. They'd been just heading into the north tower, the man answered, when a jumper landed on firefighter Danny Suhr right near them. Four of the men had stopped to help. Neil and Steve had been ten to fifteen yards ahead. They never saw the firefighter get hit, so they kept going.

Tommy led his men to a new command post on Vesey and Broadway, a few blocks from the collapse. Once there, he filled out a riding list, naming the men from his company who had responded with him. Tommy saw that the chiefs were trying to regroup and get a series of cohesive plans in motion. One of the chiefs gave Tommy and his men an assignment, to report to an area a couple of blocks south.

Walking down the dusty streets, it seemed to Tommy that everything around was burning. Cars were upended and crushed, lying on their roofs or on top of other cars, their tires burned away. Large chunks of debris flamed in the road. Some fire companies were trying to find water supplies and discovering that many hydrants weren't working. Water mains had been severed. Other men were climbing up on the outer edges of the debris pile, searching for voids that might hold some survivors.

At the second command post, Tommy and his men began stretching hose lines to get water to the ladders. Firefighters were trying to decide what to do about Building 7. A fire raged through it, engulfing the southwest corner from top to bottom, but heavy structural damage made entry too risky.

As Tommy worked, he began stopping firefighter after firefighter. He implored each man with the same question.

"Have you seen my brothers?" Tommy asked. "Seen Vinny? What about Mike?"

All morning long, the answer was no.

The bus coming from Queens stopped near the West Side Highway, and the firefighters from Rescue 4 jumped off. Both towers had fallen.

The silence was ominous. Everyone inside had to be dead, Liam thought, and everyone else had to have fled far away. There was barely a noise to be heard, save for an occasional explosion. Words passed through Liam's mind—Armageddon, World War III. A thick cloud of dust and smoke burgeoned over the entire area and reached hundreds of feet into the sky. The firefighters ran straight into it.

The first person Liam saw was a Fire Department chaplain, Father John Delendick, running toward him. The priest was covered in white dust. He'd been standing at a command post alongside some Fire Department chiefs when the first tower came down and had run for his life again after the second collapse. Many of the men he'd been with in those moments were dead, including Lt. Timmy Stackpole, Chief of Department Peter Ganci, and First Deputy Commissioner William Feehan. Delendick clutched Liam's arm and told him that Father Judge was dead. He pointed back at the smoke, where the remaining buildings around the World Trade Center towers stood but could not be seen through the thickness of the air. "That's pure evil back there," he said. Then he hurried away.

Liam kept moving forward. He passed a group of police officers, who told him there was a bomb inside the nearby Stuyvesant High School and they were fleeing the scene. Liam was skeptical. He ignored the warning. He glimpsed firefighters' gear lying on the ground—masks, breathing tanks called SCBAs (self-contained breathing apparatus) that they strapped onto their backs, and other tools. Whether guys had abandoned their equipment in their rush away from the towers or whether the owners were now dead, he didn't know. He bent to pick up items he did not have with him.

The approximately fifteen men from Rescue 4 split into two teams. Liam and his group began searching for survivors in 6 World Trade Center, also known as the U.S. Customs House. Fire had erupted on several floors of the eight-story building. Some floors showed structural damage and a partial interior collapse. Liam climbed the stairs. He didn't locate anyone inside. The air was heavily charged with smoke. He was grateful for the mask he'd found on the ground.

Some years earlier, when Liam was a carpenter, he and his uncle had constructed the ceiling and walls in the interior of an office on the 103rd floor of one of the towers. He remembered the layout of the plaza: There had been an underground shopping area near one of the subway entrances. As a rescue firefighter, he'd been trained in a six-sided approach to searching a collapse area—all four sides, top, and bottom. Now he thought of ways to get underneath, into that shopping area, to see if anyone was trapped.

As the morning went on, he lost track of the men in Rescue 4 and teamed up with firefighters from other companies. For a while he worked with firefighters from his old firehouse of Ladder 44; another time, with some men from Rescue 3. They assisted a couple of bloodied survivors, whom they found near the plaza area, and placed them in stokes baskets to be carried to safety. Liam didn't have his radio with him, but another firefighter from Rescue 3 had his. The firefighters heard Fire Captain Jay Jonas giving maydays over the airwaves. He said he was trapped in a stairway, in the north tower, Tower 1. Liam and the others scanned the debris pile. There was no telling where he could have been calling from. There was no more north tower.

At one point in the day, a civilian rushed over to Liam in a frenzy. "My sister! My sister!" the man pleaded, screaming and crying and tugging on Liam's shirt and jacket. "She was in the towers! You gotta go find her!" Liam reached for the man's hands and pried his fingers off him. "If she's alive," he said, "we'll find her."

The medical boxes were all packed. There was nothing more to do but wait. Kippy couldn't stay in the firehouse any longer. He had to do something to keep his mind off his frustration, the nagging feeling that he should have jumped on when he had the chance. Why hadn't he just gone?

Because of the recall, a few dozen firefighters would soon be arriving at the firehouse, so Kippy and a fellow firefighter drove to the nearby Fairway to go grocery shopping. When they returned, there were about forty men there—firefighters, bosses, and retired firefighters from Ladder 23 and Engine 80 who had reported for the recall. The battalion chief was still there. He told them buses would be arriving to take them to the site. Soon, he said. The buses would get there soon. In the meantime, they had to stay organized. They would report to Engine 69 and Ladder 28's quarters at 143rd and Eighth Avenue, several blocks away.

Hundreds of firefighters were already there by the time Kippy arrived. They formed a staging area outside the firehouse and piled their gear on the sidewalk. Many of the firefighters were men Kippy knew but hadn't seen in a while. Since they all worked in the same neighborhood, they were often assigned details at each other's firehouses to fill an empty slot on a shift. They shook hands and chatted.

Kippy walked into the firehouse and saw more firefighters—volunteer firemen and women, many of whom had come from companies in Long Island and upstate New York to stand by and help out as they could. The volleys, as Kippy called them, sat on the couches and crowded the doorways, blocking Kippy's way when he tried to move through. Kippy elbowed into the house watch to get a look at the TV and saw more volunteers being filmed at the scene. They were identifiable by their brown jackets and pants, lighter than the FDNY's black bunker gear. Kippy could scarcely believe his eyes. All it took to become a volunteer firefighter was to have no major felonies, to live or work in the area one served, and to be in "good" physical condition. Kippy looked at some of the heavier men lumbering around the firehouse. Obviously that health requirement wasn't too strict. By contrast, Kippy was slim and strong, a paid New York City firefighter, a trained professional and twelve-year veteran who would soon be promoted to lieutenant. But here he was, being held back from responding to the scene, while there were part-timers, freakin' volleys, right there in the center of the action—and right here taking up space on the couches in his battalion's firehouse.

Outside Engine 69 and Ladder 28, the firefighters were growing agitated and resentful. The bosses were upstairs, their office doors shut. No one knew what they were talking about in there. It would have been okay for the volunteers to stay and man the firehouses as long as the city firefighters were allowed to go. But being in the same vicinity as the volunteers, sitting there waiting for a bus that had been promised to arrive hours before, made the men aggressive and angry. "When are they gonna send us down there?" they asked each other. "Where's the bus, chief?"

The Bruntons' sister, Maryann, walked into Kathy and Vinny's house at around 3:00 P.M. The living room and kitchen were full of relatives and friends, the air heavy and tense; people anxiously rubbed each other's shoulders at the dining room table and passed tissues around. Grim voices came from the kitchen. The TV in the living room was turned on, but Kathy avoided it, blocking her ears against the panicky tones of the news.

Maryann took an apprehensive step into the living room. As soon as she looked at Kathy, she began to cry.

"Don't!" Kathy pushed out her palm and shouted in her husky voice. "Don't you do that. He's fine."

Kathy told the people in her house over and over, "He won't call me. He's busy working. He's helping people. He won't call until he's done."

Later in the day, someone finally said yes to Tommy Brunton. Someone had seen his brother Mike at the pile. Tommy and Mike found each other moments later.

All afternoon, information passed from person to person. Rumors of the dead multiplied. First Tommy heard it was 150 firefighters, then 300, then 500. Some bits were true—Ganci was dead, Feehan was dead—but even the truth was disorienting. How could the top men in the department be gone? That *never* happened. As the two brothers walked through the streets, they saw firefighters sitting on curbs, holding their heads in their hands. The devastation was too much to comprehend. Tommy had heard that Chief Pete Hayden was dead. Tommy had worked with his brother, Jack, and had known them both for fifteen years. Then he saw Pete walking toward him, out of the smoke. "I thought you were dead!" Tommy said to him, astonished. He heard Pete answer, "I can't fucking explain to you why I'm not."

Tommy and Mike came upon a fire chief who had a list of missing companies—not missing firefighters, but entire companies in which a crew of five to eleven men, as many as could fit on the truck that morning, were all gone. The officer was rattling off the missing companies' numbers. Firefighters swarmed around him in a huge crowd. They bombarded him with questions about individual men. The chief's face was stern. He had close to seventy-five company numbers before him. Names of people were not on his list.

The officer barked out, "Ladder 132, unaccounted for. Ladder 101, unaccounted for."

Tommy waited a few moments, then gradually made his way through the crowd and sidled up to the chief. Mike followed.

"What about Ladder 105?" asked Tommy.

The officer ran his finger up and down the list.

"No, 105 is unaccounted for," he said. "I'm sorry."

Mike's head fell to his chest. He and Tommy threw their arms around each other, stumbled around the corner, and wept. The noxious dust and smoke swirled over their heads.

At 5:30 P.M., the chief came down and told the men the buses weren't coming. He ordered the men of Ladder 23 to return to their own firehouse. Some vans would be arriving later that night to take them downtown, he told them.

Back at Kippy's firehouse, the long oak kitchen table was piled with trays of food, chicken cutlets and giant fruit baskets that firefighters' wives and neighborhood residents had brought by. The men sat down to eat.

Then a firefighter peeked in the kitchen door and quietly took two steps in. He was covered in gray dust. His face looked stricken. It was Steve, one of the men who'd jumped on the back of the second truck going to the World Trade Center. He gazed blankly at the firefighters sitting around the table. They gaped back at him, their jaws hanging open.

Kippy broke the silence with a joke. "Don't just stand there staring," he called out, gesturing toward the pile of dirty dishes. "Get in the sink."

Steve turned on his heel and walked out of the kitchen. The firefighters jumped up and followed him to the apparatus floor. The captain and Andy had also just returned, exhausted, unable to do any more. Those two were already talking to a couple of firefighters about what they'd seen. It was like a nuclear war down there, they said as the others gathered around. It was so messed up. Rows and rows of burned-out cars. Crushed rigs on fire. Tons of their own guys were missing. They thought they'd be getting people out, but they hadn't been able to save anyone. They struggled for words. The captain, a cool-headed leader with twenty-five years on the job, looked ready to cry. "I don't know what you're going to do when you get down there," he told the men. "It's a futile effort." Kippy listened intently, his arms folded over his chest, and studied the men's faces. Their expressions were lost and hollow. Listening to their stories made Kippy feel more acutely useless than before.

Two firefighters in the house, Rob Carlo and Brian Germain, had brothers who had responded to the scene and had not been heard from all day. But one of the returning firefighters had heard from another that Rob's brother, Michael, had been seen high up in the bucket at the end of a tower ladder, showering water on one of the burning office buildings. "See? Your brother's gonna be okay," Kippy told Rob. "Maybe his cell phone's not working. Maybe it's just crazy down there right now." Rob shook him off. He and Michael ran a roofing business together, and they were extremely close. "You don't understand," he said. "My brother would call me."

Tim Grant reported to his Bronx firehouse on the recall that morning, but his company, Ladder 33, was never called down. He and a dozen others from his firehouse eventually tired of waiting, so around 8:00 P.M. they all piled into the back of Tim's pickup truck to take a ride down to the site. When they arrived, Tim climbed out of his truck and slammed the door shut. The bang it made echoed in the silence. Wall Street was empty. Bits of dust and paper fell continuously from the air. The dark night was thick with smoke and a powdery stench of concrete and steel. A hundred million or more tiny flecks of dust and debris formed an insulation that floated through the air and muffled every sound. Tim could hear noises he wouldn't have heard before, above the din of the bustling city streets. A conversation between two firefighters taking place a few feet ahead of him. The crunch of his boots on the street. The intense quiet made Tim think of skiing during a heavy snowfall, when the silence is so absolute it almost roars.

The guys from Tim's firehouse tried to stay together at first, but it was difficult to see much more than twenty feet through the thick smoke. The buildings that continued to stand could not be seen. The firefighters all looked the same, dressed in the same gear. They soon lost track of each other.

Tim began searching for survivors. He climbed the treacherous pile and then down into a low-lying area between the two towers. He pawed at the rubble and listened for any sounds of life. He found none. Soon he began to feel numbness in his hands and feet. Gradually it spread up his arms and legs until sharp pins and needles radiated throughout his extremities. He looked up and saw a firefighter standing above him. "You shouldn't be down there," the man said, but his voice was distorted and sounded as if it came from miles away. Tim felt dizzy and drunk, symptoms that could have been caused by carbon-monoxide poisoning.

He stumbled out of the void and took a few steps away. He crouched down and tried to steady himself. He felt clumsy and tired. He'd lay his head down on the pile and sleep for a bit, he thought, then he'd be okay. A rescue worker passed by and handed him a mask, which he strapped on his face. But it was only air, not oxygen, and it did little to clear the fogginess in his head. After a few minutes, Tim rose and forced himself to walk. He thought of his one-year-old daughter, Jessica, at home and decided he should leave. He wandered across the pile for what seemed like an hour and was near the edge, almost off, when he looked up and saw a familiar face standing before him. Liam. It was Liam! Tim was elated. They grabbed each other and hugged tightly.

A lot of rescue guys are missing, Liam told Tim. Bronko had been working that morning. All the guys from Rescue 4 had gone down. No one had seen Bronko or any of the others since. Tim felt a rush of panic. Now he knew what to do. He had to find Bronko. Then a call came over a nearby firefighter's radio, an alert that a Port Authority police officer was buried alive and rescue teams were needed at the scene. Liam still did not have a radio, and he desperately needed one. All day, he'd been stopping firefighters to ask, "Did you hear any guys on the radio? Hear from Bronko?" He thought the radio he'd just heard was Tim's, though in fact Tim didn't have a radio, either. He tugged on Tim's sleeve. "Stay with me," he said.

Tim began following Liam toward the area where the officer was trapped. But then he began to reel and sway, as his dizziness returned in full force. Liam seemed to be moving much faster than Tim could possibly follow. Suddenly Liam was far in front of him. Tim thought again of Jessica. He fell away. Two firefighters grabbed his arms and brought him to a nearby firehouse. He collapsed onto a cot, and a nurse began to administer oxygen.

Liam looked back and saw Tim was no longer behind him. He pressed on alone.

All of a sudden, it was night. Dozens of rescue workers were trying to dig out the Port Authority cop, who was pinned nearly upright in an encasement of rubble. Firefighters, police officers, EMS workers, and Port Authority officers teamed up to try to save the man. One man would tunnel deep into the debris, crawling forward on his stomach into a space so tight that it left barely enough room for his head and outstretched arms. The air was thick with toxic smoke, and there was hardly room to wear a mask. The rescuer who was deepest in was followed by another close behind, then another. If one in the line were to fall unconscious, the others would be trapped and unable to retreat. If the rubble above were to shift even a couple of inches, several men would be killed. With one another's safety in mind, the rescuers traded places on brief rotations, without conflict.

Liam took a turn at the front and inched himself into the narrow opening. Those who had worked before him had been able to clear much of the debris away from the man's face, and he was now exposed down to his chin. Liam grabbed at the crushed concrete and rubble and threw it backward in handfuls, hitting the rescuer behind him in the face. The officer was screaming, "I'm in pain! I'm in pain!" Liam saw shock in his pupils and expected the man was going to die before the teams had time to get him out. He shouted that he needed an EMS worker to give this guy a shot for the pain. He cleared an inch or so of rubble, down to the man's neck, and backed out. Eventually the man was extricated, and he survived.

Long after darkness had fallen, the men from Rescue 4 grouped together again to discuss what to do. Liam turned to Billy Murphy, a fellow piper and member of Rescue 4, and said dully, "I guess Bronko's gone." They divided into two shifts. Some would go home for a rest and return to relieve the others early the next morning. Liam would stay.

More than twenty people gathered at Karen's mother's house. Friends, cousins, and siblings banded together to wait out the night, provide support, and talk about what they'd heard. Karen's mother tended to the guests while her father shut himself in another room in front of the television. He emerged every now and then to give updates from the news. Karen felt intensely sick to her stomach. The activity around her was all a chaotic blur. Something was terribly wrong. She should have heard from Bronko by now. People were confused and crying. Within earshot of Karen, some of the firefighters' wives, those who had already received word from their husbands, began to talk about Bronko as if he were dead.

By 6:00 P.M., the rumors had begun to reach the Brunton house. Maryann heard that people were being rescued from the rubble, alive.

People were guessing the total number of the dead at twenty thousand, possibly thirty thousand.

Meanwhile, the Bruntons' phone was not ringing.

Tommy's wife, Mary, looked over at Maryann. "Nobody's going to call," she whispered.

Maryann nodded and turned her head away.

By 1:00 A.M., most of the crowd had gone home for the night. Kathy stood in the kitchen, smoking a cigarette, shaking her head against the silence. Maryann was sitting on the couch in the front room when she saw a car pull up. A fireman got out, but his features were indistinguishable, and she did not recognize who it was. He moved quietly. As he started up the front steps, Maryann rose and approached the door. For a split second, he made eye contact with her. He immediately lowered his head.

Maryann began to back away from the door. It was Mike.

"No . . . No . . . ," she heard herself begging, then shouting. "No!" Mike pushed open the door and walked toward her, reaching for her with his arms outstretched. He was wearing his bunker gear and was covered in white-gray dust. The more steps he took toward her, the more she retreated. When Maryann looked in his eyes, closer now, she saw he was crying.

Mike tried to grab her arms. Maryann backed all the way through the living room, through half the length of the house, and was near the dining room table when Mike finally caught hold of her. Maryann sobbed in defeat. "No! No! I'm trying to tell you," Mike said. "We don't know anything."

"Where's Tommy?" Maryann asked.

"I don't know," Mike answered. "We got separated."

Kathy hid in the kitchen and braced herself against the kitchen counter. She'd heard Maryann and Mike shouting "No!" to each other. She was terrified of finding out the reason. Mike gently pulled away from his sister and went in to talk to Kathy.

Kathy gasped and screamed. She covered her face with her hands and turned away. Her daughter, Kelly, rushed over to Mike and grabbed his dusty coat. Kelly was twenty-two, but at this moment she was a little girl again.

"No! You gotta find him!" she wailed and pounded her fists against her uncle's chest. "Uncle Michael, no! You gotta find my father!"

"I will," said Mike through his own tears. "I'll find him, I promise."

Kelly began hitting him harder.

"What are you doing here? Go back and get him! Go back!"

Mike clutched her arms and held her still.

"I will. I'll bring your father home. Kelly, I'm your godfather. I love you. I won't come home without him."

Mike left. About fifteen minutes later, Tommy pushed open the door. He, too, was covered in chalky soot and dust. He emanated a sharp odor of burnt concrete and death. His boots left shadowy tracks on the sapphire-blue carpet, and chunks of ash fell off him as he walked. Maryann looked at the blanched ash on the floor and thought to herself: That's Vinny, right there. Kathy jumped up, shouting as she ground the ash vigorously into the carpet with her toe. "I don't want this World Trade Center dirt in my house!"

Tommy looked at his family, circled around on the couch and stairs. Tears carved muddy trails down his cheeks. The room fell silent. Someone asked, "Where is he?"

"We can't find him," said Tommy, his voice barely a whisper. "We can't find Vinny."

CHAPTER

4

DAWNING OF THE DAY

The greatest oak in the forest had crashed; it seemed as if it must destroy all life in its fall.

—Frank O'Connor (Michael O'Donovan), *The Big Fellow*

THE sun rose on September 12, casting virgin light over the funeral pyre of Ground Zero. Fliers had begun to spring up everywhere, blanketing walls and lampposts with pictures of the missing. In them were people of every race—photos of mothers with babies in their arms, the wedding poses of a bride and groom, men smiling with their young children. Each image was accompanied by details of the lost—their names, on which floor they had worked, for which company—and some included descriptions of tattoos or birthmarks. Most were titled "MISSING." Each carried a phone number and the same desperate message: "Please call."

Officials struggled to estimate the death toll. People bought newspapers and stared at the pages, transfixed. The *New York Times* front page displayed an image of the towers, burning but still standing. Thick black smoke bled upward into the blue-sky backdrop from the north tower, as the south tower erupted into billowing orange flame. "U.S. ATTACKED," the headline announced. The *New York Daily News* cover showed gaping holes on two faces of the north tower and a blurry image of a minuscule jet. The top of the page shouted in red-block words, "IT'S WAR." Below the fold and inside lay depictions of a startling new truth. A man wearing a white shirt and dark trousers, falling headfirst from one of the towers. A frail blond woman drenched in blood the same color as her short-sleeved dress. Dust-covered office workers fleeing the buildings. A man's severed hand lying in the road, index finger halfway pointing, the bones of the forearm ripped and exposed. On page two of the *New York Times,* a Reuters picture showed two firefighters, a police officer, a man wearing a coat that bore the logo of the Office of Emergency Management, and a civilian transporting an unidentified, unconscious man in a chair away from the collapse. The story just to the right of the picture was headlined, "Survivors Are Found in the Rubble."

That afternoon, Tim dialed Liam's number. He listened to the phone ring four or five times before Liam's recorded voice came on. "Hellooo. I'm not available right now." A tinge of annoyance, or maybe boredom, colored his tone. "Please leave a message and I'll get back to you as soon as I can. Thank you."

Beep.

"Bronko's alive!" Tim exulted to the empty silence. "Call me back."

News of survivors raced among the firefighters. They relied on each other's statements as truth, just as they always had.

A firefighter called Tim at his firehouse to tell him he'd heard Bronko was okay. Swept into a rush of excitement, Tim immediately repeated the news to others. He also heard that someone had called to say that Dennis Devlin, who had been the captain of Engine 75, where Tim had spent his first six years, and now was a battalion chief, was alive and had called home from his cell phone. Apparently he was under a footbridge, trapped in a car, and he'd asked for a turkey sandwich. Word was that Dennis's own son had spoken to him, though he couldn't hear very well, since the sound on the call was very muffled. The family was certain the call had come from Dennis's cell phone, because they'd recognized the number on their Caller ID. Some firefighters left to go search for Dennis, believing they could track down where he was in the wreckage. Tim and the others who were on duty waited anxiously at the firehouse, some with tears in their eyes.

That afternoon, a close friend of Karen's and Bronko's came knocking on her door. He told her Bronko had been heard of, alive, at St. Vincent's Hospital. She phoned Bronko's cousins right away to relay the good news and promised to call them later with a full update.

Karen climbed into a car with her friend and her brother, and her parents followed on the train. When they arrived at the hospital, Karen went to the desk and told them her boyfriend was there. He'd been in the World Trade Center and he might have been hit on the head and not know who he was, she said. She described Bronko, but the staffers shook their heads. No one had come in under those circumstances. She asked a policeman, and he gave the same response. She rushed around the emergency room, searching the hallways and peeking into rooms to see if he was there, but he wasn't. They drove to another hospital, Bellevue. Bronko wasn't there either.

Karen returned home at 11:00 that night. With heavy dread, she grasped the phone again and dialed the cousins.

Days later, she found out the seed that had started the rumor. Bronko had called a friend on the night of September 10 and left a brief message. The friend had picked up her voicemail on the eleventh, and when she heard Bronko's voice she was so excited that she hadn't paid attention to the date announced just prior to the message. She'd assumed it came from September 11. From there, the news spread. The farther it traveled, the less it resembled the truth.

Tim learned on Thursday that the rumors of Dennis Devlin's survival were also false. As it turned out, a friend of Dennis's had his cell phone and used it to call the family at home to see how they were holding up. He ended the call and put the phone in his pocket. Somehow, a button on the phone had been pressed, causing it to redial the house. The muffled noises the family heard were Dennis's friend standing in a deli and chatting with someone about burning cars and a footbridge that had collapsed at the site, then ordering a turkey sandwich for himself, and a bottle of water.

On Friday, September 15, Kippy went to the firehouse of Engine 54 and Ladder 4 in midtown, the company to which his rig had been sent as backup for those who'd reported to the scene on the morning of September 11. Fifteen men from 54 and 4 had lost their lives Tuesday, firefighters who were on duty and off. In all, more than a third of the firefighters who'd worked there were dead. The Ladder 4 rig was still missing. The company needed men to staff the house and a truck to stand by in case of emergency. Kippy and several men from Ladder 23 were assigned there on a twenty-four-hour tour.

Women and children streamed in and out the door. Around the kitchen table, family members and firefighters clustered in intimate groups. Kippy didn't know the names of all the men who were missing from that house. Already, he'd learned that Ladder 21 in Manhattan had reported seven men missing; some of them had showed Kippy around and broke him in when he was a young firefighter there many years earlier, just moving up from an engine to a ladder company. Kippy had stayed in touch with three of them: a robust fellow named Gerry Duffy; Gerry Atwood, at whose wedding Kippy had played his bagpipes; and Mike Fodor, who owned a house near Kippy's and occasionally barbecued with him. Friends, gone. Back when Kippy had worked in 21 Truck, from 1990 to 1995, he'd sometimes met up with firefighters in Ladder 4 at fires, since the companies were located near each other and responded to the same alarms. But six years had passed since then. Kippy knew a couple of the men from Ladder 4 vaguely. One was a kid named Mike Brennan whom Kippy had worked with at an Irish bar some years back. Other names, like Christopher Santora and Jose Guadalupe, didn't sound familiar. The firehouse was packed with on- and off-duty firefighters from Ladder 4 and Engine 54. He heard women who didn't know yet that they were widows ask the regular firefighters if they'd heard any news of their husbands. "Is it true that there may be voids, and he could be trapped inside?" Kippy and the others from Ladder 23 ate their meals with the others, all crowded around the kitchen table. Women broke down and sobbed. The other men tried to comfort them. Kippy stayed quiet. He searched his brain for consoling words, but none came. No women asked him any questions. The women stayed around the firehouse all day.

Kippy felt like an uninvited stranger in someone else's house. The tour dragged on and on. Whenever the men from 23 Truck got called out on a run, they jumped at the opportunity for action. But as soon as they rolled open the garage doors, hundreds of civilians were outside waiting for them, clapping and cheering and handing them food and money. Being showered with such attention, putting on a smile for the crowd, made Kippy intensely uncomfortable. When they were out, they stayed out as long as they could, finding other firehouses to visit, errands to run. They dreaded going back.

At one point in the evening, Kippy and the others from his company drove their rig over to the St. Francis of Assisi Church on 31st Street, to pay their respects at Father Mychal Judge's wake.

Kippy had been raised Catholic. His Irish parents enrolled him at St. Sebastian's grammar school in Woodside, Queens, when he was in fourth grade, where repeated prayers were a part of daily education, serving as an altar boy was less a choice than a duty, and sharp-tongued nuns advocated and practiced corporal discipline. One Irish-born priest still recited mass in Latin, and as an altar boy Kippy struggled to memorize the appropriate moment to chime the bells even though he didn't understand the priest's words. Once, he was a couple of seconds late. The priest reached back with a flat palm and swung hard, smacking Kippy on the back of the head as he thundered, "RING THE BELLS!" Another priest's preferred method of discipline was lifting the little boys up by the scruffs of hair near their ears till they winced in agony and their feet kicked at the air. One of Kippy's teachers was a tiny nun with a masochistic temper. When Kippy misbehaved in class, spoke out of turn, or made some unsolicited noise, she called him up to the front of the class. Then, she sent for his brother John, who was in a classroom down the hall. John was one year Kippy's senior, and bigger. When John walked in the doorway, the nun brought out her wooden paddle and commanded John to come up to the front of the room and bend over. Then, she spanked John repeatedly, each blow landing with a merciless clap, while Kippy stood there watching and wincing. When Kippy got home, his brother delivered him a pounding of his own. Such were his memories of his introduction to faith.

Still, Kippy was a believer "in God and stuff," as he put it. Faith was an obligation. Belief was drilled into him by repetition. From a young age, he learned the words to the Our Father, the Hail Mary, the proclamation of faith—"Christ has died, Christ has risen, Christ will come again"—and all the rest, until they emanated from his mouth without need for conscious thought. When he outgrew being an altar boy, he joined the people in the pews, where his daydreams were bookmarked by the act of standing, sitting, or kneeling at the right moments. He lined up for Communion, took the white wafer in his mouth, said "Amen," and crossed himself. The distant ritual was part of who he was. Churchgoing was a responsibility, a mild comfort, one that he did not question.

Kippy had never made a meaningful connection with a clergy member until he met Father Judge, who had been a friar at St. Francis of Assisi, near where Kippy worked in 21 Truck. The first time Kippy met him was during a fire in Times Square, sometime in the early 1990s.

Usually, a Fire Department chaplain would come to any major fire, three alarms or higher, since a chaplain might well be needed to administer last rites. But no firefighters were injured or killed this day. Father Judge had walked over to chat with some of the firefighters standing on the sidewalk, and Kippy had been impressed by the priest's friendly, down-to-earth manner, as well as his love of firefighting and general fire talk. Father Judge was a buff.

As the years went on, Kippy saw more of Father Judge, usually at funerals or plaque dedication ceremonies for firefighters who'd died. In 1998, when Fire Captain Scott LaPiedra sustained burns over 70 percent of his body at a five-alarm Brooklyn inferno, and later died after twenty-nine days in the burn unit, Father Judge made visits to his brothers at all the firehouses at which he'd worked during his career, including Engine 80, the company in the same house with Kippy's Ladder 23. When a firefighter in Kippy's company was dying of cancer, Father Judge came around to console the men. When Kippy's father-in-law fell severely ill with cancer, he didn't have a chance to tell Father Judge directly, but the priest got word that Mary's father was dying, and one day he showed up at the hospital. Father Judge whispered in the unconscious man's ear for what seemed like fifteen minutes. Before he left, he spoke graciously to Mary's mother. When he swept out the door, she looked after him in wonder. "Who was that?"

After they met, the only major life event of Kippy's that Father Judge didn't participate in was the baptism of Kippy and Mary's son, Daniel. "I'm not big on christenings," Father Judge had admitted to Kippy one day, and Kippy had laughed and let him off. Every Christmas, Father Judge sent Kippy a handwritten letter. His uplifting homily at Big Jim's funeral was just one reason of many that the members of the pipe band appreciated him so deeply. Father Judge had been a beacon of light through every major tragedy in the Fire Department's recent history.

Father Judge was the man being carried away in a chair pictured in the *New York Times* on September 12. Moments before the picture was snapped, he'd been alive, standing in the lobby of 1 World Trade Center, working alongside the firefighters he loved. Although rumors circulated in the media early on that Father Judge was killed by a jumper while administering last rites to a firefighter, they were untrue. After the south tower fell, a number of firefighters and chiefs discovered Father Judge laying unconscious and apparently dead near the bottom of the escalator stairs in the north tower lobby. Rescue workers carried him out and left his body near an ambulance. Seconds later, the rumbling began again, heralding the collapse of the second tower. The New York City medical examiner's office listed his cause of death as "blunt trauma to the head," though no autopsy was performed. His was one of a small number of intact bodies that were carried away from the devastation. His was the only open-casket wake.

The New York City Fire Department had its own tradition of burial, which borrowed from Irish custom and American military procedure. Funerals for firefighters who died in the line of duty incorporated handing over a folded flag, salutes, and the playing of "Taps" on a bugle, and since the 1970s the pipers skirled and the drummers pounded a dirge. In the procession, the coffin was always transported on a caisson.

Families received guidance on organizing the funeral from the Fire Department's ceremonial unit, a handful of men whose office was an oblong cubicle inside a building at the Fire Academy headquarters on Randall's Island, just east of Manhattan's 125th Street. Often, those assigned to the unit were newly promoted officers on a temporary administrative assignment. Turnover was frequent. Only a few had accumulated more than five years in the unit.

The protocol was passed down by word of mouth, not officially outlined in any book or manual. The lead officer in the ceremonial unit since 1995 had been Lt. Walter Dreyer, a compact man with a wood-brown mustache and wavy hair of the same color, and many of the traditions were recorded only in his memory. When a firefighter died in the line of duty, which happened an average of twice a year since he'd taken over the post, he consulted a series of files from the most recent funerals. They contained diagrams of the churches, maps of the streets around the area, the order of the procession, which dignitaries had attended, and so on. Police officers had to be commissioned to direct traffic, and shuttle buses were arranged to transport the thousands of firefighters—often five thousand or more—who normally turned out for a brother's funeral.

No one had ever tried to put together a comprehensive written procedure except Liam's late brother-in-law, Vinny Fowler. He had become interested in the department's treatment of its deceased members and had gone to dozens of firehouses who'd lost men, interviewing firefighters about their experiences notifying widows, working with clergy, and planning services, asking them what had worked and what hadn't. He came up with a booklet that covered every detail—notifying the family, placing the flag at half staff, securing the locker and possessions of the deceased, arranging for phone coverage at the firehouse during the funeral. It explained how a firefighter's pension would be allocated according to the circumstances of death, reminded members to clean their Class-A uniforms and perform any necessary repairs in advance of the service, and noted where to get the purple-and-black memorial bunting that would be hung at the firehouse of the deceased. Ironically, many of the procedures he'd fine-tuned were implemented at Fowler's own funeral in 1998. Liam remembered how proud Fowler had been of the work he'd done. He'd inked his initials, "VGSF," on the front page of the booklet and often said of firefighters, "We die well."

When a firefighter died in the line of duty, the department immediately sent personnel to officially notify the family. A team that included the battalion chief nearest to where the firefighter lived, a Fire Department chaplain of the appropriate faith, and sometimes a member of the firefighter's firehouse went to the next of kin's home to deliver the news in person.

Funeral planning was usually done within the next two days. During that time, a group of six to eight men from the deceased's company would come to the Fire Academy at Randall's Island for a training session with Jimmy Sorokac, a tall, bald firefighter with bulging eyes and a dark seashell mustache. Sorokac drove the department's caisson, an old-fashioned red truck used exclusively for carrying the body of a firefighter who'd died in the line of duty, with a special mechanism at the back for raising and lowering the coffin. He also trained the men in how to be pallbearers and carry the coffin into the church. The most surprising aspect of the duty, most men found, was the weight of the casket. The man might have weighed 250 pounds, and his casket, if solid mahogany, usually weighed another 300. Wood coffins were at least fifty pounds heavier than metal. Sorokac loaded a coffin with free weights from the Fire Department gym and spent three hours or more with the men as they practiced moving the coffin off the caisson, lifting it to their shoulders, marching in unison and perfecting a swaying motion that would balance the casket securely on their shoulders without touching it with their hands.

The bagpipe band members arrived at the church an hour early to tune up. They followed a standard set: "Minstrel Boy" to begin the processional toward the church, then a solo of "Amazing Grace" as the casket was lifted off the caisson and carried inside. When the service was over, the pipers assembled outside again and played "Going Home" as the casket was brought out of the church. The band escorted the family limousines for a couple of blocks, then stood to one side and let the vehicles pass. When the last car in the procession had gone, the band turned and marched back toward the church, playing a jolly military tune like "Garryowen" to a quick beat. The thousands of firefighters who remained near the church in formation would applaud the returning band. The march back signified the end of the mourning process and the beginning of celebration.

After each funeral, firefighters, friends, and sometimes family gathered for a collation, often held at the deceased's firehouse or at a public park. Tradition held that the last firehouse to have lost a member organized the collation for the next, arranging for the food to be catered and the kegs of beer to be dropped off and providing the cups and tableware. When a twenty-seven-year-old firefighter named Michael Gorumba collapsed of a heart attack at a three-alarm fire in August 2001, it had been Rescue 4's turn, since the most recent deadly fire had been the one on Father's Day in which Rescue 4 lost two men. After Gorumba's funeral, Bronko and Liam had stood side by side behind a beer table, frantically pouring drinks from a tap and handing plastic cups to the lines of waiting firemen.

Death, like most aspects of their daily lives in the firehouse, was never dealt with alone. Funerals were events that the firefighters handled together. Except those who were on duty that day, were ill, or had an unavoidable conflict, everyone turned out for a brother's funeral. Everyone.

The next morning, Saturday, September 16, Kippy returned to St. Francis of Assisi to play at the funeral for Father Mychal Judge. He changed out of his navy blue firefighting T-shirt and pants at the firehouse and put on his white short-sleeved button-down shirt, with the square FDNY bagpipe band patch on the arm just below the right shoulder, and the New York City Fire Department insignia on the left, a red, white, and blue hexagon featuring an image of the Twin Towers. In the right flap of his shirt collar, he inserted a silver metal Maltese Cross pin with a shamrock in the center; in the left, a silver pin that read "L23." He wrapped his kilt around his waist and buckled his thick black leather belt. From the side of the belt hung a small satchel that carried his wallet, cell phone, and sunglasses. To the front he attached the sporran, a long swatch of blond and black horsehair that hung suspended by a metal chain over the front of his kilt. Then he pulled on his green knee socks with the red flashes, laced up his black dress shoes, and buttoned the white spats over his ankles. He slid a six-inch knife called a *sgian dubh* (which means "black dagger"), into one sock just far enough so that the handle stayed in view. He clipped his navy blue tie casually to his shirt pocket and set off, carrying his beret and his bagpipe case in his hand.

The streets around were blocked off to traffic, as crowds of firefighters, clergy members and hundreds of people whose lives Father Judge had touched began to cluster outside. Former president Bill Clinton and Senator Hillary Rodham Clinton were among the attendees. A news crew stopped Bill Clinton on his way toward the church, and dozens of people crowded around to hear him speak. "We should lift his life up today as an example of what has to prevail in this conflict," Clinton said to the reporter. "We cannot let the twenty-first-century world degenerate into killing over religious and racial and political differences. More of us have to be like Father Mike than the people that killed him."

Everyone in the band wanted to play at Father Judge's funeral, but only thirty or so could. Three other Fire Department funerals were scheduled the same day, for Chief of Department Peter Ganci, First Deputy Commissioner William Feehan, and Engine 285 firefighter Raymond York. Under any other circumstances, thousands of firefighters would have turned out for Father Judge's funeral, but now the attendance numbered barely a thousand. Hundreds of firefighters were lost; hundreds more were still working at the site, trying to recover them. Fatigue combined with the pressure of the logistics helped Kippy push his emotions aside. There was no other choice. They would stand together and take care of this.

Tim dropped his wife, Tara, off at the church and went to the nearby firehouse. There, he brought his bagpipes out of his square case, which had the look of an odd-sized briefcase. Like the rest of the pipers in the band, he played on Scottish Highland bagpipes. The modern instrument boasted many advances over bagpipes of yesteryear. Instead of being made of kangaroo skin or cowhide, which had to be oiled regularly to prevent cracking, the bag was constructed of durable Gore-Tex that required no seasoning, the same synthetic fabric used in making waterproof gloves and coats for firefighters. African blackwood was carved to form the chanter, the blowpipe, and the three tall drones, which were strung together by a braided rope and rested over the piper's left shoulder. Small discs of ivory topped the outer edges of the drones and chanter, mellowing the sound.

He put his bagpipes together by pushing the chanter into a stock on the underside of the bag, and twisting the top halves of the drones onto the bottom halves, which were already secured to the upper side of the bag. He would have to moisten the four reeds, one below each of the drones and one in the top of the chanter, by blowing into the pipes for twenty minutes or so, so the sound would come out evenly. The pitch could then be adjusted by raising or lowering the chanter reed and sliding the drones a touch upward or downward.

The pipers gathered in a circle and played a dozen tunes together, warming up their instruments. After ten years in the band, Kippy knew the tunes so well he could blank out his mind and his fingers would keep on going. Tim blew into his own pipes for a while, then walked around to the others to check each individual's pitch in every drone and chanter. Meanwhile, the men decided on what kind of special honors they could show Father Judge. When playing at a firefighter's funeral, the band members did not always go into the church as a unit. Many stayed in the street, while a few band members who had known the man went into the church. But now, since Father Judge had been the band's chaplain, all the pipers and drummers planned to go directly into the church as soon as they had finished playing "Amazing Grace" and the immediate family had climbed the church steps and gone inside. The band members expected they would sit together near the front, since Father Judge had been so close to them. In the past, at the end of a funeral for a firefighter who'd served in the Marines, the members sometimes played the "Marine Corps Hymn." Now, Tim decided that the band should add "America the Beautiful" at the end of Father Judge's service. He spread the word about his plan, and the others agreed.

Finally, the moment came. Kippy clipped his tie into place and put on his beret. The band lined up in the street a few blocks away from the church. A procession of fire trucks began to roll forward. Kippy strode off on the left foot, stepping slowly in rhythm to the 4/4 count, skirling "Minstrel Boy."

> The Minstrel Boy to the war is gone
> In the ranks of death you will find him
> His father's sword he hath girded on
> And his wild harp slung behind him

"Land of Song!" said the warrior bard
"Tho' all the world betrays thee
One sword at least thy rights shall guard
One faithful harp shall praise thee!"

The Minstrel fell! But the foeman's chain
Could not bring that proud soul under
The harp he lov'd ne'er spoke again
For he tore its chords asunder
And said, "No chains shall sully thee
Thou soul of love and brav'ry!
Thy songs were made for the pure and free,
They shall never sound in slav'ry!"

The casket was covered in a white-and-red Fire Department flag. Kippy watched the pallbearers reach in and hoist it out. Tim began playing the solo of "Amazing Grace." Wordless, the tune sang of sorrow. The band members stood quietly while the pallbearers raised the coffin to their shoulders and brought it toward the church door. The stairs leading up to the entrance were unusually steep. The pallbearers stumbled and wobbled under the coffin's weight, blinking back tears, struggling to stare straight ahead. Family members and friars in brown habits followed the coffin inside.

Once the family was inside, the formation relaxed. Kippy, Tim, and the rest of the band walked toward the church door and joined the line to get in. They were just approaching the steps when a short, husky man clambered over the railing and blocked them. He claimed to be a retired Fire Department official and told them they were not allowed to go into the church. There wasn't room. Joe Murphy, the band chairman, stood in front of Kippy in the line. Joe shook his head and told him they were going in. Father Judge had been their chaplain, and they were going to pay their respects to him. The man's temper began to rise. His face contorted like a bruised plum. His voice grew louder. He repeated his order. The band members were not going in. The argument escalated. Joe's normally soft tone grew sharp and abrupt. The man screamed back at him. Another senior member of the band approached and tried to quell the argument. Kippy, being several inches taller than Joe, saw the whole dispute clearly. The man looked as if he were going to have a heart attack. Kippy grew furious. Why was he so adamant? Who the hell was this guy, anyway? A Franciscan priest,

Father Brian Jordan, heard the commotion and rushed over to the steps to try to defuse the fight before it erupted into blows. This is not what Father Judge would have wanted, he told the men. There had to be plenty of room in the basement of the church. The pipers could try down there.

Tim and some other pipers went through the downstairs door, but Kippy hadn't heard the priest's suggestion. He was so bewildered, he headed back down the steps and stood in the street, lost. Others filed past him and made their way into the church.

Then someone called out from the top of the church steps. "There's room in here!" Kippy and the remaining pipers rushed over and found that there was space yet to be filled. Other men in kilts, from a different pipe band, were already inside. Kippy found a seat near the back.

Father Michael Duffy, a Franciscan priest from Philadelphia, gave the homily. He summed up Father Judge's life perfectly. It seemed everyone in the church was alternately laughing and crying, enamored with the eulogy. In the next few weeks, he said, the list of names of the thousands of people who'd been killed in the attacks would become clear. "Mychal Judge is going to be on the other side of death to greet them," Father Duffy said. "With that big Irish smile."

When the service neared its end and a speaker announced that the ranks of the firefighters should step outside to line up in formation, Kippy and the others from the band left with them. They formed boxy rows near the church entrance and waited for the coffin to emerge. When the pallbearers stepped out into the daylight, the band began to play "Going Home."

Kippy looked around and saw grown men in uniform openly weeping. He fought back a wave of heat that rose from inside and threatened to topple him. He knew Father Judge was dead. He'd seen his body laid out at the wake just hours before. This was, after all, his funeral. But all the logical aspects fell apart when he saw others red-faced and crying under their gloved salutes. The state of shock that had shielded him suddenly dissipated. Father Judge was gone. Gone? As he marched past the firefighters, piping "America the Beautiful," he wondered: How are we going to get through this?

CHAPTER

5

THE FUNERALS

For the common soldier, . . . war has the feel—the spiritual texture—of a great ghostly fog, thick and permanent. There is no clarity. Everything swirls. The old rules are no longer binding, the old truths no longer true. Right spills over into wrong. Order blends into chaos, love into hate, ugliness into beauty, law into anarchy, civility into savagery. The vapors suck you in. You can't tell where you are, or why you're there, and the only certainty is overwhelming ambiguity. In war you lose your sense of the definite, hence your sense of truth itself.

—Tim O'Brien, "How to Tell a True War Story"

THE Irish have always been loath to leave their dead—hence the traditional "Irish wake." In customs handed down over the centuries, death became an occasion equally divided between mourning and celebration, and the presence of a body provided a focal point for the community's grief. Surviving loved ones stayed at the corpse's side, washing the body and preparing it for burial, saying prayers, and viewing, kissing, and touching the deceased for the last time. The area around the body was lit with candles or lamps. Village women began making the woeful crying sounds known as keening over the body as the family wept. Then more family and friends arrived to pray and bid farewell. Later, laughter and activity filled the gathering, including eating, drinking, singing, dancing, and telling stories of the life they recalled.

Finally, when three full days and nights had passed—the span of time between Jesus' death and the resurrection—the body would be laid beneath the ground. Cremations were discouraged among Catholics for hundreds of years, since the hierarchy professed that the body was sacred and would one day rise again. If people were reduced to ashes, perhaps Jesus would not be able to sort them out in order to resurrect them, and eternal life would be denied. Those who did practice cremation were considered pagans. Only heathens did not care about eternal life. The ban on cremation was lifted by the Vatican in 1963, but the basics of the funeral ritual remained the same. A corpse had to be present to be blessed correctly at the funeral mass. Only afterward could cremation occur.

The city of New York erupted into blazes of various degrees all the time, yet rescuer deaths were rare. In the 1990s, the Fire Department responded to about thirty thousand structural fires each year with an average annual loss of 150 civilian lives. From 1993 to 2000, a total of twenty firefighters died in the line of duty; 1,134 civilians were killed in or as a result of injuries sustained in those fires.[1] Even during the so-called war years of the 1960s and 1970s, when nearly 300 civilians died in fires each year, firefighter line-of-duty casualties remained relatively low, never fewer than five per year but never more than nine. Advances in training and equipment led to even fewer deaths as time went on. In 1988, no firefighters were killed on the job for the first time in the department's history. Similarly placid years were repeated in 1990 and 1997.

On June 17, 2001, when Liam heard news of the Father's Day explosion, he'd been playing with the band at a wedding. At 2:21 that Sunday afternoon, Rescue 4 responded to a fire at 12–22 Astoria Boulevard. By all appearances, it seemed to be a routine cellar fire. While firefighters were searching the building for additional signs of heat and flame, a sudden explosion let loose in the basement of the hardware store. The blast came without warning, catapulting several firefighters up in the air, throwing some men into the street and crushing others in a cascading collapse. The survivors immediately began searching for those who were missing. Capt. Brian Hickey, who was injured in the blast, grabbed his radio and began a roll call for his company members. He called for Harry Ford, who had been driving the rig that afternoon.

"Rescue Four to Chauffeur. Answer me, Harry."

Harry did not answer. The captain did not know it yet, but Harry was buried in a pile of rubble near the sidewalk.

"Rescue Four to Brian Fahey."

Brian's voice came back over the radio.

"At the scene."

Brian told his captain he was trapped in the basement under the stairwell. The firefighters tried to get near him, but there was no way to get back in the way they'd come. Bricks, wood, and rubble from the collapse completely covered the area where the stairwell had been and piled all the way to the ceiling. Brian gave a couple of maydays and repeated over his radio that he was trapped. He called for the men to come and get him. The firefighters heard a buzzing vibration during Brian's last communications: An alarm on his breathing apparatus, called a Vibralert, was sounding off to let him know he was almost out of air. The firefighters knew they had only a few minutes left. It was not enough.

As soon as Liam heard about the explosion, he threw his pipes in the back of his car and rushed to the scene. By the time he got there, firefighters had already uncovered the bodies of Harry Ford and John Downing, who lay near each other under the rubble on the sidewalk. Firefighters had made progress on the pile over the stairwell. Other off-duty firefighters from Rescue 4 had arrived, driven by the grim intent to find their fellow fireman's body as rapidly as possible. Fires continued to burn in and above the area where they dug. Some firefighters sprayed the licking flames, but the water thrown on the fire by the hoses turned to steam and scorching fluid. It dripped down on the men as they worked, seeping into their bunker gear and burning their skin. After several hours, they finally reached Brian Fahey. He was lying face up in the water, dead.

All the noises at the scene—the rush of the water bursting from hoses, the rough static voices of firefighters over the radio waves, the scratching and pounding sounds of debris being removed—came to a halt as the body was laid on a stokes basket and covered in a white sheet. Someone shouted, "Uncover!" The hundreds of firefighters all around removed their helmets. According to tradition, on those rare, tragic days when a firefighter dies at a fire, only fellow firefighters from the same firehouse bring the body out. Liam gripped one handle of the stokes, as did two others behind him and three men on the other side, all from Rescue 4. In silence, they carried Brian Fahey away from the collapse that had taken his life and tucked him into a waiting ambulance.

Later, Liam called Bronko, who was vacationing at the Jersey Shore for the weekend. Bronko answered in a cheery tone.

"Listen, you gotta come back up," Liam said.

"Why?"

"Harry's dead. Brian's dead."

"What?"

"Brother, they're gone. They just got killed in a fire."

"How?"

"I can't talk to you too much right now. I gotta hang up." And he did.

Bronko, who had been close friends with Brian, served as the firehouse liaison to the Fahey family, helping to arrange the funeral, making repairs at the house, doing anything he could to help the widow cope. Liam did the same for the Fords.

Harry Ford's funeral took place in Long Beach, Long Island, on the morning of June 21. Brian Fahey's funeral was later that afternoon in East Rockaway. John Downing was laid to rest two days later. Each time, Bronko marched at the back of the pipers' formation, drumming, and Liam led the way in front. They tried not to look at the kids—twelve-year-old Harry Ford Jr., ten-year-old Gerard, and Harry's twenty-four-year-old stepdaughter, Janna; Brian Fahey's son Brendan, eight, and his twin three-year-old boys, Patrick and James—sobbing in front of the church.

That summer, Bronko and Liam did their best to become surrogate fathers. They took the boys out to the movies and to baseball games, called them on the phone to chat, and took them to Jets training camp in August. They were happier themselves when they could see the boys cavorting and giggling. But they couldn't bring back the boys' fathers, and they knew the laughter would be short-lived.

Death had swung down like a guillotine on those in Liam's life over the past several years, taking away friends and loved ones with ruthless repetition. Brian Fahey and Harry Ford were not the first. In April 2001, band member Gene Fraher had died due to complications from diabetes. Watching the gradual amputations of Fraher's legs and arms, seeing his slow decline, had been horrifying. Yet Fraher fended off pity with humor, even in the late stages of his illness. Once, lying in his hospital bed, Fraher told a piper who'd come to visit that he was going to need to borrow some money. "Why?" the piper asked. "Can't you see?" Fraher had responded. "I'm a little short."

Three months earlier, Donny Franklin, a friend from Liam's former company of Ladder 44, had died in a fire. Franklin left behind five children and a widow. In June 1999, Capt. Vincent Fowler, Liam's childhood friend and brother in-law, had collapsed of a fatal heart attack during a fire in a Queens basement. And just six months before that, a cherished probie named Jimmy Bohan, whose parents were from

Ireland and who'd so greatly admired the pipe band that he once fawned to Liam, "I'm so lucky to, like, know you," had been killed in a fire on Vandelia Street that also took the lives of two other firemen. Including the three lost in the Father's Day fire, that was nine brother firefighters Liam knew personally, all gone in a period of barely three years. His maternal grandmother had recently died, too.

Longer ago, Liam's only brother had waged a brief battle for life and lost. John Joseph, born when Liam was nine, was sickly and suffered from weak lungs. His abbreviated existence was spent mostly in the hospital. While John struggled, his parents took Liam and his two younger sisters there every day. The children weren't allowed near the baby, so while his sisters played, Liam found his way around the maze of hallways and memorized every detail of the waiting room, the chairs, the side tables, the swinging doors, the walls and flooring. During the funeral, seeing the tiny white box at the front of the church, Liam wept violently. As he grew, his family never talked about it again. His mother was inconsolable in private; his father was consistently a rock. The child was dead. What was there to say? They focused their attention on Liam, their only son, their future.

Not since that childhood death had Liam cried so. Now, when tragedy occurred, he modeled his action after his father's. His father just got on with it. He had lost his own mother when he was a toddler and was raised by his older sisters near the coasts of Galway Bay. Liam had never heard him complain about his youth or beg for attention by going on about how the tragedy had affected him. Emotions were destructive. Pain caused hurt to others. Breaking down was selfish and therefore useless.

Every man from Rescue 4 who had climbed on the rig the morning of September 11 was gone. Lt. Kevin Dowdell, Pete Brennan, Billy Mahoney, Pete Nelson, Terry Farrell, and Bronko. Al Tarasiewicz, from Rescue 5, who was detailed at Rescue 4 for that tour. Michael Cawley, who'd been filling in at Engine 292 and had wanted to become a member of Rescue 4. And Capt. Brian Hickey, who had been filling in at Rescue 3 that night and responded to the scene with that company. Nine men altogether, more than an entire shift. A full third of the company's men. One half of the company's officers.

At Rescue 4, the surviving men's focus turned to recovering the bodies. They went to the site every single day to dig for their men. Early on, they came up with names for landmarks within the pile, so they could describe to others where they were at a given moment or explain the general area where recent recoveries had been made. The giant reaches of metal that stuck out over the West Side Highway were the "Fingers." The looming crane that was visible from miles away they called the "Crane from Space." And the triangular remnants of a tower facade that had stayed sticking up they named the "Christmas Tree."

Liam and others from Rescue 4 made a pact: They would stay until the end, no matter what. He dug countless days and nights alongside fathers who were searching for their sons, like Dennis O'Berg Sr., a long-limbed, silver-haired man, whose son Dennis, a probie in Vinny's company of Ladder 105, had changed careers from accounting to firefighting only months earlier. O'Berg spoke little, and when he did the words came out in a near whisper. When he paused from his work, his pale blue eyes kept moving, side to side, far into the beyond, forever searching a landscape known only to him. Brothers were searching for brothers, like Tommy and Mike Brunton, unable to focus on anything but bringing home Vinny's body. One man Liam saw, sensing he knew exactly where his dead brother was in the sixteen-acre disaster, climbed up the pile to where a cluster of bones lay, gathered them in a pail, and carried them down. When the DNA analysis came back, science proved him right.

These firefighters placed their responsibilities at the site above anything or anyone else in their lives. Their families were neglected or ignored for days on end. They shrugged off the physical pain they felt. Liam told himself that if there was one thing in life that could be controlled, it was his thoughts. He admitted to no weakness of spirit or body, and he couldn't bear to hear others complain. The way Liam saw it, the kind of emotion that caused some firefighters to bow out of the recovery effort had no place in the department. They'd all known what they were getting into when they signed up for the job. There was no way a firefighter would have ever left his brother at the scene of a fire before, regardless of the scale of the fire. This one should be no different.

By some estimates, 1,200 to 1,500 firefighters worked at the site daily in the first weeks after September 11.[2] As time passed, the numbers dwindled. Liam watched as men around him grew exhausted and upset over digging out hundreds of body parts. Some firefighters who had spent only a few days at the site hacked and wheezed and complained that they'd come down with "World Trade Center cough." Liam scoffed at the term, but he, too, felt the physical effects—a burning sensation in his lungs, a poisonous taste in his throat, a constant ache that seeped through his muscles. He fought the symptoms some of the time and was grateful for them the rest of the time. The presence of physical pain was a relief. It gave him proof that he was being affected by the disaster, when inside he just felt hollow and empty.

Liam never returned Tim's call about Bronko being alive. He'd known it wasn't true from the very first night. The rumor mill wielded the power to create devastating hope. Talk circulated of earthquake survivors who'd supposedly lived for six days or more without food or water, and had been rescued alive. Some beliefs—for instance, that cafeterias lay undisturbed deep within the rubble, where people might be surviving on sandwiches and soda—he knew were absurd. One lieutenant recalled reading a newspaper article that described voids in which survivors had etched messages on walls before they'd died. He became enraged at its falsehood, clenching his fists until veins protruded from his neck.

Talk of potential suicides among recovery workers also began early, as firefighters and construction workers guessed at the numbers who would take their own lives after witnessing such a grisly aftermath or experiencing the loss of relatives, friends, and colleagues. There were conversations about how many Oklahoma City rescue workers had committed suicide after the truck bomb ripped into the Murrah Federal Building, killing 168. The story persisted that Chris Fields, a firefighter who had been pictured in the national media cradling a dead baby in his arms, was one of them; he was not. Liam believed most people were more resilient than they were given credit for.

Liam took pride in the level of commitment that he saw in other firefighters who stayed at the site after the weaker ones fell away. Some likened working at the Trade Center to going to church. There was something spiritual about it, a feeling of mission, of doing the right thing just by being there. In many ways, the work there was a ritual, both of punishment and of redemption. Surrounded by a violent new terrain, they forged new alliances and clung desperately to the old ways—the relationships, the trust, the knowledge that no one would ever be left behind. There were days of triumph when they found bodies, and days of discouragement when they didn't. Every day blended into the next. When they took breaks, the firefighters would lift each other's spirits by telling amusing stories about the men who were dead. Sometimes, while patrolling the pile, Liam would implore the missing men in his head: Where are you guys? Tell me where you are, Bronk.

Liam pushed himself to the point of sheer exhaustion at the end of each day, then started it all over again the next. When he and the core group from Rescue 4 were away from the site, all they could think about was going back. Liam's mad pace gave him a focus and helped to suppress the anger that boiled inside.

The afternoon of September 11, after Tommy and Mike were told that Ladder 105 was missing, their thoughts quickly turned to finding Vinny's body. Many firefighters were held back from searching near Building 7 as it burned, but once that structure collapsed, they were permitted into the area. Chiefs began dispatching two and three companies to search together, to see if there were any civilians who couldn't get out and to try to extinguish any localized fires as they encountered them.

As night fell, someone came over and told them that they'd discovered Ladder 105's rig, partially covered and damaged by the force of the towers' fall. The truck had been parked on the West Side Highway near the Marriott Hotel. Tommy, Mike, and a crew of firefighters from Ladder 105 and Engine 219 converged on the scene. They dug frantically at the debris all around, searching for any signs of life inside. There were none.

In the days that followed, Tommy and Mike continued to search for Vinny every day. Sometimes they worked together; other times they joined separate teams.

The debris field was gargantuan, twenty stories or more of huge steel beams and girders twisted on top of each other. A few broken shells of the towers still teetered. A thick layer of dust coated the streets for blocks all around. Papers were scattered everywhere. Tommy thought that pictures of the site on television gave no indication of what it was like to be there. The camera was able to back up and, from far away, encapsulate the scene in a neat box with no senses or emotions to clutter the frame. When you could see the whole site at once, the scale was entirely thrown off. Up close, the enormity was incomprehensible. The air was thick and repellent. Fumes from the fires that were still burning deep under the debris pile poured out in putrid smoke. The smells were not like the sickening-sweet charred-pot smell of a cooking fire or the wood-and-paint aroma of a house fire or the rubber-and-oil stench of a car fire. The combination of smells at the site was entirely foreign—a nasty, noxious mixture of red-hot steel, diesel fuel, concrete dust, scorched chemicals, and who knew what.

Dozens of rescue dogs patrolled the debris, one type searching for cadavers and one for live bodies. Tommy heard other men at the site commenting that they hadn't seen so much as a desk in one piece, much less a phone. Many, many fragments were the size of a fist, or smaller. Everything seemed to be coated in the same light-gray dust. Since all the bits looked the same, it was difficult to tell a chunk of flesh and bone from a rock of broken cement. As Tommy dug through the debris, he paused to sniff any piece he wasn't positive about. A dry scent of steel or cement meant it was nothing. A repulsive whiff of dead flesh meant it was a piece of a scalp or a part of a leg; he'd cover it in plastic and tuck it gently into his bucket.

Tommy took the body parts he found to the makeshift morgue near the site, where workers catalogued the remains. Once when he took his bags to the table, someone asked him what he had found. "I don't know," Tommy snapped. He held open the bag. "What the fuck do you think?" It was impossible to tell.

Tommy's anger ran through him like a surging subterranean river, always present but usually unnoticeable. Mike's anger turned into gushing fury, a tsunami of rage and spitting hate for the bastards that did this to him and to all of his Fire Department brothers. The notion that terrorists could have obliterated his brother Vinny, taken away his enormous smile and crushed his life into tiny pieces, added to the stress of seeing the remains day after day and trying not to wonder, Is this part of Vinny?—it was as if the Al Qaeda terrorists had engaged him in a deeply personal and violent battle, and Mike was on the losing end. A lot of the men felt that way; one firefighter who'd dug at the site said of Osama bin Laden that fall, "I want to bite off his nose and dig his eyes out with my thumbs." When Mike's rage swelled, his eyes glittered and his mouth refused to let words come out. As the days pressed forward, a truth Tommy did not feel prepared to face nagged at him. His actions were fruitless. They were never going to find Vinny. Mike, on the other hand, outwardly ignored any sense of doubt he may have had. He became absolutely and utterly resolved to find Vinny and give him a proper Christian burial. It was the only reasonable retribution Mike could envision.

Every night, the brothers stopped by Kathy's house, either alone or together. Kathy would rush out onto the front porch and wait for them. "Did you find him?" Friends had tried to lift her spirits by saying that Vinny was probably stuck in a giant void far beneath the rubble. There were drugstores down there, they said, so Vinny would have his pick of whatever he wanted. He was probably down there running a card game, drinking bottled water, and chomping on Junior Mints. She hoped that one day his brothers would come back and tell her they'd found Vinny trapped and he was in the hospital but he was going to be okay. But Kathy's hope was a form of denial, a way to push back the day when she'd have to deal with the truth.

Then, one afternoon in late September, Tommy was digging when someone nearby recognized the fabric of a firefighter's bunker gear and glimpsed a bit of a boot. They lifted the debris to uncover the body.

Someone gasped.

The firefighter's entire body lay on the ground, but he'd been so severely crushed within his bunker gear that his body looked to be barely an inch thick. He wasn't decapitated, but his face and skull were a mass of bloody flesh and bone. Seeing the body made Tommy think of a cockroach someone had just pounded on with a heel and squashed.

Someone turned and choked.

A friend turned to Tommy and said, "What the fuck are you doing here? You don't want to find your brother like this."

Tommy looked at him, and down at the body.

"You know what, you're right." He turned and left the site. The next day, he rejoined his brothers in the band.

On Sunday, September 16, 168 Fire Department officers and firefighters were promoted in order to fill the ranks of the missing. Seventy firefighters became lieutenants, sixty-one lieutenants rose to captain, twenty-nine captains were now battalion chiefs, and six battalion chiefs assumed the positions of deputy chief. Daniel Nigro, who had served as chief of operations, became the chief of the department to replace Peter Ganci. The promotion ceremony took place under the blazing sun in the plaza outside the department's Brooklyn headquarters. The shell-shocked soldiers rose in turn, wearing their old uniforms for the last time, and raised their right hands. Mayor Rudolph Giuliani spoke at the ceremony. "In the last great attack on America," he said, his voice cutting like a clean razor through the air, "the attack on Pearl Harbor, the first casualties of that war were the members of our United States Navy. They wore a uniform, like you do. In this war, the first large casualties are being experienced by the Fire Department of New York City."[3]

Meanwhile, the task of burying the dead had begun. But circumstances had stripped the ritual of its core traditions. Countless bodies were decapitated, burned, or mangled beyond recognition. None of the World Trade Center dead, other than Father Mychal Judge, would have an open casket. The list of the missing swelled, and the total toll was estimated at more than six thousand during the first few days. Most of the dead were crushed to pieces, entwined together with steel and concrete and toxic chemicals. Blessing and burial in family plots at cemeteries after three days was possible for only four of the thousands lost. The rest of the funeral dates extended days and weeks beyond the death.

Twenty-nine funerals for firefighters were scheduled the first week. Five were held the first Monday after the attacks, then five on Tuesday, four on Wednesday, eight on Thursday, two on Friday, and five on Saturday.

Seventy new officers, mostly lieutenants, were assigned to the ceremonial unit to help with the funerals. Lt. Dreyer divided the men into eight teams, so they could cover eight funerals a day. On the first Monday after the terror attacks, September 17, Dreyer held a meeting of all the new officers and handed out a booklet that detailed the kind of information they could provide the families. Most firefighters had had little experience with the ceremonial unit, and indeed many did not even know it existed, so individuals were calling friends from the Police Department to arrange escorts or phoning members of the band to let them know about a family that wanted to schedule a funeral. Many efforts were being duplicated. Dreyer proposed a liaison system, like the one Rescue 4 already used. Each firehouse would assign one firefighter to each of its bereaved families, and that person would be the conduit between the ceremonial unit and the family. At first, band chairman Joe Murphy handled all the scheduling for the band. He adapted a phone tree system that had been established some years before, so men could notify each other about the next day's funerals and pass messages along. The band split into groups according to where the pipers and drummers lived—upstate guys, city guys, Long Island guys—and each group covered the nearest services. Kippy traveled with the upstate group, Tim with the Long Island group. When a group of pipers and drummers arrived at a church, one of the more experienced pipers went around and tuned everyone, the way the pipe major and pipe sergeants once had, back when the band had all played together. With Liam working at the site, they now marched without a drum major. The entire department was operating on an A/B chart—twenty-four hours on, twenty-four hours off. For the first few weeks,

Band led by drum major "Big Jim" Corcoran, St. Patrick's Day, 1978. Photo courtesy of Frank O'Rourke.

"Without that kilt, I'd be just another fat man at the bar." Bronko at Danny and Jeannie McEnroe's wedding, September 8, 2001. Photo courtesy of Jeannie McEnroe.

"When they were four." Young Tommy Brunton holding baby sister Maryann, Mike (center), and Vinny, January 1962. Photo courtesy of Tommy Brunton.

"Could I still wear a white dress?" Vinny and Kathy Brunton on their wedding day. Photo courtesy of Tommy Brunton.

"Tommy and Vinny led parallel lives." Tommy, left, and new daughter Aileen; Vinny and new daughter Kelly. 1981. Photo courtesy of Tommy Brunton.

"He always had the right words." Father Mychal Judge and Kippy Walsh, September 9, 1995. Photo courtesy of Chris Walsh.

"The last summer." Vinny, Tommy, and Mike Brunton, July 2001. Photo courtesy of Tommy Brunton.

"Oh, Captain. My Fire Captain." Vinny's mass card.

"Going Home." Tommy escorts sister Maryann, December 13, 2001. Photograph by Kerry Sheridan.

Bronko's funeral, November 8, 2001. Liam leads the band up the street. Tim is pictured behind him, left. Photograph by Alan Simpson.

"Inside the coffin lay their beloved friend." Bronko's pallbearers carry his coffin into St. Patrick's Cathedral. Photograph by Alan Simpson.

Firefighters and civilians line the streets around the bagpipe band as they wait to play the final set at Bronko's funeral—"Going Home," and "America the Beautiful." Photograph by Alan Simpson.

"Riding in a fire truck for the last time." The band stands to the side as the fire truck carrying Bronko's coffin rolls up Fifth Avenue. Photograph by Alan Simpson.

"Farewell, Brother Bronko." Liam pours whiskey over Bronko's coffin as Billy Murphy (far left) and Kippy Walsh look on. Photograph by Alan Simpson.

"Tuning up." Tim helps piper Tom McEnroe Sr. tune his instrument before the St. Patrick's Day parade, March 16, 2002. Photograph by Kerry Sheridan.

"We just wanted to do our own thing." Band kneels in prayer at Ground Zero, October 7, 2001. Photo courtesy of Sandy St. James.

"Closing Ground Zero." Bagpipers march up the ramp leading out of the site during closing ceremonies, May 30, 2002. Photograph by Kerry Sheridan.

"The last piece." A girder covered in black and draped with an American flag is driven out of the World Trade Center site, May 30, 2002. Photograph by Kerry Sheridan.

"Flag bearers." Color guard members approach the site on the anniversary, September 11, 2002. Mike Brunton is pictured at center. Photograph by Kerry Sheridan.

the fire commissioner did not consider playing at a funeral as time on duty, so the band members continued to work their full shifts, too, either at their firehouses or digging at the World Trade Center site.

Sometimes they would arrive at a service to find that pipers from different bands had shown up to help them play. Though meant as a courtesy, this was not regarded kindly by the Fire Department pipers. Playing with new members on the spur of the moment was a potential musical disaster: The new pipers' tunings might be set slightly differently, or they might have learned a tune with an extra half beat here or there. But beyond that, the firefighters wanted to bury their own men. They were grateful to a number of other local bands, who'd filled in at services when no member of the Fire Department band was able to attend. But when the newcomers asked to play along with them, they viewed it as disrespectful of Fire Department traditions. Even if the department was so strapped it could only provide a couple of pipers at a funeral, the FDNY pipers were adamant that it be them and only them.

Murphy made repeated calls to the commissioner's office, asking him to take the band members off regular duty so they could focus on the funerals. His calls weren't returned. No manpower could be taken off duty. So the men carried on.

A couple of weeks after the attacks, the *New York Times* published a two-page spread that showed every lost firefighter's face. Three hundred and forty-three head shots, each firefighter's official portrait. A piper named Bobby kept the sheet and circled the faces he recognized with a highlighter. He haloed at least fifty head shots in iridescent yellow. Some were men whom he worked with on occasion and could recall by sight, not name. Others were friends, close ones. Some nights he would come home and lay the paper out across the table, studying the faces. One night, he came home to find that his wife had thrown it out. She didn't think it was good for him, she said. The paper was gone. There was nothing he could do.

The September 11 deaths were rapid, and frighteningly random. Firefighters survived to tell of other men they had seen ten feet in front of them who'd died. Within seconds, they'd lost track of a friend and he'd disappeared forever. Others had switched shifts, as was so often done in the department, and found that those who had filled in for them were killed. Many were young, with small children at home. Just as many were skilled professionals with years of knowledge that could never be replaced. Fate was nonsensical. The survivors could only wonder: Why him, not me?

After the first week, the idea that somehow people might have survived began to dissipate. Some families began consulting their parish priests to discuss options for funeral services when there was no body to bury. Dreyer anticipated a flood of questions on the matter, so he contacted Father John Delendick, a Catholic Fire Department chaplain. He told Dreyer that any remains would be acceptable; even dust or dirt from the site could be considered remains and be blessed at the ceremony and buried. Another priest, Father Brian Jordan, a Franciscan from Father Mychal Judge's church, had begun working at the World Trade Center site minutes after the towers came down and had been there almost every day since, blessing remains and providing support to the recovery workers. Father Jordan wrote a paper in which he explained how the Roman Catholic church had always adapted liturgical rites to the pastoral needs of the people. He noted previous disasters in which blessings were given to the deceased without the body present, such as the sinking of the *Titanic,* the world wars, the Korean and Vietnam wars, and major earthquakes. He also outlined his own perception, emphasizing that funerals exist primarily to pray for the dead and to comfort the living.

On Monday, September 24, almost two weeks after the attack, another meeting was scheduled at the ceremonial unit, to inform officers of a new protocol regarding funerals with no body. Two families had already decided to hold memorial services, and both were held on Tuesday, September 25. By Wednesday, the ceremonial unit had sixty requests from families who planned to do the same.

The pace built into a frenzy. Now, every day of the week, funerals and memorial services were scheduled in growing numbers. On Thursday, September 27, there was one funeral and three memorials. On Friday, September 28, six funerals and three memorials. The band had no protocol for setting priorities. In the beginning, they treated funerals and memorial services alike. Later, they might send one or two extra men to a funeral, if they could. Band members rushed from service to service. Each small group split into smaller units, playing at two or three services each day. Police escorts sped the players through the streets. Sometimes, band members would play the "in" at one church—marching up the street playing "Minstrel Boy" and then stopping for the solo of "Amazing Grace"—then, when the family disappeared into the church, rush off to another church to play the "in," then head back to the first church to play the "out"—"Going Home" and "America the

Beautiful"—to escort the procession away, then go back to the second church to do the same thing again.

Tim Grant, the pipe major, knew thirty-five of the firefighters who had died. Eight were men he counted among his friends. Dennis Devlin, who'd been a captain at his firehouse before being promoted to battalion chief; Billy McGinn, who'd helped him study for the lieutenant's test; Tommy Foley, his hunting buddy; and Bronko, the closest of his friends who had been taken in the collapse. During the first few weeks after September 11, Tim cried often. One Sunday, driving to work, he dialed a local radio station and requested "The Fields of Athenrye," to be dedicated to Bronko.

> By lonely prison walls, I heard a young girl calling.
> "Michael, they are taking you away.
> For you stole Trevelyn's corn
> So the young might see the morn.
> Now the prison ship lies waiting in the bay."
>
> Low lie the Fields of Athenrye
> Where once we watched the small, free birds fly
> Our love was on the wing
> We had dreams and songs to sing
> It's so lonely 'round the Fields of Athenrye.

He and Bronko had been in a pub in Ireland once when the whole room began singing the mournful ballad. Now, alone in his van, Tim began to weep, his face twisted, tears streaming down his red cheeks. He wondered what people would think if they saw him crying like that as he drove by.

He slept poorly at night, intervals of exhausted sleep interrupted by nightmares of the towers collapsing on top of him. In one, he was Tommy Foley, scrambling to escape the spewing dirt from the tower as it fell, diving under a vehicle while the debris pummeled him from all sides. The avalanche slowed, leaving Tim (who was really Tommy) to think he had made it, only to realize he had not. He was lying there, dead.

Tim moved through the days in a numb state and tried not to look too far ahead. He didn't get involved with scheduling the rest of the band. His e-mail in-box filled up with good wishes, requests for interviews, inquiries about how to buy the band's CD. The mass of trivia overwhelmed him.

Saturday, September 29 was the busiest day yet—two funerals and thirteen memorials.

Tommy Foley's funeral was being held at 10:00 A.M. in Nanuet. Dennis Devlin's memorial service was scheduled to start at 11:00 A.M., thirty-five miles away in Washingtonville. Tim had to choose between two close friends. He was unsure which was more important—a memorial for a top chief or a funeral for a young friend? Tim hated to miss either, so he attempted to do both. He played the opening set at Tommy's funeral, then drove to Devlin's service. He left before Tommy's eulogies began and arrived too late to hear Devlin's; he saw his company from the firehouse all seated together there, but the church was so packed he could not join them. Tim played his bagpipes at the close of Devlin's service. He berated himself for showing up at the end. Splitting himself in two had not made the situation any better. He told himself he should have been there for the whole service. For both of them. Somehow.

By the end of September, the band had played at sixty-five funerals and memorials. The band members had been officially removed from firehouse duty in order to focus on the funerals. This was referred to as being "off the chart," a term firefighters also used to describe any event that was bad beyond imagination. Most decided not to go to the pile anymore. Still, some persisted, particularly those who had lost a number of men from their firehouse; among them were Liam and Billy Murphy from Rescue 4, Al Schwartz from Ladder 4, and Frank McCutchen from Ladder 5. Some of the band members felt guilty about their decision to leave the site, but most determined that their better place was with the band. The dead needed to be buried with honor.

The number of New York City firefighters attending funerals dropped lower than it had been in decades. With hundreds gone, hundreds at the site, and every single man and woman in the Fire Department grieving, attending funerals every day of the week was neither emotionally or logistically possible. Most days, out-of-town firefighters from Chicago, Boston, Los Angeles, from all over the country, and even from Canada showed up at funerals to thicken the ranks.

Former pipe major Tom McEnroe took over the scheduling and made himself the point man for inquiries regarding the band and the services; a drum sergeant named Teddy Carstensen assigned drummers. McEnroe decided "Minstrel Boy" was too banal—every piper in the whole world, it seemed, knew "Minstrel Boy" and played it in parades—and changed the opening tune to "Dawning of the Day." In Irish, this traditional air is known as "Fainne Geal an Lae." A number of different lyrics have been adapted to the rhythmic tune. One is an Irish rebel song.

> For the fields your blood has hallowed
> O you host of Irish dead
> In the light of Freedom's morning
> Men of Ireland yet shall tread.
> When the foemen reel before them
> In the thunder of the fray
> They shall shout your name in triumph
> At the dawning of the day.

One is about a sweet maiden.

> One morning early I walked forth
> By the margin of Lough Leane
> The sunshine dressed the trees in green
> And summer bloomed again.
> I left the town and wandered on
> Through fields all green and gay
> And whom should I meet but a colleen sweet
> At the dawning of the day.

Another, titled "The Ballad of William Bloat," is about murder.

> In a mean abode on the Skankill Road
> Lived a man named William Bloat.
> He had a wife, the curse of his life,
> Who continually got his goat.
> So one day at dawn, with her nightdress on,
> He cut her bloody throat.

And the most recent was a poem about heartbreak and an angel's impossible love, written by the Irish poet Patrick Kavanagh in 1946, and titled "On Raglan Road."

On Raglan Road on an autumn day I met her first and knew
That her dark hair would weave a snare that I might one day rue;
I saw the danger, yet I walked along the enchanted way,
And I said, let grief be a falling leaf at the dawning of the day. . . .

On a quiet street where old ghosts meet, I see her walking now
Away from me so hurriedly my reason must allow
That I had wooed not as I should a creature made of clay—
When the angel woos the clay he'd lose his wings at the dawn of day.

"Dawning of the Day" had first entered the band's repertoire as a buoyant quick march. But when played as a slow march, the sounds were dramatic, sorrowful, and unique.

Each day the band members dressed, marched, and played the exact same way. Their presence was a symbol of strength to the onlookers at a funeral. They strode confidently, swayed in rhythm, and maintained stony expressions. When the tunes finished, the silence left them alone with their thoughts. Though they stared straight ahead, appearing to notice no one, they could see everyone around with their peripheral vision. From a distance, they appeared as a surge of honor and meaning. Up close, the tang of stale beer wafted from their mouths with each breath.

Playing at two, three, four services one day, then the next, then the next, they lost their grasp on time. A month passed and it felt like one second; two minutes of silence, like days. Each firefighter knew anywhere from twenty to two hundred of the men who died, yet somehow, most days none of the pipers knew the people they were playing for. When McEnroe made his rounds with his clipboard, he shouted out the location of the next service, not the man's name. Pipers and drummers would come up individually to peer over his shoulder at the clipboard to see if there was a particular guy they wanted to play for—even though playing for someone they knew was the worst.

As long as the band members had no time to think about what they were doing, they could pretend the task was manageable. Family life was set aside. One piper admitted to letting his grass grow wild on the lawn, leaving his pool uncovered, and allowing the bills to stack up. He mentioned "trouble at home," rising tension over his nightly drinking and constant bickering with his wife, a situation that others were surely experiencing but rarely talked about. His eyes grew damp and red at the slightest mention of funerals, and he shuddered constantly, even on warm days. His anguish was more visible than anyone else's in the band. He drove to services in his car, alone, while many of the others carpooled. Most of them talked little with him. Some steered away from him entirely.

One drummer's wife came home a couple of days after September 11 to find her husband in bed, curled in a fetal position under the covers, weeping. In more than ten years of marriage, she'd never seen him cry. Later, when she asked him what was the worst thing he'd seen down there, expecting him to say a bloody body part, she'd been shocked by his answer. It was the voices on he'd heard on the radio, he said, during the last seconds as one of the towers was coming down, the cries of "Mayday! Mayday," the desperate cursing mingled with the anonymous pleas for their mothers, their kids, to tell wives of their love. But after weeks of playing at funerals and memorial services, he'd grown numb to the suffering of others, even bored by the repetitive ceremony, and it frightened him.

One young piper called the funeral detail a "recurring nightmare." Another likened it to *Groundhog Day,* the 1993 movie in which Bill Murray is trapped into living the worst day of his life over and over. But that was comedy. This was reality.

On September 29, a fire lieutenant named Michael Quilty was memorialized in Staten Island. Shortly after his family finished the service, his body was identified. He was given a funeral two days later, on October 1. The pipers began to wonder, in horror, how many of these repeat services lay ahead.

Firefighters age quickly. They join the department in their twenties and are eligible to retire after twenty years. In their youth, endless reserves of stamina and adrenaline sustain them through battles with fire. Over time, the smoke and harsh conditions take a toll. Kippy was only forty-one, but his hair had recently lost all its hazelnut color to pale gray and white. One side of his lower lip grew swollen from pressing against the mouthpiece of his blowpipe; one eyelid ballooned. Mary watched her husband aging before her eyes. She'd half expected it, but now that it was happening, it seemed too soon.

One day while out grocery shopping, Mary ran into the widow of a firefighter friend. Mary asked how she was. The woman's eyes were glazed. "He always does the grocery shopping," she said to Mary, still talking about her husband in the present tense. "I don't know what I'm doing here."

Kippy was bearing witness to the wives and kids of the dead, day after day. Worse, he saw their suffering increase the moment the music began to float through the air from his pipes. The pain he saw in their faces began to show on his own. The group of pipers was smaller than ever before, which forced the band members closer to the mourning families. Pipers who might have habitually taken a spot near the back, and drummers, who always marched behind pipers, suddenly found themselves a few feet away from the widows and children. They practiced fixing their eyes on a point on the ground in front of them, in order not to meet the eyes of the grieving.

After every memorial service there was a collation, in the firehouse or at a bar or in the basement of a school or church. On October 6, after Kippy had played the solo of "Amazing Grace" at his friend Gerry Duffy's memorial service, he'd wanted to stay around afterward to meet some of the men from 21 Truck he'd worked with and to check on Gerry's family and see if they needed anything. But he didn't have time. He had to rush off to play at another service.

Many nights, Kippy would crash in an open bed at his firehouse, rather than drive more than fifty miles back to his home in Warwick. On evenings when he did come home, he slipped into the bedroom for a nap. Mary tried to keep communication open with her husband, but he didn't confide easily, the way he used to. Some nights, Mary would overhear Kippy talking on the phone, scheduling services with other pipers for the coming days. Now and then, she'd catch snippets of his conversations, and wonder: Why isn't he telling me this?

For the most part, every day was the same. Death after death. Funeral after funeral. He didn't want to talk to Mary about it.

Half a dozen years earlier, when their son, Danny, was born, Kippy had considered leaving the band for a while in order to spend more time at home with his wife and the new baby. But Mary had insisted that he stay with it. She saw how much fun Kippy had around the guys, and the pride he took in being a member of an elite group. She didn't want Kippy to abandon something that he loved.

Now Danny was six, bright, sensitive, and old enough to want to know the answers. "Daddy, are you going into burning buildings anymore?" he asked one day. "I don't want you going into burning buildings anymore." The Walshes weren't the only ones struggling to make sense of the tragedy for their children. Other pipers in the band sometimes talked of their kids' most trying queries, including "Do all firemen die when they go to work?" One friend of Bronko's was crippled to tears when his five-year-old son asked, "Why did the bad men kill my friend Bronko?" A profession that had once seemed glorious to young ones now turned frightening. Mary tried to shield Danny from the images of the collapsing towers on television, but one day she discovered he'd learned to master the remote control: She found him sitting in front of the set, watching reports on the disaster. In the first few days after September 11, as she talked to friends and family on the phone, Mary was aware that Danny could hear the concern and sadness in her tone, and she was unsure how to protect him from it. She didn't want to lie to him, but could his young mind handle the honest truth? The less Mary said to him, the more anxious he became. His father was rarely home, and the boy didn't understand why. "Where's Daddy?" he cried. "He promised he would play with me!" Eventually, Mary told him that a lot of firemen had died in those buildings and that his daddy was doing what he could to help. "How many people died, Mommy?" he asked. "A lot," Mary answered quietly. "A lot of our friends died."

Mary was thirty-seven, and for the better part of four years she and Kippy had been trying unsuccessfully to conceive a second child. Danny deserved a sibling. They didn't want to adopt. Time was slipping away. In late summer, she and Kippy had gone to a fertility specialist to begin discussing their options.

When Tommy returned to the band after a couple of weeks, people from the neighborhood—other firefighters, too—sometimes remarked to him that they couldn't understand how he did it. Everyone had lost large numbers of friends, whom they'd called "brothers." But Tommy had lost his brother, the only one in the band who had lost such a close relative. Yet here was Tommy playing nearly every single day at funerals for those who'd been found and could be finally buried by their families. How was that not an unsettling reminder of the fact that Vinny had not yet been laid to rest? The remarks Tommy heard weren't really questions, or if they were, they were purely rhetorical, but Tommy knew what they were getting at. It was like when other firemen asked how he was doing; something in their voices told him they weren't asking the same question they'd asked before, while Vinny was alive. This was new, a query filled with sympathy and caution. Behind it was a morbid curiosity to which they dared not give words. Was he a monster at home? Beating his wife? Drinking too much? More often than not, the askers didn't want to be burdened by the real answer.

Tommy didn't consider the funerals and memorials exhausting, as so many of the pipers did. Exhausting, to Tommy, was the fruitless torture of digging. But if he wasn't going to be at the site, he had to do something. Downtime was just time to sit around and stew over what the terrorists had taken from him and so many others. Instead, he concentrated on blowing, pressing and fingering the notes, marching forward and back, again and again. He would do what he could to help bury the ones they had found, or memorialize the ones they hadn't, with the honor the men and their families deserved. To Tommy, he was merely remaining faithful to an unspoken reciprocal agreement—some firefighters would dig for the missing, and some would pipe for the dead. When people asked, Tommy gave the same line again and again. "This is the job. We're just doing what has to be done." He didn't want anyone's pity. The duties were only two parts of an honor all men had agreed to when they became firefighters. To give up their lives for others, and to take care of their own when they died.

When—if—Vinny was found, other firefighters would guard him while Tommy and Mike rushed to the site to help carry their brother's body out. Tommy trusted the firefighters there and knew that they would handle every brother with the same care and dignity. But Tommy had always sensed that such an event would never take place for him. No matter how many small pieces he and others pulled out with their hands, no matter how the pile shrank before him, none of it would be Vinny.

Kathy became the focus of the Brunton brothers' attention. She'd quit her jobs at the school and the hospital. Most of the time, she stayed in the house. She kept the door to the master bedroom upstairs tightly shut. She rarely went in there anymore, just long enough to blow-dry her short brown hair and grab clothes from the closet. She had not slept in the bed since September 10. The sheets remained unchanged. She had picked up the running shorts and sweaty T-shirt Vinny had worn on his Monday morning jog and wrapped them in a plastic bag to preserve his smell. She lived mostly downstairs now. During the day, she often sat at the head of the dining room table, in a central location between the kitchen and the living room. As morning faded into night, a rotating cast of family and friends filled the chairs around her. Tommy and Mike came by to check on her every day. Time passed, but she took little notice. Kathy felt like she was frozen in a block of ice. Everything in her life was on hold until Vinny came back.

Maryann kept a close watch on her older brothers. She saw Mike's fury growing day by day. He'd stopped working at the site a couple of weeks after Tommy did, and his family and friends had supported his decision, but he was deeply upset at not being able to keep the promise he'd made to Vinny's daughter. His temper was on a short fuse. He became bitter toward his own family. He'd always been a drinker; now he drank more, maybe to numb his pain, maybe to punish himself. Maryann began to fear that Mike was dangerously depressed.

Tommy, too, was drinking more, but he had shown little emotion since the early morning of September 12, when he'd come in the door dust-covered and weary. He tended to the needs of Kathy and the kids, and Maryann, and stayed quiet about his own sadness. He'd comforted, hugged, soothed, handed out tissues, shushed, and gently scolded, but hadn't cried. Maryann worried about Tommy playing at all the funerals and memorials. She knew what he said he was doing it for, but she wondered if he wasn't hiding behind his uniform—if playing with the band at services, dressing up in an ornate kilt and tunic, marching with them as a separate and distinct unit, "doing what has to be done" in the name of honor, was really just a complicated way of not dealing with his own grief.

By the end of September, forty-three firefighters had been memorialized and twenty-two buried. In October, the overwhelming majority of services were ones in which no body had been recovered. In that month alone, 129 firefighters were honored with memorial services and twenty-seven had funerals. As the end of October approached, none of the five missing members of Ladder 105 had been recovered, but three were given memorial services. Kathy and the rest of the Brunton family had attended all of them. Firefighter Tom Kelly was memorialized on September 29, Henry Miller on October 1, and Frank Palumbo on October 20. One other firefighter who'd lived in the Bruntons' neighborhood, Peter Vega, had not been found, either, but his family held a memorial service on October 6. By the end of October, while only fifty-seven of the missing 343 firefighters had been recovered, close to two-thirds had received some kind of service, as families tried to move on.

Never before had entire shifts of firefighters from the same company been simultaneously lost. There was no Fire Department tradition to dictate whether there should be an order to their services, who first and who last. Kathy thought that the way Vinny had put the needs of others before himself, he might have wanted to be memorialized or buried last, after all his men had been laid to rest and their families taken care of first. But the other missing member of 105 Truck was a probie named Dennis O'Berg Jr. Kathy knew his father was holding a vigil at the site, digging every day in hopes of recovering his son. The O'Bergs would wait until, as many said, "until the last guy is pushing the broom" through the site before relenting and holding a service. Kathy respected their decision, though it made her even less sure of what to do. Did that mean she should wait until after the O'Bergs? Or what if she had a memorial service, like most families were now doing, but then something of Vinny's was found? Would that taint the whole service? Would she be able to go through the wrenching ceremony twice? She wanted to do the right thing by Vinny, she just didn't know what that was. When it came right down to it, all Kathy wanted was a body to bury. Hosting a memorial might send a message that she'd given up hope that Vinny would come back. Worse, it might make true her nightmare that Vinny would never come back. She decided against it. She waited, in the hope that the problem would solve itself.

In the beginning, all of the Bruntons had expected, to varying degrees, that they would some day bury Vinny. As October wore on, Maryann felt more and more strongly that the family should have a memorial service. As the two-month anniversary approached, Maryann saw the need to put an end to the waiting. The chances of recovering him seemed slim. She feared in some way they were letting Vinny hang, preventing his spirit from finding peace. She and her brothers had been raised Catholic, and Maryann believed Vinny should have a Christian burial—prayers said over his body, a casket draped in a white cloth, the evocation of a full and rich life, and a ceremony that included the purification of the soul. Once that was done, his spirit could rise to heaven as his body was led to its final resting place. She asked her parish priest how they could do this if they didn't have a body? Could they use ashes from the World Trade Center site, or other mementos of Vinny's, and bury that instead of a body? The priest said yes, they could do it that way if they chose.

People kept asking Maryann if the family had decided when the service would be. So many people posed the same question, Maryann quickly grew tired of it. The circle of expectation was pressuring her to do something she already wanted to do. She was family, and she wanted a service. She became adamant.

She started bringing up the topic of a memorial service to Tommy and Mike. "When should we do it?" she asked them outright. Refusing to memorialize him held everyone in limbo. Worse, it seemed to be implying that nothing had happened, or that Vinny didn't matter. She and Vinny were the two youngest, Vinny was her closest brother in age. She wanted to be able to take care of him. She wanted a place where she could go and kneel and plant flowers, see "Vincent Brunton" etched in stone, and grieve. Maryann felt she was the only one in the family who was saying, "We have to sit down and talk about this." If she didn't, it seemed everyone would just let it go.

Maryann had known Kathy for more than two decades, and she believed she knew instinctively the way her sister-in-law was seeing the situation. Kathy would never make this big of a decision on her own. She'd always looked to Vinny, and waited for his direction. After more than twenty years of marriage, those habits didn't just vanish overnight. "Kathy is just waiting for someone to tell her what to do," Maryann pleaded with her brothers. "It's okay to go ahead and start planning."

Tommy, too, had begun to feel like it might be time to have some kind of service. Vinny was his brother, yes, and Maryann's and Mike's. But he had been Kathy's husband, and now Kathy was the only one that mattered.

One day, after Maryann had pressed, Tommy finally told her. This wasn't their decision to make. "We can't force her to do something she's not ready to do," he said. "We have to wait."

He wrestled to balance Kathy's optimism, Maryann's insistence, Mike's drive to recover a body, and his own sense that Vinny was never coming back. Still, some of the old rituals were harder to let go of.

One afternoon, Tommy stood at the edge of pipers' formation, resting his mouthpiece on his shoulder as he waited for someone to call the start of "Going Home" to finish the funeral set. He glanced at the line of firefighters who were assembling themselves into a solid row, looking at their feet as they set their toes to the white line at the side of the street. In the distance, he caught sight of a slim captain with reddish hair under a white hat. *Vinny?* Tommy snapped his head downward and stared at the tiny individual rocks that formed the smooth pavement at his feet. No. No. It couldn't be true.

As the weeks wore on, Liam began to feel a hundred years old. The company shifted from the twenty-four hours on, twenty-four hours off schedule to an ABC chart—twenty-four hours in the firehouse, forty-eight hours off. Liam and many of the other Rescue 4 firefighters spent their forty-eight hours off working twelve-hour shifts at the site. When they returned to the firehouse for a twenty-four-hour tour, they paced the apparatus floor, unlaced shoes flapping and scraping against the cement. They heard dispatchers on the system talking about emergencies or fires to which rescue units would normally have been assigned. But rescue wasn't being called out on any fires. They were powerless to engage in the kind of firefighting and rescue work they once had. Day after day, they listened as a call came over announcing a four-five: 5–5–5–5, the code for a fallen firefighter. Every firefighter in the house would stop what he was doing and bow his head, listening to a voice relay the names of more firefighters who had been killed on September 11. Sitting around like this, captive for an entire shift, guys got on each other's nerves. Even Liam sometimes blew up.

The first week after September 11, Karen waited anxiously for news that someone had found Bronko, either alive under the rubble or unconscious at a hospital. At two weeks, she wondered how long he could have survived. He was big and hardy; two weeks wouldn't have been out of the realm of possibility. She returned to work. Some widows went to visit the site, but Karen was too afraid. Even after a month had passed, Karen refused to let herself believe that he was truly gone. She continued to have dreams of Bronko striding out from the smoke and debris and saying, "I'm fine! What are you worried about? You're crazy. You're such a worrier."

The women who had lost husbands in Rescue 4 included Karen in their circle. Everyone knew Bronko would have made her his wife if he'd had the time. They grieved together, along with Denise Ford and Mary Fahey. Some of the widows joined support groups, where they shared their thoughts and experiences with other women in similar situations. But in those sessions, the widows talked about situations that did not apply to Karen—helping young children understand the death of their father, running a household without a longtime husband, how to apply for victim's compensation money and how to deal with the shadowy prospect of suddenly becoming financially well-off because of the horrible circumstances in which their husbands were killed. Karen had been told there were secondary funds that offered money and other benefits to girlfriends of the deceased, and on occasion such gifts were offered to her, but she abruptly turned it all down.

She was grateful to the widows for the kindness they showed her, but she knew her grief was different from theirs. They were trying to piece together the remnants of a life and a home they'd shared for years. Karen was trying to come to terms with the idea that the man she'd hoped to start a life with and have babies with was gone forever, before they ever had a chance to begin. Karen chose one-on-one sessions with a therapist instead.

Bronko's friends and Karen had considered themselves Bronko's family, since his parents had both passed away and he had no brothers or sisters. But Bronko had a cousin, Nina, on his father's side who lived in the New York area and five other cousins who lived in Indiana. Suddenly, the cousins thrust themselves into the picture, seeking their legal rights as blood relatives and their right to claim the legacy of having lost a family member in the greatest terrorist tragedy ever to take place on American soil. Bronko's friends hadn't heard much about these cousins. They'd assumed he was not close to them. The cousins felt the opposite.

When it came to the question of a memorial service, everyone had a different idea. Nina wanted a memorial service at a small church in Long Island, in a parish near where he had grown up. Liam had planned from the beginning to hold the service, preferably a funeral service, in St. Patrick's Cathedral. Bronko had too many friends to squeeze into a village church. Karen deferred to Liam. She, too, hoped they would have a body before they made a final decision. Nina began to talk of planning her own memorial service, regardless of what the others wanted. Liam did his best to alleviate the tension. He suggested they just wait a bit and see. Maybe Bronko would be found.

One night, a TV crew from ABC news came to Rescue 4 to interview some of the men about how they were coping with the loss of two men from the house on Father's Day and nine on September 11. Liam had slipped through the garage door of the firehouse late that evening after a long day at the site, having slept little in the past twenty-four hours. He was dirty, and his chin was littered with stubble. A producer begged him to sit in front of the camera for a few questions. After some pressing, Liam relented. He answered questions about the work at the site; no, no men from his house had been recovered yet. When it was over, he barely remembered what he'd just said. He'd been asked something about closure. He didn't even know what that meant anymore. He hated the word and the vacant meaning it carried. His eyes were burning. The sharp fragments in the air were scraping at his corneas. His vision wasn't what it used to be. He climbed up the long staircase, found an empty bed, and fell asleep.

New men had taken assignments to replenish the ranks at Rescue 4. They cringed at the word "replacements." One was a bright-faced young firefighter with bristly black hair, whose late father had been a member of the pipe band. Another had been a friend of Michael Cawley's from Ladder 136. Like others before them, they came to the elite group with their connections and expertise. But they could not avoid the fact that they'd come after. They were not a part of the original firehouse. Their presence reminded everyone of the loss. Most of these new men would not stay long, opting for another transfer after a couple of months.

One of the new recruits was Richie Schmidt, a slim, quiet firefighter with enormous hands, blue eyes that tilted down at the outer corners, straight brown hair and a bushy mustache. At first, Richie had come by Rescue 4 almost daily to check in and see if there was any news of their missing men. He soon fell in among the firefighters there. He began working at the site every day with them, spending every bit of his off-duty time digging as they did, and eventually he officially transferred to their firehouse. The other men later found out that Richie had been very close to Terry Farrell. He was digging to recover his lifelong friend. As weeks went by, Liam, Richie, and another burly Rescue 4 firefighter named Eddie Zeilman became inseparable.

Liam also met and befriended a bald-headed fellow named Jimmy Miller, who was close to Liam's age and fit into the category of "construction worker" at the site. Actually, Jimmy's role there was unique. He owned a company that provided equipment for movie sets, including lighting rigs and rainmaking trucks. Jimmy had been friends with Rescue 4's Harry Ford for eighteen years. Because of Ford's side job, they were members of the same union, the International Alliance of Theatrical Stage Employees, Local 52. But their families had known each other much longer: Harry's father was vice president of the union and best friends with Jimmy's uncle. After Harry was killed in the Father's Day fire, Jimmy fell into a deep depression. He locked himself in his apartment on Manhattan's Lower East Side and rarely ventured outside. He couldn't sleep at night. He lost thirty-three pounds.

Within hours of the terrorist attack on September 11, the city revoked all filming permits. That meant Jimmy's company was out of business, indefinitely. Later that night, a union representative called to say trucks were needed at the World Trade Center. Jimmy made some phone calls and arranged to have several of his trucks driven there. Then Jimmy and his brother, who had come by Jimmy's apartment to watch the news, drove to the site together—all the streets in lower Manhattan were barricaded, but there was an emergency route that led almost from the door of Jimmy's apartment directly to the site—and began to work, setting up tents to serve as temporary morgues.

The next day, Jimmy offered his generators, trucks, and lighting rigs to help in the relief effort. Some of the same water trucks that had created rain for the movies now perched near areas of the burning debris, creating a deluge of water to put out the fires, while others tooled around the site, serving as sprinkler machines to reduce the dust in the air. The powerful, multi-bulbed lighting rigs illuminated massive areas of the rubble and became beacons of light for the rescuers as they worked through the night. Jimmy also donated a fleet of his vans to the pipes and drums band, so they could travel together to funerals instead of racking up mileage and wear and tear on their own vehicles.

Jimmy sensed a bond with many of the firefighters at the site. He more than understood the firefighters' pain at losing men they'd considered to be their brothers. He had lost Harry and, two years before that, a brother of his own. Jimmy also knew what it was like for the families who couldn't bury their loved ones because they hadn't recovered a body. When he was ten years old, he woke in the middle of the night to discover that his twenty-three-year-old sister had committed suicide by plunging into Niagara Falls. Her remains were never found. Jimmy knew why many of the rescue workers who'd lost a son, brother, or father were afraid to leave the site, fearing someone would find the body when they weren't there. They were like Jimmy, still afraid to go to sleep at night in case something terrible would awake him again.

With work to do at the site, Jimmy gained a new focus. He put back on twenty-five of the pounds he'd lost. He ordered a thousand hard hats emblazoned with the American flag and handed them out free to the rescue workers. He bought Trade Center pins in bulk and made T-shirts to raise money for his new friends at the site. One of the things that Jimmy learned early was that firefighters were a territorial lot. When they glimpsed a part of a firefighter's uniform, a boot, or a tool in the debris, they pushed the construction workers away and took charge of the digging themselves. When that happened, Jimmy rushed around the outskirts, making sure they had enough drinking water or adjusting the lights so they could see far enough into the voids within the debris. He soon began calling Liam his good friend. They ate lunch together, and some nights they went out for drinks. Anyone seeing them talking and laughing with one another in rhythmic tones would have thought they were lifelong buddies.

As of October 6, the medical examiner's office had logged 5,927 body parts. Of all the missing, 265 people had been identified. Ninety of those were firefighters.[4] The only sign recovered at the site of any of the nine men from Rescue 4 had been a lone halligan tool, engraved with the initials "KD." It was Kevin Dowdell's. No remains had been found. In early October, those families began to hold memorial services. Liam went to his first memorial service on October 1, for Pete Brennan. He did not join the band. He stood in the honor guard with the men from his company instead, dressed in his navy blue Class-A uniform.

Liam was working the night shift at the site on October 6 when, around 4:00 A.M., someone came upon a crushed helmet bearing the shield number 4. Liam looked inside and saw that the headpiece had belonged to his company's captain, Brian Hickey. Liam turned it around in his hands and studied it. A helmet was a cherished find. It bore each nick and dent of a lifetime of fires and was entirely unique to the man who'd worn it. He wrapped it in a sheet and kept it, hoping that some of Brian's remains would be found nearby. One day soon, when he was recovered, he would give the helmet to Brian's wife, Donna, as a valued memento of her husband's life.

The bagpipers were facing the most demanding day yet. Nineteen memorials and two funerals were scheduled. Among them were services for Peter Vega, a firefighter from Tommy Brunton's neighborhood in Brooklyn, and two of the men counted in Rescue 4's tally of the dead—Pete Nelson and Al Tarasiewicz, the detail from Rescue 5. The band split into even smaller groups to cover them all. Most played for at least three men that day, some managed four. Liam brought out his bagpipes to play at Pete Nelson's memorial. Marching as drum major would have made no sense—only three band members were there, including Liam. At some of the services, there were only two pipers.

Liam still sensed he knew precisely where Bronko was, buried deep beneath the pile of debris that had been the south tower. But with fires still burning below, there was likely to be nothing left by the time the recovery workers reached that area. He slowly became reconciled to the probability that Bronko's body would not be found.

On October 7, the city organized a prayer service for families of all the victims lost at Ground Zero. Over the previous few days, word had spread among the band members that they would be playing at the site that day, all together for the first time since September 11. Many assumed that the service would be small and that only the FDNY band and a collection of family members would be there. The idea of the ceremony carried great meaning to the men. Memorial services disrupted their sense of order. With no body, there was no coffin, and no tangible object around which to base the ceremony. Of course, their presence meant a great deal to the families, and they bestowed honor on the dead through their music. They were part of a group that had always focused their efforts outward. Now, the more they looked away from themselves, the more it forced them to glance inward. In the midst of the onslaught, they fought for some control. Like finally being able to visit a grave, today they would be going to play in close proximity to the majority of the dead, and to their friends and brothers who lay in the smoldering ruins, including Bronko. These were their men, and this would be their service. Something real, for once. And they would be all together once again. They dressed up for the occasion, putting on their red wool tunics and plaid shawls instead of the navy blue sweaters they'd been wearing with their kilts at services.

When they arrived, they discovered the event was entirely different from what they'd expected. Politicians had shown up, including Mayor Giuliani and a number of dignitaries. The Police Department pipe band had also come to play. Two chaplains, one from the Fire Department and one from the Police Department, waited at a viewing stand. The firefighters were told that they were to stand at attention during the speeches and then play at a certain time. They weren't the headliners of the event. Suddenly, the ceremony had a cheap ring to it. They sensed they were just there for the show.

The band had little choice but to go along with the program. Tim and a couple of other Fire Department pipers circled up with four Police Department pipers to tune their instruments to match. They lined up in formation next to the Police Department pipers and drummers and played, as they'd been asked. They stood and listened to the speeches. When it was over, Liam growled at one of the officials, "Is it done?" The man nodded. "Now we're going to do what we came here to do," Liam snapped. He turned and began marching in toward the site. Liam hadn't prepared the band members for this. But he glanced back and saw they were all following him, in single file.

The destruction around them was vast. The rubble pile rolled and peaked in dangerous hills and valleys. A remnant of the facade of one of the towers still stood upright near the western side, reaching 100 or so feet in the air. Several plaza buildings remained around the edges, half destroyed and visibly pummeled, with metal shards protruding from gashed edges. Banging metal and roaring excavators and shrill backing-up alarms filled the air with noise. The band members climbed a makeshift road, overwhelmed in places by the rocky debris. Gray-brown dust settled over the pipers' white spats. After nearly half an hour's journey, they arrived at a flattened plateau, fifty or sixty feet above the ruins of the south tower.

Machine operators and ironworkers all around stopped their work and removed their hard hats to watch. The band formed a large circle. Liam planted his mace in the ground, gripped it at the top, and called the tunes—"Shenandoah," "America the Beautiful," and "Marine Corps Hymn." Sounds never heard before at the site soared across the mountains of debris, replacing the grunts of the machines and the screams of scraping metal with beauty and sorrow. The bagpipes cried out the loss of lives, sounded the call of patriotism and the unity of battle. Then came the joyous tune they'd often played to end a funeral, "Garryowen." The skirl of the pipes brought tears to the faces of the brawny, dirty construction workers. When the tune finished, Liam hollered to out to the pile, "Well done, Bronko!" One of the drummers tossed his sticks high over the edge for Bronko, and they circled and soared through the air. Tim Grant jettisoned his *sgian dubh.* Inside Liam's left sock, pressed between skin and fabric, rested the knife Bronko had once carried.

Then all the pipers got down on one knee, grinding skin into the unforgiving ground. The Rev. Everett Wabst, a retired firefighter and an honorary Protestant chaplain for the Fire Department, rose and spoke a brief prayer. Wabst was a Lutheran minister. As a recovering alcoholic, he had befriended Father Judge years earlier, and together they spearheaded the department's twelve-step anonymous programs. Wabst had worked at the World Trade Center site ever since September 11, blessing bodies as they were removed from the debris, talking with firefighters and rescue workers, and handing out business-size cards with Father Judge's special prayer printed on them.

> Lord,
> Take me where you want me to go

Let me meet who you want me to meet
Tell me what you want me to say
And keep me out of your way.

With wispy black hair combed over a balding crown, full dimpled cheeks, and a rapid laugh, Wabst was a clergyman whose feet trod the same ground as everyone else's. Liam especially gained a special appreciation for the man. Wabst understood the firefighters' anger. Sometimes he told them to imagine their brothers in heaven, active, not motionless, dressed in full spiritual armor, ready to do battle with the evil that had accosted all of them. He reminded them that Father Judge was with them and that their spirits were no longer in these broken bodies. Today, as Wabst spoke in his soothing tones, the pipers bowed their heads, and in an extended moment of silence, each prayed.

Tommy crouched on the outer edge of the group and stared at the gray ground before him. He squeezed his eyes shut and prayed, wished, hoped that Vinny had not suffered when the tower came down. That the tumultuous force of the collapse had taken him before he had a second to be frightened. He imagined the rush of debris throwing Vinny up and down and around, and he prayed that it was fast. That he hadn't had an instant of suffering. Or even to know that this would be his end.

When it was over, an older piper walked over to Tommy and told him he was sorry about his brother.

"This was for Vinny, too," the man said.

"I know," Tommy answered.

One week and eighteen services later, Kippy set his face in a tight-lipped scowl as he stood in the front row of pipers on the street in the Woodside neighborhood of his youth. The late afternoon sun fell gently over the stream of mourners as they emerged from the church. Kippy glared at the fire truck parked near the church entrance, the one that blocked his view of firefighter Mike Brennan's mother as she came out to accept the folded flag offered in memory of her son.

"Detail!" bellowed a lieutenant from the ceremonial unit. "Hand salute!" Kippy snapped his fingers to his forehead and bit his lip.

Silence.

Then the band of twenty played "Going Home" and turned their backs to the church as they led the procession away. When the song finished, Kippy walked back up the street past the church toward his car. He wove through the crowd, pausing to shake hands with firefighters he knew, men who had also known Mike, back when Mike was a young busboy in a local Irish pub. Back when Kippy was a bouncer at that pub, working part-time to supplement his income as a firefighter. Back when Mike had wanted to be just like Kippy.

"You remember how he always used to ask us how he could get on the job?" one firefighter said to Kippy. "What a good kid."

"Yeah, he was a real good kid," Kippy said, and backed away.

After Mike's service, which was the second and last service scheduled that day for Kippy and this group of pipers, they went to that same Irish pub for dinner and a few beers. Those eating in the restaurant suspended their forks and stared as the pipers walked in. Kippy found a table at the back where they all could fit. He told the others about the days when he, Mike, and Liam had all worked in this place. With his finger, he traced out the path that Mike used to follow, from the front to the back of the restaurant, carrying armloads of plates and glasses. From time to time, Kippy got up from the table to talk with bartenders and staff he knew in the restaurant. They all told Kippy how glad they were that he was alive.

"I'm glad I'm alive, too," Kippy answered back, trying his best to retain a jovial tone. "I guess it's not your choice when you go, right?"

Kippy came back to the table and slid into the booth seat. The waitress asked if anyone cared for an after-dinner drink. Kippy nodded; the others shook their heads. She came back with a voluptuous glass containing a cognac and port mixture, sweet and potent. Kippy told the men at the table that this was the drink they used to give the Irish-born guys after a fight broke out in the bar. The "donkeys," as Kippy called them, were always less menacing than the Woodside boys, and often smaller, yet they always went after the biggest guys in the pub, like him. Kippy laughed as he spoke in their Irish brogue, "'I'll burst your nose,' they'd say." He'd eject one of the offenders, then sit the other one down and get him this drink. As a device for mellowing a belligerent drunk, it worked every time.

Kippy drained the last drops from his glass and ordered another.

CHAPTER

6

DISCOVERY

I will be as harsh as truth and as uncompromising as justice. On this subject I do not wish to think, or speak, or write with moderation. No! No! Tell a man whose house is on fire to give a moderate alarm; tell him to moderately rescue his wife from the hands of the ravisher; tell the mother to gradually extricate her babe from the fire into which it has fallen; but urge me not to use moderation in a cause like the present.

—William Lloyd Garrison, *The Liberator,* January 1, 1831

As October wore on, Liam and many of the men from Rescue 4 remained among the hundred or so firefighters who worked at the site just about anytime they weren't at their firehouses. Some fire chiefs complained that certain firefighters were spending too much time there. The Fire Department counseling unit feared that constant exposure to the grisly recovery effort would have negative consequences on the firefighters' mental health, and some firefighters from Rescue 4 were told outright to leave. They didn't. Instead, they sneaked around, stopped wearing any gear that would identify them as firefighters, and disguised themselves as regular construction workers, wearing hard hats and coveralls. If they caught sight of a chief who they knew was opposed to their presence, they darted away in order to avoid a confrontation. One day, a firefighter crouched in one of the valleys of rubble, wearing a white bucket over his head with a hole cut out at the front so he could watch the equipment operators and survey the contents being torn away. From a distance, he hoped, he would look like an upturned bucket in the debris. It worked. He wasn't caught. Given the circumstances, the Fire Department brass probably wouldn't have penalized the firefighters for not obeying orders, but still, the men felt juvenile and ridiculous.

The firefighters' main job was watching construction vehicles called grapplers, dozens of powerful diesel excavators that roared across the piles on tank-like treads. By some estimates, one grappler could do the work of twenty men in eight hours. Vast chunks of steel and debris were removed from the site and dropped at a transfer station near the firehouse of Ladder 10 and Engine 10 on the south border of the site, where the rubble was sifted and raked for signs of remains. The firefighters studied the mouthfuls of rubble that the grapplers pulled from the pile, searching for flecks of color that might be clothing. They stood perilously close to the excavators, sometimes less than ten feet away, digging with shovels at any areas that appeared to hold remains.

Special Operations Command (SOC) oversaw the recovery efforts on a long-term schedule. Two rescue or squad companies within SOC served as specialty teams and rotated to remain there on call night and day. The rescue firefighters assisted in void searches and complicated extrications. They extended their tours to overlap the 7:00 A.M. and 7:00 P.M. change in task forces. The SOC teams arrived at 5:00 or 6:00 A.M. to relieve the night crew. They passed along information to each other about progress during the night, and often stayed until 10 or 11:00 P.M. Rescue 4 was one of the companies that maintained a constant presence. Most worked six or seven days a week. They knew every detail of the site—who was recovered, when and where.

New York City police officers and Port Authority officers also worked side by side with firefighters in the recovery effort. The police officers' duties at the site extended beyond the firefighters'. Some dug through the debris; some oversaw the makeshift morgues or stood guard at checkpoints around the exterior of the site; others were in charge of investigation.

Tensions began to rise between the firefighters and the law enforcement officers. With large numbers of firefighters around, treating the terrain as if it were their own, the Port Authority officers became understandably territorial about the operations at the site. Liam noticed that some of them were wearing a new sticker on their hard hats, which read "WAM," as in "What About Me?" Other Port Authority cops took to saying, "Remember, this is our house." Liam scoffed at their display. Whenever he passed someone wearing a WAM sticker, he muttered loud enough for the other to hear, "It may be your house, but we paid the mortgage."

Firefighters and police officers had publicly called one another "brother" for decades, but the purported similarity in their missions to serve the public now turned rivalrous. Some of the anger came down to an essential difference in their lifestyles and cultures. Cops were individuals. They worked with one partner and slept at home in their own beds. Firemen were collective. They lived together, rode everywhere together, never even went on so much as an errand alone, and wanted to be brought home together when they died. In the wake of the devastation, dormant resentments resurfaced. Firefighters were smaller in force—about eleven thousand compared with about twenty-five thousand police officers—had a less influential union leadership than the police, and generally assumed the underdog's role whenever the two agencies were compared. Now, there were more firefighters at the site than cops. The firefighters' role at the scene of a disaster had always been rescue and recovery. Each firefighter, it seemed, now remembered a moment when a cop had blocked him in some way—a cop who'd stolen credit for rescuing people or property at a fire, or a cop who'd waited longer than necessary to secure the scene of an emergency before calling for fire rescue assistance, thereby chipping away at what rescuers call "the golden hour," the space of time when rescue is most critical for a victim's survival. One firefighter in the band saw a group of cops in a pizza parlor near the site one day, relaxing and laughing. The scene raised his hackles so much he cursed them bitterly for lapsing in their duty and huffed out. The rest of the divide—the so-called Battle of the Badge—came down to numbers. Twenty-three NYPD officers and thirty-seven Port Authority police officers died at the World Trade Center. The firefighters had lost 343. Their sense of ownership was rooted in the dead.

By October 23, the toll of the missing in the World Trade Center attack had fallen below five thousand for the first time. Duplicated reports of the lost had contributed to the early inflated figures, which had risen as high as 6,729;[1] on further review, officials determined that the total dead now numbered 4,964. The medical examiner's official death count, of bodies or parts recovered and identified, remained at 324.[2]

Eight thousand sixty-one remains had been counted at the morgue, 4,121 over the count of one month earlier. Eighty firefighters, six Port Authority officers, and one New York City police officer had been found. Only 186 "whole bodies," as the medical examiner's office classed them, had come in since September 11. A determination of "whole body" was a subjective assessment, made by an intake pathologist, and was accorded to remains that bore resemblance to a human body.[3] A foot was a "remain." A corpse missing a head or a couple of limbs was a "whole body." A torso could fall into either category, depending.

The work was moving faster due to the grapplers. Firefighters working in one area of the site could tell if a recovery had been made somewhere beyond their view by the reports that they heard over the radio. A call for a tool van, rebar cutters, or partner saws—digging tools, not fire tools—meant some part of a body had been spotted. Then, all the machine work stopped. Firefighters assembled at the scene, some dug, others watched. There was no hard-and-fast rule as to what sort of remains were given an honor guard and which weren't. The recovery workers figured out what to do when they got to the area and saw the remains. During the first couple of weeks after September 11, firefighter remains were placed into black body bags and spray-painted "FDNY." Now, any significant piece of a body, civilian or uniformed personnel, was tucked in a stokes basket and covered in an American flag. Smaller remains, like bones, were usually not. When the remains were removed from the debris, an officer on the scene would call, "Uncover!" and the workers around the area would remove their hard hats and hold them to their chests as a priest said a prayer. When the prayer was done, they put their hats back on. If the remains were clearly civilian, a crew of construction workers grasped the handles of the stokes while the firefighters, policemen, and other recovery workers formed a thin double line and saluted as the body passed through the ranks. If the remains belonged to a police officer, fellow police officers carried them out. If the remains belonged to a firefighter, firefighters—from the man's company, if he'd been identifiable—carried him out. An honor guard of all the different groups at the site—construction workers, police officers, and firefighters—always formed for each recovery, stretching a long line of saluting men from the site of the discovery all the way to the door of the waiting ambulance. Peace among the clashing parties reigned fleetingly in the presence of the dead.

Liam had stood in such honor guards at least a hundred times. He'd covered bodies with flags. He'd helped carry out the remains of firemen on stokes. He'd stood on the edge and held his salute, like the rest, long after the body passed his line of vision, until his arm started to tremble. But never had he been able to do this for a man from his own company. The firefighters in Rescue 4 decided that they would have a code to alert the widow if one of their men were found. They were fiercely protective of the widows, and they literally shivered at the notion of rushing to notify and unintentionally giving someone a false identification. Many men had borrowed one another's gear in the rush to the site, so a positive ID could not necessarily be made by simply checking the name on the gear. They determined the best thing would be to make a phone call only when they were 99 percent certain, and when they did, they'd say simply, "We need to talk."

The firefighters in Rescue 4 took control of every aspect of the recovery that they could. They waited for the day to come when they'd be able to use this phrase, instead of the fishing metaphors they'd been using lately, like "It's cold right now. No bites." So far, the occasion had never presented itself. Hope of recovery faded with each passing hour. The pile obeyed no one.

On the morning of October 26, Liam was leading a class called Firefighter Rescue and Removal Techniques at the Fire Academy at Randall's Island. The department was having some difficulty finding instructors to teach the rescue courses, in part because every firefighter from the city's five rescue companies that had initially responded to the scene on September 11 had been killed there—forty-two in rescue, thirty-six in the squads, nine in Haz Mat, and four top chiefs, ninety-one total in all of SOC. About a third of the department's specially trained force was gone, so Liam had agreed to help. Being trained in rescuing or recovering firefighters from a fire scene was a key element of a rescue firefighter's job. One had to have the strength of mind to be able to perform in spite of the shock and grief that such a moment would involve, as well as the skills necessary to extract a person. Liam covered all eleven methods listed in the text for pulling a trapped firefighter, dead or alive, out of a confined space. He used a live firefighter crouched in a stairwell to demonstrate for the students. He had two volunteers position themselves at the head and feet of the trapped firefighter, to show the right way to move a man up a flight of stairs. For another exercise, a member of the class climbed into a hole that would replicate a rubble-covered stairwell. He showed the class how to fold a hose line and drape it down in front of the firefighter, then push the man to lean in and hook his arms over it so he could be lifted up. "The biggest thing with rescue companies is being able to innovate. That's what makes a good rescue guy," Liam told them. "It's not like you can't do it, it's a matter of figuring out how you're going to do it."

During a break, the firefighters in the class remarked on Liam's bloodshot eyes. He looked like he'd been beat up, they told him. He'd been working twelve-hour shifts at the site all week. He was supposed to take Saturdays or Sundays off, but he usually didn't. The rescue techniques he was teaching bore little resemblance to the kind of work he'd been doing lately—digging at debris with gloved hands and garden tools, pulling buckles, shoe soles, and pieces of bleached bone from the rubble.

That morning, a grappler had been snatching enormous chunks of debris from the lobby area near the inner core of the south tower when a nearby firefighter had spotted a torso in its grip. Someone yelled and waved his arms to the machine operator, signaling him to stop. When the firefighters approached, they saw a small radio attached near the chest area. The radio was marked "Rescue 4."

Liam was about to get into his car when his cell phone rang, shortly after class had ended in the early afternoon. Lieutenant Freddy Scholl, who was Liam's partner at the site, was on the other end. Scholl had worked at Rescue 4 until 1994, when he'd received his promotion to lieutenant and was assigned to Ladder 150. Liam had started at Rescue 4 in 1996. They got to know each other after September 11, at Ground Zero.

"We got a radio from Rescue 4," Scholl said. "Better get down here."

Liam tore out of the parking lot and made his way down the FDR Drive. The normally clogged highway was free of traffic. The ten-mile trip barely took ten minutes.

He parked on the corner of Washington and Liberty streets, as close as he could to the area that used to be the south tower. He opened his trunk and pulled out his knee pads, gloves, pile helmet, and respirator, then dashed across the street and into the site.

Billy Murphy had been standing near the site's edge with Rosellen Dowdell when he heard a garbled call over his radio. Rosellen didn't understand the words Billy had heard. He hustled her away and rushed to the scene of the recovery.

The area was near where a set of elevator banks had been. As the firefighters climbed down a hill of debris to inspect, they found a small void, where a four-foot-wide steel box column had crashed and bent upward over the lobby floor, creating a kind of shield. Above was a mountain of twisted debris, thirty feet high. Underneath it was a low-lying cave filled with loose debris, about ten feet wide and fifteen feet deep. The entrance was a few feet high, just large enough for two or three men to crawl in close. As the firefighters pushed away the dust and dirt at the opening, they could make out the shiny gray-flecked pieces of the lobby floor, chunks of white marble that had lined the walls, and twisted silver metal that night have come from elevator doors. The firefighters filled buckets with debris and passed them out and away from the area. As the entrance cleared, they glimpsed arms, legs, tools, masks. There were bodies in there, several of them. They were all dressed in firefighters' heavy coats and pants. To find a cluster of complete bodies was extremely rare, especially in an area like this one, so far into the inner core of the south tower.

Other firefighters from Rescue 4 arrived, and more were on their way. Though their firefighters' helmets were normally too heavy to wear during digging, they now put them on, so the 4 on the front would make them identifiable as men from the company. A small group dug to clear away the mouth of the cave. When they found chunks of white marble, they dug downward. When they saw the silvery terrazzo, they dug horizontally. Eventually the pieces gave way to a slick horizontal slab. They realized they were actually on the lobby floor. Now they progressed faster. They reached in with outstretched hands, scooped the loose dirt and debris into armfuls, and slid it backward, where the men behind filled buckets and passed them away.

Liam climbed up the outer hill of rubble and then descended into the area where the bodies were. Twenty or twenty-five men were passing out buckets along either side of the void's entrance, and four firefighters were kneeling in the center, with several other men behind. He pushed past the men working the bucket brigade until he reached the handful of firefighters who were at the center of the digging. He looked down and saw one black body bag already laid out. Inside lay the torso that had held the company radio.

Liam shoved his way to the front and got down on his hands and knees to inspect the cave. Smoke was pouring out, releasing fumes from a fire that was still burning somewhere deep within the rubble. The steamy air was unbreathable, hot and thick with carbon monoxide. The decomposing bodies emitted a stench of ammonia. Scholl was sprawled on his stomach, digging alongside another firefighter. Liam called the other firefighter out. "This is my company," Liam shouted. "Step back."

The firefighter retreated, and Liam crawled alongside Scholl, who had already uncovered the midsection of one firefighter near the right side of the crypt and was working up to the head area. Liam set to work on the lower half. After lying there for more than six weeks, the corpse was now mostly skeleton with some remnants of shrunken and charred flesh. Though not much mass remained, Liam could tell it had been a big man because he wore an extra-large turnout coat. His helmet had fallen off, but his skull was intact, his unrecognizable face still covered with a mask. A thermal imaging camera was strapped around one arm. Liam had a feeling he knew who this was. He looked inside the thick coat, and saw the name.

Durrell Pearsall.

Liam said nothing. He saw his hands digging, but his mind no longer commanded them. Behind him, someone shouted that one of the guys was Bronko. Liam heard but stayed silent. He looked at the deteriorated, motionless shell that had been Bronko—his best friend, uproarious, laughing, animated. Liam could not put the two together. The stink of ammonia was overwhelming, and Scholl began to feel sick. He told Liam he had to step away for a minute. Liam nodded and kept digging.

Since the body was covered in loose debris, it came out with relative ease. Scholl returned to the cave to help Liam. When they were ready, someone slid a black bag next to the body. This time, Liam picked up Bronko's shoulders while Scholl took his legs, and together they gently rolled him on top of the body bag. Liam tucked Bronko's helmet inside, then pulled up on the edges and zipped the bag shut. He slid the body out into the light as delicately as he could. "Do not take them down," Liam yelled to the firefighters nearby, "until we get out."

Inches away to the left, another skeleton lay on its back. The man had removed his turnout coat and was untouched by any of the falling shards of metal. Scholl wondered if he had been alive for awhile after the collapse. The men removed that body next.

The last body was near the back, behind where Bronko had been found. His was the most difficult removal, because his foot was trapped under a steel bar. Liam tried to cut away at the steel with a Sawzall, but it wasn't powerful enough. As Liam maneuvered around to try to figure out a way to untangle the foot, firefighters behind him called out suggestions. Liam was starting to feel woozy from the ammonia and the carbon monoxide. Adrenaline surged and subsided, keeping his body moving, but then leaving him flagging and confused. Scholl saw Liam moving faster, growing frantic, almost panicky. He was trying to do everything too fast. Scholl suggested he take a break. Liam snapped at the men to give him some time.

In the end, five body bags were placed in stokes baskets and covered in American flags. When Liam stood up, he removed his mask and took a breath of the less toxic air. He knew there was no logic governing which guys were recovered. He knew that no matter how much he searched, he might never have been able to get Bronko. But if his friend hadn't been recovered, Liam felt, the guilt would have eaten away at him forever. Tonight was a minor triumph, a personal victory over the pile. He felt a rush of relief for the first time. He could scarcely believe it. They had him.

Liam looked down at the body bags. "Which one is Bronko?" he asked one of the firefighters. The man pointed at the stokes basket that held Bronko, and Liam grabbed the front right side. Five other firefighters gathered to lift the body. Someone shouted, "Uncover!" The men marched down the pile, through two long rows of firefighters who held their hard hats against their chests and bowed their heads as they passed.

Several ambulances awaited the rescue workers when they arrived at the edge. Liam paused as a priest shook holy water over Bronko's body and said a prayer. Then Liam climbed into the back of the ambulance with Bronko, alone. The driver turned on the flashing lights, no siren, and drove slowly down the block to the temporary morgue. Liam looked down at the body bag and started thinking ahead to the funeral. Now it would be sooner than they had anticipated. He imagined more struggles with the cousins over when and where.

The ambulance stopped at the makeshift morgue. The body was brought out for a brief initial inspection. After the coroner was finished, the body was loaded back into the ambulance, and Liam climbed in again, this time heading to the city morgue on 30th Street.

He pulled out his cell phone.

By now, Karen had stopped obsessively checking her messages at work, scanning her Caller ID for numbers of firefighters who might be phoning her. In the beginning, someone from the Fire Department had called every day to check on her. Then the calls came every couple of days. Lately there were fewer and fewer. That afternoon, she left work at 4:00. An hour later, she wearily decided to check the voicemail, just in case. There was a new message from Liam.

"Karen, you need to call me right back," said Liam, abandoning the code words they'd established. "It's important."

She called him right away.

"Karen, we got Bronko," said Liam.

"Are you sure?" she asked.

"We're pretty certain."

Karen was silent. For the first time, it was real.

"This is a good thing, Karen," said Liam. He told her he would be in touch later, and hung up.

As she waited for Liam to call again, Karen thought for hours about the finality of it all. She kept pushing it away. She still hoped that Liam might call her back and say Bronko was alive.

The New York City Medical Examiner's Office, which many called the "city morgue" for short, sat in a six-story square building in midtown Manhattan at First Avenue. and 30th Street. A hundred-foot-long alleyway on the south side of the building served as the office's wartime death classification camp. At the front, near the entrance, a giant white tent stretched over the southern facade of the blue brick building. Looking in, several rows of tables lay waiting for remains to be rested upon them for examination. An inconspicuous gray door led inside to cream-colored hallways and stark rooms, where in other times all forensic work on bodies that arrived there had been done. But now, the entire operation of identifying World Trade Center victims took place outside in the chilly air, shielded from the elements only by this massive tent and several smaller square hut-like tents with triangular tops, where work on multiple recoveries could take place at the same time. The remains that came in from the site never intermingled with the bodies of New Yorkers who'd died of other causes.

All kinds of professionals trolled the alleyway, day and night. Odontologists, biologists, pathologists, a DNA team, and photographers, all of whom sported the word "forensic" before their titles, performed sophisticated analyses to try to identify the dead. They did not perform autopsies to determine the cause of death. That was the same for all—"blunt trauma." The manner of death was "homicide." Police officers and fire marshals collected personal items like rings, wallets, and watches and stored them in sand-colored trailers with forest green tops and bottoms, which lined the middle section of the road like train cars. Funeral directors, ambulance drivers, and volunteers from the Red Cross and Salvation Army were always on hand. A chaplaincy truck was parked near the far end of the road, where clergy offered words of healing to the distraught. Each person played a necessary role in the society of this miniature city. Just like the rescue workers at the site, who fought depression on days when no remains were recovered, the morgue workers' morale sagged when no body parts came in for them to work on.

By the time the ambulance carrying Bronko's body pulled up, several of his closest friends were already there. Liam climbed out of the back door, and several firefighters reached in to carry out the stokes. The spinning red lights of the ambulance flashed an intermittent glow over a group of men and women in white coats and white surgical masks who waited solemnly as the body was removed, some raising their hands to their heads in salute, others covering their hearts. The body was carried into the intake area and laid carefully on a table.

At the last second, Liam realized he'd forgotten Bronko's helmet was still inside. He quickly unzipped the body bag and yanked it out. He reached behind him and slid it into the hands of one of Bronko's friends, Tommy Cunneen, who was also a piper in the band. A fire marshal saw him and protested. He needed the helmet to classify and store under lock and key. Liam pretended he didn't know what the fire marshal was talking about. The actual helmets that widows and family members were handed at funerals were not the helmets that the firefighters wore on a daily basis. The funeral helmets were brand new, shiny and emblazoned with the man's company number, but did not bear the characteristics that made each helmet absolutely unique. Bronko's helmet was the most intimate relic anyone would ever have of him. Liam didn't trust the fire marshals to take care of the helmet and return it. When Vinny Fowler had been killed, his family had requested the helmet, but they'd never received it. Liam didn't want that to happen this time. He thought he might give it to Karen if she wanted it. Maybe he would keep it himself. He didn't know exactly. He just didn't want to let go of it yet. The helmet reeked of death, but Liam knew he could clean it up, by soaking it in coffee grounds and water to remove the smell.

The fire marshal scolded Liam. He told him he'd seen him take the helmet. He threatened to arrest him if he didn't give it back.

"Arrest me?" Liam demanded, his eyes wild. "Fine. I could use the rest."

The fire marshal was acquainted with another of Bronko's friends who was there, a red-haired fire lieutenant named Mike Meyers. He spoke softly with Mike about the situation. Mike negotiated with Liam. The fire marshal promised to give the helmet back. Tommy gave it to Liam, and he handed it to the marshal.

The other firefighters' remains that had been found that day arrived, and the identification process began. The firefighters from Rescue 4 stayed close to their men, telling jokes and stories about them while they waited. Some peeked in the tent at the white-clothed workers hunching over the bodies; others walked right inside and looked over their shoulders. A light board was set up on one side of the tent, where the odontologists could compare antemortem dental X rays with postmortem samples. The firefighters were fascinated with the process. "Whatcha doin' that for?" asked Tim Kelly, a friendly, gray-haired lieutenant from Rescue 4. The medical examiner's staff explained, step by step. There had been times when firefighters had been able to identify a man to the morgue workers by his tattoos or other physical characteristics. With these recoveries, such input was not possible. These were skeletons in turnout gear. "You could tell that was Bronko," someone offered, "because of his big-sized head."

The identification process finally finished around 2:30 A.M. They had brought in one firefighter from Engine 214, who was sped through the identification process and then whisked away by a funeral director because his memorial service was scheduled for the following day. Five sets of remains had come in from Rescue 4, but in the end forensics had identified them as belonging to four—Terry Farrell, Pete Nelson, Al Tarasiewicz, and Bronko. The men were mildly disappointed, but not surprised. That sort of thing happened often.

Another honor guard formed along the edges of the long alley as the bodies were covered again in American flags and carried down to the opposite end, to another mountainous white tent looming just underneath the elevated highway. The back ends of eighteen refrigerated tractor-trailers poked through the tent's edges into the interior, each with a ramp leading up to its back door. A gigantic American flag hung at the far end. The vehicles were the resting places for all remains not immediately taken away by funeral directors. The morgue staff had named this tent "Memorial Park," even though it looked more like a loading dock and the frigid air carried the sickly honey aroma of decay mingled with the meaty smell of a butcher shop. Memorial Park was a sort of purgatory. Some inside had been identified, others not. Some bodies remained for a few days; fragments of remains might wait there for months. Family members could arrange to visit the refrigerator trucks if they wished, but they were not allowed to view the remains.

The firefighters from Rescue 4 loaded their men into the trucks. They saluted again as the bodies were placed inside. Lt. Kelly paused and told one of the morgue officials he wanted to have one more look. The official hesitated. Was he sure he really wanted to see this? "Come on," Lt. Kelly shot back. "Who do you think brought them out?" He slid down the zippers for a last look at each of them. His eyes scanned them, up, down and around. He imprinted them on his memory.

When it was over, Liam and the others stepped outside. The gusty night air was cold and biting. Mike and another one of Bronko's friends headed to Karen's house on Long Island to give her the official notification. When they got there, they told her he was intact. They'd been able to recognize him. He'd looked like he was singing.

Liam returned to the site. He climbed the rubble again and descended into the area where the bodies had been found. There were men still working there, digging deeper into the void. Liam holed his way back into the cave with the others, and together they dug until the sun came up.

On the morning of Friday, November 2, Liam was working at the site with Freddy Scholl and Rescue 4 firefighter Eddie Zeilman. Eddie was in his forties, six feet tall with sinewy muscles, bristly curled hair, and a thriving mustache that dripped over his cheeks and onto his chin. Several other firefighters' remains had been found in the same area over the past few days. They continued to dig and widen the area around the void until the top space rose so high they could stand up inside and walk several feet in. Hearing chants and cheers coming from West Street, they paused in their work and headed over for a look. They didn't expect to stay long. Eddie absentmindedly carried with him his short halligan, a wood-handled tool that stretched a couple of feet long and ended with a pointed metal tip.

Inches away from the site, near the corner of West and Chambers streets, outside the orange-brown brick P.S. 89 building, a protest was in progress. A pack of about two hundred firefighters shook their fists and shouted toward a man standing far in front of them. Protesters had come dressed in the range of firefighter clothing. Some wore jeans and navy blue FDNY shirts with company crests on the chest; others wore sturdy bunker coats and helmets. One firefighter wrote in chalk around the letters "FDNY" on the back of his black coat, "Dignity for the Dead, Safety for the Living." A peppering of signs bounced above the crowd. One made out of cardboard read, "Don't Shut Us Out." A square banner flapped in the wind: "Rescue 3 Bravest. Never Let Us Forget Our Fallen Brothers." The leader in their midst, a round-bellied union official, hollered into a bullhorn, his silver hair increasingly offset by the flush that rose in his cheeks. Whenever he paused, the hordes cheered and barked a variety of chants back, including "USA! USA!" and "Bring the Brothers Home!"

By the time Liam and the others got there, the protest was multiplying. Soon there were more than five hundred firefighters. From the back of the crowd, Liam and Eddie squinted in the sun and looked around at the bobbing heads and pulsing fists before them.

Days earlier, the mayor's office had issued an order to reduce the number of rescue personnel at the site to twenty-five firefighters, twenty-five Port Authority police, and twenty-five NYPD officers, due to safety concerns. Until now, anywhere from 80 to 150 firefighters[4] had worked daily at the site. The night before, the firefighters' union had issued a fax to all its members, alerting them of a planned rally to garner public support for the firefighters' opposition to the mayor's plan. The firefighters' frustration sprang from multiple roots. Firefighters never left the scene of a fire without all the men from their company, dead or alive. They deeply resented being ordered to abandon their brothers' remains. If fewer firefighters were there to watch the grapplers lifting out debris, there was a greater chance that remains would be missed and carried off to the Staten Island dump at Fresh Kills Landfill. Many felt that the excavation effort was being pushed too fast, and they sensed tension from the construction overseers every time the entire operation was stopped and a recovery was made. Some firefighters, realizing that a significant number of man-hours was being lost as a result of their determination to bestow dignity on the dead, grew certain that some higher-ups were fighting to stop their process.

In addition, there was anger at this newly proposed equality in the numbers of uniformed services. Twenty-five police officers was nearly the same as the number of police officers who'd died there. If the city was going to extend that courtesy to the cops, then why not do the same for the firefighters? Then 343 firefighters should be working at the site at all times. The medical examiner had publicly hinted that many bodies were never going to be found, but the firefighters and many of the rescue workers knew that bodies were still being uncovered. New proof had just come, when the men from Rescue 4 and Engine 214 were discovered in the south tower void. Between October 26 and November 1, 367 more pieces of remains were logged at the medical examiner's office, plus eight whole bodies. In those six short days, thirty-one people were identified, including ten firefighters but no additional police officers. Yet the rush was on, and the firefighters felt cheated. So many were yet to be found. The ground was slipping away from beneath them. They revolted against the orders to relinquish their grip.

The speeches finished, and the sentiment in the crowd changed. The angry throng decided to march south and say a prayer at the site, then continue on to City Hall to rally some more against the mayor. The fire union had obtained a permit to gather near the site, but not inside it. The firefighters turned as they began to walk en masse toward what had been the back of the demonstration, where Liam and Eddie were standing. The march surged with new momentum. Suddenly, Liam and Eddie were at the front of the flock.

Liam rushed ahead to alert a few of the police officers who stood behind metal barricades on West Street. He called them "brother" and told them that the march was proceeding their way. The officers stood fast. They had orders to stop them.

A pulsing stream of firefighters rushed the barricades. Police officers in navy blue struggled to hold up the metal barriers between them and the swarm of black-and-yellow-coated firemen pressing against the fences with increasing force. Some firefighters elbowed against the chests of the cops, and the cops pushed back. The firefighters burst through.

Liam lost track of Eddie in the crowd. The march carried on toward a second barricade. Again, officers were waiting to prevent the crowd from entering the site. At this, Liam grew angrier. "You should be marching with us," he yelled at one lieutenant. "We're looking for your brothers, too."

Eddie was caught in the swell moving toward the site when he felt a sudden tug at his shoulders, then a knee in his back. His chin hit the slick, muddy ground. He heard a man growl, "Drop your weapon!" He opened his fingers and let his halligan go. Then he scrambled back to his feet and kept moving.

A group of firefighters carrying a long white banner that read "New York City Firefighters" carried on toward the barricade. Many of the police officers were now each caught up in trying to subdue a group of a few. The banner-carriers pushed through the flimsy barricade and stepped over it. One stumbled. Another paused to help him up. The banner became entangled in the stampede. One firefighter struggled to hold up a Fire Department flag, a mesh of red, white, and gold that wrinkled and jerked in the chaos. When he teetered, a firefighter from behind reached forward to help him steady the pole.

Six feet tall and wearing a bright red construction hard hat with an "I Love NY" sticker on it, Eddie made terrific footage for the TV cameras. His fury showed in his eyes. A police officer tried to shove him backward, to no avail. Eddie barked out, "You're not stopping me! You're not stopping me!" Eddie yanked his arms from the officer's grasp. A white-haired firefighter next to him screamed in the officer's face, "My cousin's in there!" Skirmishes between cops and firefighters were erupting all around. Some fire officers in white coats were pushed against trailers and handcuffed.

In the end, five police officers were reported injured, some as a result of punches being thrown, officials said. Twelve Fire Department members were transported to the 28th Precinct in Harlem, a processing station more than a hundred blocks north of lower Manhattan, and arrested on charges that included inciting to riot, criminal trespass, and disorderly conduct.

Mayor Rudolph Giuliani, Police Commissioner Bernard Kerik, and Fire Commissioner Thomas Von Essen held a press conference that night to denounce the actions of the firefighters.

Kerik promised more arrests after police officers had an opportunity to review tapes of the fracas. The *Daily News* quoted Mayor Giuliani, who was not present at the rally, as saying that afternoon, "Leadership requires sometimes doing things that maybe people as an emotion can't understand. Nobody would like to see, I don't think, anyone die and get seriously injured in this effort. Firefighters will continue to have a role. But what they're not going to be allowed to do, and they were doing it in the past, is to take over the whole site."[5] Giuliani cited one example he claimed to have witnessed at the site, when a colleague tackled a firefighter who stood dangerously near an approaching crane, saving him from imminent demise. As the days passed and the story was recounted and reinterpreted, every player had a different truth. Some police officers said the cops had not wanted to arrest the firemen. Some firemen said no cops were ever punched. The fire unions claimed that "a few police brass provoked what happened."[6]

Soon after, the recovery work at the site was divided into four (and later, three) sectors according to the grid that the construction companies had originally devised. In an effort to ensure that each branch of the services would oversee each area in rotation, firefighters were assigned to one sector one day, Port Authority officers to another, police officers to another. But there was one sector where firefighters believed there were no recoveries to be made, and they were angered at being assigned to spend time searching that area. Soon, City Hall agreed to allow fifty firefighters at the site instead of twenty-five. Some of the fire chiefs established new aide positions for the rescue firefighters, so that one or two assistants from a rescue or squad company could oversee the work alongside a chief. The fire unions issued a formal apology. But the protest, and the newly prescribed rules, changed little about the tense circumstances.

Recoveries continued under the south tower. Between November 1 and November 12, 647 body parts and four whole bodies were removed from the pile. Rescue 4 firefighter Billy Mahoney was recovered. On November 4, Michael Cawley was found, a few dozen feet from where the others had been. He was identified, in part, by the Father's Day fire T-shirt he wore and the claddagh ring on his finger.

On November 7, Eddie Zeilman and two other firefighters turned themselves in to police. They'd been spotted on video.

Liam heard that Eddie had been arrested when he was at Bronko's wake, on the second and last night of the visitation. He was at once furious, despondent, and paranoid. But his best friend was about to be buried, and there wasn't time for that. That night, Liam, Tommy Cunneen, and Mike Meyers waited until all the family members, friends, and firefighters who'd come to Bronko's wake left. They were alone in the funeral home with the casket. In turn, each approached the casket alone, each carrying mementos, which they placed inside. Bronko's favorite picture of himself and his parents. Bronko's kilt and band shirt. A Notre Dame jersey and helmet. His Class-A New York City Fire Department uniform and his uniform from when he was a Hempstead firefighter. A picture of Bronko and nine of his closest buddies vacationing at Club Med. His fire helmet. Liam took out a bottle of Irish Mist and poured a shot into a glass from Bronko's parents' wedding. In turn, each man did a shot. Bronko had performed this ritual at his own father's coffin several years earlier. They tucked the glass and the rest of the bottle inside the casket for Bronko and said good-bye.

CHAPTER

7

LAYING TO REST

No rising column marks this spot
Where many a victim lies,
But oh! the blood which here has streamed,
To heaven for justice cries.

—Robert Emmet, "Lines on Arbour Hill"

KIPPY'S wife was scheduled to begin fertility treatments in the first week of November. The day her menstrual period began, she would go to her physician's office for an ultrasound and a blood test. Based on those results, she would receive the proper dosage of a hormone to inject into her thigh every night for the next two weeks. As a veterinary technician, she administered shots to animals all the time, and she felt certain she could do it to herself. But as the time approached, she grew skittish and queasy. She decided Kippy would have to do it. He agreed, though he was uneasy about the idea, too, which made Mary even more unsure. He wasn't trained to give injections. What if he did it wrong? That needle was an inch and a half long. They dreaded the whole idea of it.

Her cycle was so regular that she scheduled an appointment with the doctor ahead of time. When it didn't begin the day she'd expected, she phoned the office apologetically to schedule an appointment for the next day, sure her period would come. It didn't. She rescheduled again. She seemed unusually late this month. She attributed the delay to stress. But then five days passed and she began to wonder. Could it be? She mentioned it to Kippy, and together they shrugged it off. After four years of trying, the idea now didn't seem plausible. Still, Mary bought a pregnancy test kit at the drugstore, just in case.

On the morning of November 7, Mary awoke early and slipped into the bathroom. When she came out, Kippy was still in bed, and Danny lay next to him. Tears streamed down her face. She showed the strip to Kippy. He looked at her in disbelief, then swept her up in a tight hug. Danny bounced up and down on the bed. Together, they screamed and laughed in excitement. A miracle.

The next morning, mild sun rays and a November chill took turns falling over Fifth Avenue outside St. Patrick's Cathedral. The eight firefighters who would serve as Bronko's pallbearers arrived early to meet Jimmy Sorokac from the ceremonial unit, who was there to review the protocol. He arranged them according to height, four on each side. He told them that the coffin would be covered in an American flag and would slide off the fire truck with the striped end coming first, where Bronko's feet were. The two shortest men would take the casket at that end, and the tallest would handle the top end. When the coffin had been brought all the way off the fire truck and each pallbearer held it in his hands, Sorokac would stand behind, at the head of the casket, and whisper, "Ready, shoulder." Then they'd raise the coffin, pivot toward the church, and wedge a shoulder underneath. Their hands would drop to their belt buckles. The two men in front would step off on the left, watching each other's feet to set a rhythm. He advised them not to attempt a shoulder carry on the stairs leading up to the cathedral entrance—the risk of gravity causing the coffin to slide from their shoulders was too great. They should raise it only while standing on flat ground, and bring it down to their waists for the trip up the stairs. After giving hundreds of such training sessions, Sorokac was well aware of the wrenching emotions this duty provoked. He did his best to steer their focus to the movements and procedures, away from thoughts of their beloved friend who lay dead inside the box, so near to their hands when they held it at their waists, and when they lifted it to their shoulders, so close to their heads as the cold wood pressed against their cheeks.

Across the street from the cathedral, the pipers began to tune up. Most had their uniforms half on. Kilts, sporrans, hose, and spats were all in place, but unbuttoned red tunics swung open, shoulder drapes remained unfastened, and heads were covered in baseball caps or left simply bare. They stood in groups of three or four, talking among themselves. Wives came by to chat and smooth their husbands' collars. Kippy stood off to one side, alone. He told no one of his news. Mary was not there. He hadn't wanted her to come. The sounds of squealing pipes, a dozen different tunes being played at once, created a noisy complication in the scene of activity.

Jimmy O'Neill loitered around the edges of the circle, unmotivated to tune or warm up. A handful of blocks from this spot, years ago, he'd met Bronko for the first time, when Bronko had lifted his kilt and torn off his boxer shorts. This was the department's 255th service. Jimmy anchored his feet on the pavement and grumbled, "I'm so sick of doing this." His bagpipes hung from one hand like a stray mitten. After a few moments, he sighed, pulled up his pipes, and joined the others.

Gradually, a few pipers began patrolling around the circle, carrying square, hand-size tuning instruments, holding them high at the mouth of each drone. Hatless, Tom McEnroe stepped to the middle of the group and hollered the names of the tunes the band would play while Tim and others checked the accuracy of each piper's pitch. Then Tim put on his tall feather bonnet and took over the center circle, calling more tunes. Today, the enormity of the task before them, of burying one of their own, made the pipers unwilling followers, more rebellious than usual. When they didn't all snap to readiness and play on his command, Tim barked at them. "We need to get going!" In response, a couple of pipers muttered to each other, "We need a new pipe major."

Eventually the pipers were all in tune. They helped each other wrap, pin, and fasten their shawls so they cascaded suitably off their shoulders. The pipers took off their baseball caps and replaced them with their busbies. The drummers secured their berets. The wives rushed across the street to find a spot on the steps where they could watch. Liam whisked up to where the pipers stood practicing, flanked by Billy Murphy and a few officers. Liam answered last-minute queries about the procession, and the band members began to line up. They could prolong the moment no more. They stepped into formation and marched away from the cathedral. In the middle of the group, on the outer edge, strode Kippy. His face suddenly gnarled in a frown. He struggled to fend off a wave of tears. But the breeze of the march was soothing. He made it, with the others, to a corner about four blocks away, and waited.

The engine rumble of police motorcycles percolated and gently revved. The procession began.

A bay horse with no rider, cloaked in a black crocheted covering, was led toward the cathedral by two young soldiers from a local military academy. The animal's lower legs were covered in glossy red bands. In each stirrup, an empty black boot faced backward. The reversed boots symbolized a hero who would never ride again. A hush fell over the crowd. The clip of the hooves against pavement was the only sound. When the horse neared the cathedral, it reared up on its back legs and whinnied as if in anguish.

Rescue 4's giant rig crawled a short distance behind.

Then came the pipes, heard before they could be seen near the church. From far away, the melody of "Dawning of the Day" rolled upward in triumph, then downward again in sorrow.

At the front of the pipers' procession, one of the band's drummers carried Bronko's snare drum, covered entirely by a fitted black-and-purple mourning cloth. Behind him, seven members of the color guard in their dress blue trod carefully. The center four held their flags high: the American flag on their right; the tricolor green, white, and orange of the Irish flag; then the green-and-gold Emerald Society flag; and on their far left, the red-and-white Fire Department flag.

Behind them marched Liam. With the color guard ten feet ahead and the band ten feet behind, he was alone in an island of his own. His expression was set like porcelain, grim and purposeful, yet untelling. The real Liam was far within. He stepped one foot ahead of the other in slow motion, right fist extended, then retracted. Again and again. The repetition pulled him forward. Behind him to his right, on the far edge of the front line, Tim blew mightily into his pipes.

Separately, each band member's face looked stricken, skin sagging earthward. But taken together, the band marched up the cement plain as a solid block, with a distinct left-right sway. The seventy musicians strode forward with the grace of unity and pride, dexterous fingers evoking the spirit of the lost in the notes they played. Behind them, the body of their fallen brother, now shielded in metal and covered in stars and stripes, was riding in a fire truck for the last time.

The tune ended. The slow pounding of the drums continued, echoing like gunshots off the surrounding buildings.

The band continued a dozen yards past the church and then did a countermarch, turning and walking through their ranks until they once again faced the cathedral. Silence. Liam faced the band, held his mace horizontally at a level just above his forehead, and with four dips signaled the end of the drummers' dirge. He pivoted on a heel and faced the fire truck that held Bronko's casket. The pallbearers slid the coffin off the rig. Each pallbearer wedged a shoulder beneath the casket's weight and hoisted it to his neck.

An officer called out over a microphone, "Detail! Hand, salute!"

The thousands of mourners gathered in the street remained silent while Tim alone piped the keening notes of "Amazing Grace." Liam was motionless, his hand resting sharply at his eyebrow. Then came a skirling symphony, as every piper in the band blew the lilting notes in refrain, not once, but twice. They puffed laboriously to weave a continuous fabric of music, their brows furrowed in concentration.

The pallbearers, still balancing the coffin on their shoulders, gripped the edges for stability. The rhythm they'd rehearsed was lost. They shuffled their way up the steps, past a sea of white-glove salutes, and through the ornate golden doors of the church.

Inside the cathedral, the pallbearers lowered the coffin onto a rolling dolly and removed the American flag. A priest shook holy water over the bare casket. Then the pallbearers covered it again with a beige cloth. They lined up again, four on each side of the coffin. Each man placed a hand on top, and they guided the casket toward the front of the cathedral. Besides the clergy, they were the only ones inside the silent echoes of the church's expanse. Four right hands, four left hands. When they reached the altar, they stopped.

The four men on the right stepped out to form a straight line, shoulder to shoulder, each facing the altar. The men on the left did the same. In unison, they genuflected. Each man bowed his head and took his hat into his hand. They stood up together and tucked their hats under their left arms. Pivoting on a heel, they proceeded to a side-aisle pew designated for pallbearers.

Karen and Bronko's family members followed. Karen's shoulders were hunched. Her hair hung loosely around her face. She looked down at the ground in front of her.

When the melancholy chorus evaporated and the sound of nothingness hung in the air, the squadron of musicians tucked their pipes under their arms or slung their drums around their waists and followed the casket into the church. They marched with a steady gait. They stared ahead with fixed eyes, grown hazy from battle—this one and the hundreds that preceded it.

Relatives took their places in front, and the band members followed close behind, filing into the first several pews of the church. They stacked each row, shoulder to shoulder, and bowed their heads.

Behind them swept a sea of thousands—firefighters and police officers in dress blue uniforms; brothers, fathers, sisters, and sons. Step by tiny step, the massive crowd filed into the century-old pews. Those who could not find a place to sit stood around the edges.

A youthful, round-faced priest named Father Kissane gave the opening remarks. He spoke conversationally of how he and a friend of Bronko's had talked recently of scenarios. If the terrorists had waited just a few minutes longer, Bronko would have been driving his truck home, listening to the Wolfe Tones, perhaps "The Streets of New York," or perhaps "Big Strong Man." He would not have heard the news on the radio. He would have arrived safely home.

Then the actress Christine Ebersole walked to a microphone at the front of the church. A friend of hers had lost a firefighter boyfriend on September 11, and Ebersole had sung at his service some weeks earlier; impressed by her moving performance, the band had asked her to sing today. She bowed her head for a moment. Then she began to put words to the tune the pipers had played incessantly over the past weeks. She sang unaccompanied, in a tender tone.

> Amazing grace, how sweet the sound,
> That saved a wretch like me

Kippy lowered his head and wept.

> I once was lost, but now am found,
> Was blind, but now I see.

Gradually, an organist began to accompany Ebersole ever so lightly, and she raised her voice in a haunting crescendo.

> Through many dangers, toils, and snares
> We have already come.
> T'was grace that brought us safe thus far
> And grace will lead us home.
>
> The Lord has promised good to me.
> His word my hope secures.

He will my shield and portion be
As long as life endures.

The organist stopped. Ebersole finished in the near whisper with which she'd begun.

Amazing grace, how sweet the sound,
That saved a wretch like me.
I once was lost, but now am found,
Was blind, but now I see.

Ebersole stepped down to a chorus of applause.

Bronko's cousin Nina spoke next. She told of how Bronko had been like a little brother to her, how making people laugh was what he did best, how his dream had been to become a lieutenant. By way of farewell to the last surviving cousin on her father's side, she ended with an Irish blessing:

May the road rise up to meet you
May the wind be always at your back
And until we meet again
May God hold you in the hollow of his hand.

Then Mike Meyers stood up. He'd been a member of Rescue 4 for a time and had played on the FDNY football team with Bronko. His hands were empty as he walked up to the microphone.

"When I sat down last night to prepare a speech, I looked up to Bronk in the sky and said, 'What should I say?'

"And he said, 'Do like we did in college. Put down that piece of paper, and let's go get a bite to eat and a beer.'"

The audience chuckled. Mike continued.

"He would want everyone to thank Rescue Company 4 and all the people there at the site."

He swallowed, and his voice grew grave.

"If they have to arrest every one of us, we're going to continue to dig until we bring each of these guys home."

Anger over the riot of days before now spilled into the cathedral. The thousands of firefighters sprang to their feet and pounded their palms together in vociferous applause. The clamor lasted several minutes.

When the roar finally quieted, Mike told of how Bronko used to stand up in the FDNY football team's locker room after every game and sing "Wild Rover." Bronko had felt about the University of Notre Dame the way many Catholics felt about the Vatican, he said. One year, he went there for his pilgrimage. Within minutes of arriving at campus, Bronko befriended an equipment manager. Before Mike knew it, they were getting a personal tour of the locker room and strolling on the field. As they left, Bronko touched the "Play Like a Champion Today" sign that all Notre Dame players touch before they head onto the field.

"He was probably the biggest hero that ever walked on that field or touched that sign," Mike said before he stepped down. "On September 11, 2001, he played like a champion, and he will always be a champion in my mind."

The crowd gave him a standing ovation.

Liam rose from his pew and walked up the steps to the pulpit. He pressed his lips together and nodded briefly at the coffin as he passed. He stood tall and unwavering as he looked placidly over the masses before him.

"I also prayed to Bronko for inspiration," Liam said. "And he told me, 'You better pray. You need a script.' "

The churchgoers laughed politely. Liam resumed. When he spoke into the microphone, his baritone voice was calm and even.

"Tough times."

He thanked the two units in which he and Bronko had had the privilege to serve—the Emerald Society Pipes and Drums, and Rescue 4. He continued.

"There is a kitchen not too far from here. I believe WFUV is playing on the radio. And in that kitchen, there is a group of men sitting around a huge table. As you look to the right side of the table and begin to pan left, you immediately notice Harry Ford smoking a huge cigar, lost in his crossword puzzle. As you continue to gaze down the table, there is Brian Hickey with a small chalkboard, explaining the finer points of roof ventilation to Pete Brennan and Pete Nelson. Terry Farrell is extremely busy balancing the commissary books. He grunts something about guys opening up a new Hershey's syrup before the old one is finished. Kevin Dowdell looks up from his copy of the *Irish Echo* and smiles, as his gaze fixes on the show going on down at the other end of the table. Brian Fahey, Billy Mahoney, Mike Cawley, and Al Taz are all belly-laughing as they listen intently to 'Himself,' the great entertainer, spin one of his countless yarns.

"Sounds like a great place."

He shifted his weight from one foot to the other, pumping his soles slowly against the ground.

"In heaven, I believe that we will see everybody in their ideal state," he said, a smile lightening his voice. "Bronko's ideal state would definitely have to go something like this. Picture walking into a sports bar that specializes in chicken wings. As you look around, you notice that all the TVs are tuned to a Notre Dame game, and they're winning, 49–0. The bar is packed with firemen, and they all seem to be looking at something other than the game. It is then you notice a rather annoying sound, piercing through your ears. You turn to look at what everyone is staring at, and the source of the noise becomes apparent.

"There he is, in all his glory, with one arm around Father Judge and the other around Gene Fraher. He's wearing his kilt with an FDNY football shirt that is two sizes too small. The sleeves are rolled up, of course. He has a glass of Guinness in one hand and a microphone in the other. He's belting out a rendition of 'The Wild Rover,' and he's telling Jesus that He's singing the wrong words."

A ripple of laughter arose from the pews.

"On the outside, Bronko appeared to be the ultimate tough guy: rescue firefighter, football player, snare drummer for the band with an incredible admiration for military pomp and circumstance. But on the inside there was a warmth and kindness larger than this cathedral.

"A month ago, the pipe band went to Ground Zero to pay tribute to our fallen. Before I went, my mother handed me a bottle of holy water and asked me to sprinkle some on the area of the pile where I thought he might be. In the hectic pace of that day, I totally forgot about the holy water, but today, it's in the casket with my brother. I'd like to thank God for giving him back to us."

He took a breath.

"Now, my brother, your Rescue 4 family took you the first part of your journey out of that smoking crater. Today your band family is going to take you the rest of the way home."

Liam paused.

"One night after taking up from the World Trade Center," he said, "I was driving up West Side Highway heading back to Rescue 4's quarters. It had been a rough day. We had recovered eight of our brothers. Although in these dark days that would be cause for some solace, I could not shake the lack of feeling that welled inside of me. Emptiness would express it best.

"As I drove north, I saw a woman holding up a sign with one word on it. I read the word, and not one day has gone by since that I have not thought about it. The word on that sign changed my focus, from my emotionless state to thinking about my wonderful FDNY family. Even though we were working in what might be described as hell on earth, I opened my eyes and began to see the beauty of it all. I saw my brothers at their absolute best when everything, everything was at its absolute worst. I saw brothers climb mountains of unsteady twisted steel and dive down into crumbing voids that went many sublevels below ground. I saw brothers put their family lives on indefinite hold so they could tend to the needs of their missing brothers' families.

"I saw guys don kilts and Class-A uniforms to pay homage to our fallen at hundreds of services, tirelessly driving hundreds of miles to make sure each brother was sent off with the dignity and respect he deserves.

"I saw brothers gather on West Street in a peaceful and civilized manner to show solidarity and voice their disagreement with City Hall. Let us bring them home with the same dignity that they went into those buildings with."

Applause had threatened to break out several times as Liam spoke. Now it erupted.

"The word written on that sign," Liam shouted above the din, "was UNBROKEN. Hold your heads high, my brothers."

Eventually the cheering quieted.

"Last but not least, here's some advice, until we meet again. Don't spill Guinness on your spats. Make sure Gene Fraher eats and gets his rest. Give your mom and dad a big hug, and be careful not to squeeze too hard. And save singing 'Wild Rover' until we are all together again to cheer you on. Tumac."

At Liam's mention of the inside joke, a chuckle broke out in the front pews.

Before Liam stepped down, he said, *"Slan leat a chara."* As some in the pews knew, those words meant "Good-bye, my friend" in Gaelic. To the rest, amidst the echo of the cathedral, the phrase sounded like "So long ago."

When the service was over, the band members filed into the street and lined up on the north side of the cathedral. The firefighters streamed out after them and re-formed their line up and down the block. Liam kept his eyes on the church entrance. Inside, the pallbearers were again alone with the casket. But now it was over. Mike Meyers felt the sting of approaching tears, and he tried not to meet anyone's eyes. The moment they'd so looked forward to for all this time was over. Now he had to lead the casket out. When Liam saw the priests emerge from the door, he called "Going Home," and the pipers played for Bronko as his casket was loaded again into the waiting fire truck. They marched the coffin down Fifth Avenue to "America the Beautiful." When they'd gone a few blocks, they turned off to the side and watched the rig and coffin pass. Then they climbed into three tour buses and rode to the Holy Rood Cemetery in Westbury, Long Island.

The band marched the coffin straight to the grave, where they played "Amazing Grace" for Bronko for the last time. Then the hundreds who had come to the cemetery lined up in pairs to approach the coffin, to touch it or drop a flower on top.

Once all had a chance to wish Bronko a final good-bye, the crowd dispersed and the pipers converged around the coffin. They passed around bottles of Irish whiskey and gulped deeply. Liam took an open bottle and poured the amber liquid over the glossy surface of the coffin.

A few steps away from the grave, piper Bill Duffy Jr. played a mournful solo of a tune he had written, "Our Brother Bronko."

> Farewell Bronko
> Fireman's hero
> Your life's flame burned bright and brief
> War's first fury
> Took you early
> Too early, indeed . . .
>
> Valor, strength
> You embody
> Bold and true, the brothers knew
> Bronko, friend
> How we miss you
> Only God can tell.

Then the band members erupted into an a cappella rendition of "Wild Rover." Their singing voices were off-key and rocky and did not carry far through the cemetery air. They stamped their feet and laughed through what had been Bronko's favorite song.

> I've been a wild rover for many a year
> And I spent all my money on whiskey and beer

And now I'm returning with gold in great store
And I never will play the wild rover no more.

And it's no nay never
No nay never no more
Will I play the wild rover
No never no more.

All the pipers and drummers, friends, and family headed to the Hempstead Country Club for the collation. A collage of photos stood on a table near the entrance to the reception hall. Hors d'oeuvres were served in the front room; the small bar nook filled quickly, and hundreds of people filed into the main hall and found seats at circular tables. At one end, numerous silver dishes held chicken, pasta, and vegetables.

Later that evening, everyone gathered around a giant screen at the front of the room. Many of the pipers sat on the floor in half-circle rows; others watched from their tables at the back. A hush fell over the room, and a video that Liam's sister Maureen had put together began to play.

First, a still image came on the screen of Bronko's black-and-white portrait. He wore a black mock turtleneck and gray suit jacket with a thick gold chain around his neck. Under his chest were the words: "Durrell Bronko Pearsall. August 19, 1967–September 11, 2001." Next came his Tostitos commercial, set in the Jets locker room. In the foreground, coach Bill Parcells was singing, "Groovin', on a Sunday afternoon"; in the background was Bronko, wearing a white towel, swaying and singing with a chip in his hand. A burst of laughter and cheers cascaded through the room.

The Partridge Family's "I Think I Love You" came over the speakers, and snapshots of Bronko with his parents and other family members flashed on the screen. On came a picture of Karen and Bronko, sitting on a couch and grinning widely. Whistles and catcalls filled the hall. From her table in the back of the room, Karen laughed and wept. Tears glistened on her cheeks. She wiped them away with her French-manicured hand. Then another picture of the two of them sitting in a garden, Karen's slim hand resting on Bronko's chest. The room erupted into more excited cheering and hollering. Everyone in the room turned and looked at her, smiling at her, joyous for her, as if Bronko were alive and the two had just announced their engagement. Karen turned her eyes down modestly. For those few seconds, he really had only stepped into the next room.

The tape moved on to a home video shot during Liam's thirtieth birthday party. Gene Fraher was leading a small group in the song he'd written about his namesake, the cowardly fireman. Bronko was kneeling on the floor next to Fraher, who stood cradling a cigarette in one hand and balancing himself with the other on Bronko's shoulder. Of the half dozen men circled around in the shot, Bronko was the only one who could come close to singing with Fraher on anything more than the chorus.

> Now the Deputy's directing, the Safety's inspecting,
> The FieldCom performs with a grin.
> 'Cause no matter how bad the fire may get,
> They know they will never go in.
>
> So don't go into the building, Gene.
> They're calling you on the air.
> 10–75! Say, that's no jive,
> I wouldn't go in on a dare.
>
> Yes, the searchlight is shining, the marshals are whining,
> We'll ruin our suits, they all pout.
> And SOC's on the air, but they really don't care.
> They won't show till the fire goes out.
>
> So don't go into the building, Gene.
> The brothers are in on the line.
> Genie dear, please stay out here.
> We'll keep those lungs pink and fine.

At this, Bronko could no longer contain himself. His eyes darted across the circle at Liam, who crouched just under the person holding the camera. Bronko broke into a wide smile and giggled, then paused to rub his eyes for a moment. Liam's throaty chuckle could be heard offscreen. The men standing around behind Gene leaned back, drank from their beers, and laughed.

Every eye in the room at the country club was transfixed on the images. Tears glistened. The spectators relived the moment as if it were happening right there and the two stars of the show were not dead but alive, performing for them again. When the song ended, everyone in the room again clapped and whistled. A new photo slide show began to roll by in the screen. Bronko in probie school, dancing with a mannequin. Bronko with his face squeezed against Tommy Cunneen's, double chins bulging as they snapped a close-up photo of themselves. More shots of Bronko's trips with the boys. Liam was next to him in almost every one. They raised giant half-filled steins of beer in Munich. They stood in the street in New Orleans, laden with beaded necklaces, Liam laughing, Bronko shouting, a red string tied across his forehead. Bronko with the football team. Bronko in his red scuba gear. Bronko in Ireland on the day Tim proposed to Tara on the Cliffs of Moher. Bronko in the back of a bus fooling around with a red napkin over his face. In one of the last shots, Bronko stood between Liam and Tim, his arms around both of them, all three of them wearing navy blue Fire Department T-shirts. Bronko was smiling. Tim and Liam looked grim for some reason and just stared back at the camera.

The tape ended, but when the party resumed it replayed again and again through the night. Tom McEnroe finished his rounds with the clipboard, making checks on the paper, verifying the next day's attendance—five memorials and one funeral. Tomorrow was a few hours away.

CHAPTER

8

THANKSGIVING

Here our murdered brother lies
Wake him not with women's cries;
Mourn the way that manhood ought;
Sit in silent trance of thought.

—William Drennan, "The Wake of William Orr"

EVERY Thanksgiving, Maryann hosted an early afternoon dinner at her house for the Brunton family. The first year after their father had died, they'd held Thanksgiving in the old house, where Mike, Maryann, and Vinny and Kathy all lived. For the next few years, they tried taking turns, hosting dinner at different houses, but that system became too disorganized for Maryann's liking. She had the most time to get the cooking together, so she became the regular host. That morning, she hustled around her own pale pine kitchen, lit in warm rose hues, jostling familiar pots and pans full of simmering food and setting out plates for all nineteen of them—eight adults and eleven children, who now ranged in age from ten to twenty-two. Given the nature of the brothers' firefighting schedules and Kathy's rotating hospital hours, it was not unusual for one of the adults to be missing for dinner. Now, the entire family faced the holiday with reluctance. They were forever one fewer.

The Bruntons' mother had come from an Italian lineage, and so antipasto and homemade ravioli had always been part of their holiday meal. Tommy brought the antipasto. Mike carried desserts and a huge bottle of Chianti wine, wrapped in a wicker basket. Maryann cooked the turkey. Kathy baked stuffing in a pan.

Maryann's small living room and kitchen filled quickly as her brothers and their wives and kids came through the door, their arms laden with food. They kissed and hugged each other. Kids darted around their legs. The noise level rose. They were all together in the same place for the first time since September 11.

Tommy and Mike went to check on Maryann's progress in the kitchen. They grabbed beers from the fridge and peered into the pots on the stove. Then they remembered. The garlic bread. That had always been Vinny's contribution, and he'd excelled at making it. Maryann wiped at her reddening eyes, and the three siblings began to prepare it together. One chopped the garlic; another sliced butter and dropped it in the pan. They banged elbows, gave each other orders, chuckled and cried in turn. Finally, they slid the bread into the oven. Maybe not as good as Vinny's, they decided, but he would have been proud of their effort.

The adults gathered around the oval dining room table, and the kids sat at the table set up in the living room. The conversation moved around from topic to topic—how everybody was coping, recent events in the news, how the kids were doing in school and at work. The food was tasty. They complimented each other. But no matter how savory the meal, the holiday was bland without Vinny.

When the meal was over, they cleared the table, rinsed the dishes, and piled them into the dishwasher. Maryann walked over to Kelly. She had some home videos of Vinny. One had been filmed during Kelly's eleventh birthday party. She asked Kelly if she'd like to watch them. Kelly tilted her head away, suddenly anxious, and said no, she thought it might be weird. She and Tommy's oldest daughter, Aileen, took out photo albums instead, and together they looked through them.

Soon after, Kathy announced to the room that she wanted everyone to gather around the table. She had something she wanted to say. Maryann sent the younger children to the basement to play. The adults pulled their chairs around.

"I've been giving this a lot of thought." Kathy said. "I think it's time to start thinking about having a memorial for Vinny."

Maryann released a quiet breath of relief. Tommy told Kathy he thought it was a good idea and asked her when she wanted to do it. Kathy wasn't sure, preferably before the end of the year. That way, they might have some hope of starting off the new year free from some of the grief and uncertainty. Doing it too close to Christmas would be hard on everyone, so Tommy suggested December 13. He was pretty sure there were no other memorials scheduled that day. He didn't want firefighters to have to choose between attending Vinny's service and another man's.

Then he began talking about the logistics. They would notify the ceremonial unit, which would handle the Fire Department end of the ceremony and schedule the mayor and other dignitaries. Visiting hours should be held for two consecutive days prior to the service, since so many people from the neighborhood and Fire Department would want to pay their respects. On the day, the pipe band would march the family into the church and play again when the service was over. Early on, Liam had promised Tommy that his brother would get the full band, top honors for one so close to the group. A group of men from Ladder 105 would form an honor guard. The family could have a coffin if they wanted, or flower boards, or an urn, or just go into the church without such a symbol.

Mike had been sitting quietly, but now his fist began rapping against the table, moving down harder and faster, like a hammer acting on its own volition. When someone mentioned what other families had chosen to do, Mike burst out. "We'll do what we want to do." He glanced at Kelly and bent his head down. "I'm sorry," he said. He'd made a promise. He couldn't do anything to bring back her father. He could barely look her in the eye.

"Nobody blames you," Kelly said to him. "You're not Superman." Kathy spoke up, too, and Maryann and Tommy, each trying to comfort Mike.

Kelly spoke again. "Uncle Michael, it's okay," she said. "Yes, I wish that you could have brought him back. But I know you did everything you could do. You didn't let anyone down. It's not your fault. You can't control this."

Mike shook his head and stared at his lap.

December 13 dawned drizzly and gray. All morning, Tommy's stomach twisted in knots. A few nights earlier, he'd begun jotting down notes about what he wanted to mention when he stood up at the mass to deliver his eulogy. He wanted to convey the significance of Vinny's unpretentious life and give an accurate depiction of the man so many had respected and loved. But he also intended to be brief. He didn't want the memorial to turn into a marathon of tears. Short was better. It kept the dignity in the service. Though most of his thoughts flowed easily onto the page, he'd had trouble finding the right words for the end.

On the two previous evenings, he'd stood for several hours at a stretch inside the funeral home across the street from Holy Name Church, surrounded by giant floral arrangements occupying the space where a casket would otherwise have stood. A table held relics of Vinny's life—a golf club, a sweat-stained Yankees cap, a pair of running shoes, and a large photo of Vinny covered in soot, looking skyward after a fire. A line of friends and firefighters stretched out the door and down the street as hundreds came to pay their respects to the Brunton family. Tommy had stood in front of the pungent flowers shaking hands, thanking people, introducing Maryann and Kathy to firefighters they didn't know. Everybody had gracious things to say about Vinny. In one of those conversations, Tommy found the final words for his eulogy.

Inside Farrell's pub, on the corner near the church, the lights were dark. An enlarged picture of Vinny hung in the window. The bar had closed for the day. The owner had only shut his doors once before, after his own father had died. Now he did the same to honor Vinny, his cherished bartender.

The pipe band arrived early. Every member dressed in his full red regalia, and they lined up several blocks away from the church. Soon the narrow streets and mottled brick sidewalks around Prospect Park West were jammed. Vinny had thousands of friends in the neighborhood, from Holy Name grammar school, from Bishop Ford High, from Farrell's, and from companies throughout the Fire Department. They had all come to bid him good-bye.

Twelve ladder trucks paired at intersections on the six blocks leading up to and away from the dark brown brick church. Their ladders reached high into the air and met at the tips, dangling enormous American flags.

An officer called out over a microphone, "Colors, post."

The men in the front row of the honor guard, facing the church entrance, lifted their flags high.

"Detail, ten-*hut.*"

The formation snapped to attention.

Vinny's brothers, sister, wife, and children—Kelly and Thomas—lined up in the wet street, behind the band, and held onto each other's arms. The Ladder 105 rig rolled slowly forward. The band began to march to the drum dirge. At the church, they continued past, until the group of family members stood right in front. The band counter marched, turning their ranks so they faced the family. The drummers tucked their sticks into tight pairs and held them over their drums. The pipers rested their blowpipes on their shoulders and waited.

"Detail, hand salute."

The men in the formation lifted their hands in salute. A member of the color guard dipped the American flag and held it forward, a few inches below the rest.

"Amazing Grace" began. The notes sounded so shrill, so sad, to Maryann. She couldn't remember ever hearing the bagpipes for any other reason than a death. Now they were sounding for her. For her brother. Kathy, too, began to cry.

The solo ended, and the rest of the band struck up their pipes and joined in for a second refrain, just as they had for Bronko. The notes rebounded loudly off the shop fronts. At that moment, it seemed, there was no other sound in the world.

When the tune finished, a voice over the mike called, "Ready, two." The firefighters dropped their salute.

A hymn sounded from the organ inside. Kathy and the family turned and shuffled up the short flight of three stairs, past two unlit black lampposts, into the 123-year-old redbrick church. The gray limestone of the steps was worn away in places. Their dress shoes scraped against the sharp surface.

Behind the family, the mourners streamed in. The church seated only about 350, so many were diverted toward a door that led to the basement, where they could watch on a large television screen. When seats could no longer be found, upstairs or down, people lined the walls.

Tommy, Mike, Kathy, Thomas, Kelly, and Maryann walked quietly across the thin beige carpet up to the front pew. The inside walls of the church were painted in pinks and purples. A tall crucifix hung high on the wall at the front, framed in a glowing circle; Jesus' head lolled to the left. Below stood the boxy rectangular altar, stained dark to resemble mahogany. Tommy glanced at the lectern to the left of the altar, its microphone curving upward into the empty air. When the entrance hymn had finished, Tommy's eldest daughter, Aileen, rose to speak. She read from the Old Testament Book of Wisdom (4:7–15).

> The just man, though he die early, shall be at rest.
> For the age that is honorable comes not with passing of time, nor can it be measured in terms of years.

Rather, understanding is the hoary crown for men, and an unsullied life, the attainment of old age.
He who pleased God was loved; he who lived among sinners was transported,
Snatched away, lest wickedness pervert his mind or deceit beguile his soul.
For the witchery of paltry things obscures what is right and the whirl of desire transforms the innocent mind.
Having become perfect in a short while, he reached the fullness of a long career; for his soul was pleasing to the Lord.
Therefore He sped him out of the midst of wickedness.
But the people saw and did not understand,
Nor did they take this into account.

"The word of the Lord," she finished. The response rose from the church. "Thanks be to God."

Father John Gildea, who had married Vinny and Kathy in this same church more than twenty years earlier, read from the Gospel of John. During Communion, a favorite performer of Vinny's, whom he'd often gone to hear while he and Kathy vacationed on the Jersey Shore, sang "Danny Boy."

Finally, it was time.

Tommy took a deep breath and walked up to the lectern. He pulled the folded sheets of white paper from his pocket and glanced out at the packed church. He pressed the pages out in front of him. Every face was close enough to be recognized, every pair of eyes close enough to be met. He lowered his head and thanked the hundreds of friends for coming. His voice rang solidly from the speakers as he began to draw a picture of Vinny as the nucleus of the family—loving husband and best friend to Kathy, beloved father, uncle, nephew, cousin, and brother, "the finest brother you could have."

"He was a good and decent man," Tommy said. "I guess in the common vernacular of a Brooklyn neighborhood, Vinny was a stand-up guy. That simple phrase speaks volumes about the person it is describing. It says that he instinctively knows how to do the right thing, that his honesty and integrity are beyond reproach, that he is respected by those that know him. So I guess that phrase fits Vinny to a tee, and it's not surprising since he came from a neighborhood that produced so many other stand-up guys. He was an uncomplicated and unassuming straightforward guy, not prone to blowing his own horn. In fact, I'm sure he'd be a bit embarrassed at what's going on here today."

Vinny had outscored him on all the tests in probie school, Tommy said, leading the instructors to refer to Vinny as the "Smart Brunton" and Tommy as the "Stupid Brunton." He told about the night Vinny attended a Yankees game after receiving a medal for rescuing a handicapped woman in Bedford-Stuyvesant. Some friends had arranged for a congratulatory message to be flashed on the big screen at the stadium. Tommy said he was sure Vinny got a bigger charge out of seeing his name on the scoreboard than out of being awarded the medal.

"For the past two days at the visitation across the street," said Tommy, "a steady stream of men who knew and worked with Vinny spoke of him only in superlatives. I heard them murmur phrases such as 'He was the best' or 'Vinny was a natural' or 'I'd follow him into any job.' I can't tell you . . ." Tommy's voice cracked, and he faltered for a moment. When he spoke again, his tone was high and unsteady. ". . . how much pride it fills you with when you hear guys with huge reputations speak of your brother that way."

He hastily brushed away his tears. Hundreds of people who'd crowded into the church bent their heads and did the same, sharing the pain of this excruciating moment.

"I just regret that Vinny can't be here to expand his own reputation further. He was a great firefighter, an even better officer, and he left his world as a hero along with 342 other brave souls who steadfastly and courageously did their duty. And although his passing will leave a gaping hole in the lives of those who knew and loved him, we can take some consolation in the knowledge that he and others have arrived at the destination we all strive to attain someday, and that the face of God is smiling down on all of them in that perfect place. I could probably stand here and regale you with stories about Vinny all day, but I promised I'd be brief, and I guess some of those stories shouldn't be repeated in a church anyway.

"Last night, before I went home, I was having a conversation with one of Vinny's close friends. We were talking about Vin, and I remarked to the friend that Vinny was a 'home run.' His friend got a little indignant and corrected me. He said, "Your brother wasn't a 'home run,' he was a 'grand slam.'

"I couldn't have said it better myself. Until we meet again, Vinny, rest easy, brother."

Applause thundered throughout the church and filtered in from the street as the hundreds who could not fit inside listened intently to speakers near the church steps. Tommy folded the papers and stepped down from the pulpit.

Vinny's friend John Atwell stood in front of the microphone and opened by saying, "Aloha." Many in the church chuckled, recalling the luau they'd celebrated when Vinny first became a captain.

He told a few quick stories about working with Vinny at the firehouse. Then he read from a Robert J. Hastings piece called "The Station." Kathy had arranged for the story to be printed on the back of Vinny's memorial service program, but Atwell hadn't noticed until moments before he rose to speak.

"If you go to the back of the booklet, there's a passage from an article that appeared in the *Daily News* in 1991, that was found in his wallet. It was something that he cherished."

The article was a reprinted parable that told of how people often waste their lives waiting to arrive at a destination that will provide true happiness, looking for the station that marks success—turning eighteen, buying a car, paying off the mortgage, getting a promotion. "However, sooner or later we must realize there is no one station, no one place to arrive at once and for all. The true joy of life is the trip. The station is only a dream. It constantly outdistances us." Now, since most of the mourners had the words in front of them, Atwell read just the parts he thought related most closely to Vinny.

"'Relish the moment' is a good motto, especially when coupled with Psalm 118:24: 'This is the day which the Lord hath made; we will rejoice and be glad in it.' It isn't the burdens of today that drive men mad. Rather, it is regret over yesterday or fear of tomorrow. Regret and fear are twin thieves who would rob us of today.'

"No regrets," Atwell said. "And Vinny would have no regrets. Being in the Fire Department was who he was, a part of his identity, not just a job.

"As of right now, Kathy doesn't know this, but I gave this passage to him. I said, 'This is exactly who you are.' Sometimes, if we were sitting in the firehouse and heard someone griping about his lawn being unmowed or some other minor annoyance, one of us would say, 'Have you read "The Station" lately?' I had no idea that he kept it in his wallet. It puts life in a nice perspective. 'Stop pacing the aisles and counting the miles. Climb more mountains, eat more ice cream, swim more rivers, laugh more and cry less. Life must be lived as we go along.'"

As Kathy wept and applause echoed through the church, Atwell stepped down and took his seat.

Billy Burke had been Vinny's mutual partner at Ladder 105 and had often switched shifts with him—as he had on the morning of September

11. He spoke on behalf of the firehouse and recalled the firefighters' love for working with Vinny and learning from him. He explained that he'd had difficulty finding the right words for this speech and that in the end he'd been inspired by a poem written by Walt Whitman and had adapted the words to suit Vinny and the Fire Department. He cleared his throat and began to read in his thick, muddy voice, boyish but deep.

Oh, Captain! My Fire Captain! Your dire trip is done.
Your ladder company death endured, the treasure sought is won.
25,000 that day released from death's grasp
Tell the tale of fallen fiery towers of steel
The world's bravest stayed till the last
Our world's fresh breath they no longer feel.

Oh, Captain! My Fire Captain! Where is it that you rest beneath this labyrinth of steel and stone?
Your loyal crew has come to the crest and labors to carry you home.
Home! Where the world is true
Where your loved ones stand awaiting!
They need not fear for you are here forever within their hearts a-staying.

Oh, Captain! My Fire Captain! Rise up!
Rise up! For you the flag has flown, the bells are rung.
For you the pipers wail, the drummers drum.
The streets they are a-crowding, swaying masses.
They turn their heads to see you so proudly marching.
For you are theirs forever more urging deep within their breast
"Move on, men, move forward bravely
For life we give our best!"

Oh, Captain! My Fire Captain! He answers not.
Oh, father! Oh, husband! Oh, brother! Oh, friend!
Why? Oh, why did you come to this brutal end?
"For my soul to be true, to the sacred duty I do.
For God's freedom to endure!
For country! For family! For friend!"

The service ended. The firefighters left the church first, to re-form the line in the damp street. Their formation stretched back a full block. The friends and neighbors filled the sidewalks, a mass of people, all ages, some strangers, most familiar, standing very close together, wearing overcoats in blacks and browns. All up and down the street, the enormous flags flapped in the wind.

The Bruntons walked out of the church last. Kathy, Kelly, and Thomas shuffled down the steps past the men in the honor guard and came to a stop on the edge of sidewalk. Tommy, Mike, and Maryann stayed five feet behind. Three officers emerged from the lineup and approached Kathy and her children. Burke handed a white captain's hat to Kelly. Another officer gave a shiny firefighter's helmet to Thomas. Atwell handed a triangular folded flag to Kathy. He struggled to hold back his tears, breathing fast and raggedly. He thought maybe he was supposed to say something, like "On behalf of the New York City Fire Department, please accept this flag in recognition of your loved one's faithful service." But he couldn't. He knew Kathy so well. The words wouldn't have meant a thing. He reached his hands forward and lowered his eyes. Kathy wrapped her fingers around the flag, and took it gently from him.

When Liam witnessed the exchange, he called "Going Home." The firefighters snapped to salute, and the pipes began to wail.

When they finished, a bugler stood on the rooftop of a building across the street, tilted his instrument skyward, and played "Taps."

A trio of police helicopters flew very low overhead. The pummeling sounds of the chopper reverberated in the mourners' chests.

The band countermarched until every member now faced away from the church. Kathy, Maryann, Kathy's friend Maureen, and Tommy's wife, Mary, climbed into the first limousine. Other family members filed into a series of limos behind.

Tommy and Mike stayed outside on the street. As the procession began to roll forward to the sound of pipers skirling "America the Beautiful," the brothers marched ahead of the first limousine. They walked side by side, facing front with austere eyes. Between them, an empty space. Room enough for a man to have walked.

Kathy covered her face with her hand, grateful for a moment of shelter. Maryann sat facing backward and watched the lines of saluting firemen they'd already passed. The limousine slowed to a stop.

Suddenly, Mary gasped. "Oh, my God! Look!"

Tommy and Mike had joined the line of firefighters and were standing next to each other, saluting. Saluting them. The car began to move again. Tommy and Mike looked straight at the windows of the car, unwavering, as the family rolled past.

CHAPTER

9

END OF THE LINE

If every second of our lives recurs an infinite number of times, we are nailed to eternity as Jesus Christ was nailed to the cross. It is a terrifying prospect. In the world of eternal return the weight of unbearable responsibility lies heavy on every move we make.

—Milan Kundera, *The Unbearable Lightness of Being*

THE morning after Vinny Brunton's memorial service, Liam left his apartment in the Bay Ridge neighborhood of Brooklyn around 10:00 A.M. and drove through a chilly December rain that pecked persistently at his windshield. He headed north, on a twenty-minute trip to the Greek Orthodox Church in Corona, Queens, where the memorial service for another firefighter, James Pappageorge, would be held at 11:00 A.M. Pappageorge's service marked the 348th for a firefighter killed on September 11. There had been 234 memorial services, 86 funerals, and 28 more funerals for those already memorialized.

Liam had attended fewer than ten of these services—only the ones for Rescue 4 and a couple more. This morning, as Liam drove by the church, he noticed that about a hundred firefighters had gathered in the street. A handful of them had brought umbrellas to shield themselves from the rain. The rest let the drops fall on the shiny brims of their hats and seep slowly through the fabric covering their shoulders. The usual mangled concert of dozens of pipers all blowing different notes at once was nowhere to be heard.

He turned into a parking lot around the corner from the church, bounded by a tall chain-link fence, and glanced at the clock on the dashboard. The memorial service would begin in about fifteen minutes. Inside the parking lot, thirty bagpipers hovered in groups inside their donated passenger vans. The wet weather made it impossible for them to tune their bagpipes with any degree of precision, and too much moist air could cause the joints in the drones to swell, making them prone to breakage. Besides, standing outside too long in the rain would also cause their stiff wool coats to shrink. So the pipers fumbled with their slim plastic overcoats, new royal blue ones that had been imported from Scotland and were tightly bound into square bundles. They unwrapped them and slipped their heads into the holes and their arms under the flaps, then laughed as they wondered how they would bind them back up again. Liam pulled into the lot as the pipers were climbing out of their vans and getting ready to line up. He parked his minivan next to Kippy's and sat inside, alone.

Kippy smiled and came over to greet him. For weeks, Kippy had been calling Liam and suggesting that he come back to the band. But whenever Kippy had brought up the idea that Liam should start marching with the band again, Liam had always refused, saying he had to stay at the site and dig for Bronko. Once Bronko and four of the others missing from Rescue 4 were found in late October, Kippy had begun pressing harder.

Kippy was concerned about Liam's state of mind. Over the years of their friendship, Liam had been the one who was always teasing and perpetually shooting off jokes and wisecracks to make Kippy laugh. Kippy, who was six years older than Liam, had viewed himself as the jaded one in comparison. But since September 11, he had begun to see a reversal in their attitudes. Liam was more sarcastic than he used to be, and angry. Kippy became the joker of the group, and charged himself with the duty of sparking up conversations, making up humorous banter out of thin air, and trying to keep others' spirits up during the dark days. Kippy had seen how deeply Liam had been affected by his brother-in-law Vinny Fowler's death two years earlier, how much Liam fought to preserve his memory. He'd started a charity softball tournament in Fowler's name and promoted it nearly all year round. In a short time, it became one of the most successful charity events in the entire Fire Department. That was the way Liam did things these days. Everything to the extreme.

Kippy told Liam he couldn't shoulder the burden of finding all 343 men by himself. If he'd come to the funerals, maybe he could unwind some, and just being around the guys again would be good. Playing the funeral detail would, in fact, be a break, compared with the work Liam was doing.

Eventually, in early December, Liam relented. Ground Zero was gradually becoming less of a recovery area and more of a construction site. With less specialized digging to be done, he was feeling less effective in his work there. He made a minor compromise with himself. He decided he would split his duty three ways: the firehouse, "the pile"—which they were now starting to call "the pit"—and the funerals. That way, he could lead the band through a funeral or memorial service in the morning, change clothes, and be at the site by the early afternoon. This was the second day in a row that Liam had made it to a memorial service, and Kippy was relieved to see him.

When Liam returned to the band, he discovered a very different atmosphere at these services than he'd been accustomed to in previous years. After so many line-of-duty deaths, a ceremony that had once been rare and somber was now routine, almost mundane. Firefighters who formed the lineup outside the church used to snap to attention early, but now they conversed with each other until the last second before the procession was to begin. He habitually made a quick head count whenever he arrived at a service, and he saw that the firefighters in attendance numbered fewer than two hundred on most days, out of over eleven thousand. Liam couldn't understand why. He couldn't understand why so many things were different now. Even the idea of honoring the dead brothers didn't seem to mean what it used to—or as much as it used to.

The whole pipe band didn't play for services now, even when there was only one scheduled. The pipers seldom went inside the church, unless they knew the man being memorialized. They didn't rush from service to service anymore. In the second week of December, for instance, only one service was scheduled per day, and the band members had received one day off. The routine was predictable. They'd arrive at the church at 9:00 A.M. for a 10:00 A.M. start, then the family would lag and the service wouldn't get started until 11:00. The ceremony would last at least two hours; they might not play the ending set until 2:00 P.M. or 3:00 P.M. Then they'd go to the collation.

The eulogies were getting longer, and there seemed to be more of them than before. Now, just one funeral or memorial took up an entire day. At the funeral for firefighter Christopher Santora on December 1, the pipers sat in their vans so long they ran out of things to talk about. There were fourteen eulogies that day, including a number of musical interludes. The service dragged on for four and a half hours. Santora's body had been misidentified on September 24 as Jose Guadalupe,[1] another firefighter in his company, Ladder 4 and Engine 54, the house that lost fifteen men; Kippy had gone there to fill in during the days following September 11. The body had been recovered a couple of days after the collapse but was not identifiable by sight. However, with the help of a flat gold chain that Guadalupe always wore, and an X ray that revealed a congenital defect in his neck, the medical examiner's office was confident the remains were Guadalupe's. The Guadalupe family held a funeral. Later, DNA samples taken from Santora's toothbrush matched the body that the Guadalupes had buried. Further investigation revealed that both men wore similar gold chains, and both had the same bone anomaly in the neck. Dental records confirmed the medical examiner's error. The corpse, like Santora, had no eye teeth. The body was exhumed, and the Santora family held his long-awaited funeral.

At every service, firefighters would hear family and friends step to the podium and glorify the deceased—"He was the best this, he was the best that"—which left them wondering, "Are they talking about the same fella I knew? He wasn't all that great." To avoid the torrent of emotion, once the beginning procession was over and the family was seated inside the church, the officers in the ceremonial unit would go on "half-time," as they called it—out to a deli for a bagel and coffee, in order to avoid hearing the prayer service and the eulogies. The band members and many of the firefighters in attendance usually did the same. But some churches had begun to broadcast the service over giant speakers that sat outside the church doors. Then, the men couldn't get away. They'd talk louder in their groups outside, or make sure to hang around farther from the church.

There were additional causes of anxiety among the officers in the ceremonial unit. For instance, doves. Some families wanted to release them after the service, as a symbol of their loved one's soul taking flight. A man in Pennsylvania had sent a fax to the FDNY offering his birds for use at services. When let out of their box, they would instinctively fly back to their roost in Pennsylvania. But if they were kept in the box too long, sometimes they would become lethargic and wouldn't fly. The result—a crew of lazy doves, pecking around on the ground after a heart-wrenching funeral, refusing to fly away. And if the firefighter assigned to release them did so too early, the birds could get sucked into the helicopter rotors during the flyover and chewed up, sending thousands of bloody bird parts raining down on the mourners' heads. Considering such scenarios of potential disaster, the officers grew to regard the doves as more trouble than they were worth. Someone in the ceremonial unit scribbled on the bird owner's fax, which was posted on the side of a filing cabinet in the ceremonial unit's office, "FDNY Rod and Gun Club called. Will shoot doves for ceremonial purposes if necessary."

Before September 11, the department had followed strict rules regarding the caskets. Only FDNY members or veterans of the U.S. Armed Services received American flags over their caskets. The rest got the Fire Department flag. Now, every firefighter killed on September 11 was given the American flag. The stars of the American flag draping the coffin were supposed to lie over the heart, the striped end over the feet. The deceased was to be carried into the church feet first, except in the case of a clergy member, who would be carried in head first. But with such small amounts of remains being identified and placed in the coffins for burial, Jimmy Sorokac had to adjust the procedure. Sometimes the casket was completely empty. Other times there were just a few files of a man—the medical examiner called the remains "files," instead of "pieces" or "parts"—which could have been anything, a couple of rib bones, a part of a femur, a thumb. It was impossible to know how to arrange the files "feet first," so he didn't try. He just oriented the flag to the shape of the coffin, draping it with exquisite care, tucking in the corners, and securing it perfectly each time.

Sorokac rarely had adequate time to practice with the pallbearers before the service. Instead of coming for a three-hour session at Randall's Island, they often met him at the funeral parlor a couple of hours before the service was to begin. If the service called for an empty casket, Sorokac would give them a quick rundown of the procedure, miming the movements in the air. *When the casket comes down, you take it out. Then you take it toward the church, either on a hand carry or a shoulder carry. Then you stop in the foyer of the church.* It made more sense than having them actually practice carrying the coffin especially in plain sight of grieving family members.

The band and the ceremonial unit grew familiar with the idiosyncrasies of different belief systems. Lutherans tended to sing every verse of the hymns, while Catholics usually shortened them to two or three. Jehovah's Witnesses did not allow pipers, American flags, or the playing of "Taps," but a helicopter flyover was usually permissible. Atheists held services in secular locations; the one for Capt. Frank Callahan took place in Lincoln Center. That day, the family asked the pipers to play "Dawning of the Day" continuously as they marched up the street and back for the countermarch. Normally, the pipers would have stopped by that point and only the drummers would have played, but no matter. The band obliged. The members were let go right after the beginning of the service. Inside, the word "God" was not mentioned. Music played, and family and friends stood up to tell stories about the deceased.

For the families, planning a funeral or memorial became similar to planning a wedding, to such an extent that to an outsider there seemed little difference between the two events. Widows who'd attended funerals or memorials for other firefighters would see elements of a friend's ceremony that appealed to them and want it for their husband's service. Certain songs became popular, like Eric Clapton's "Tears in Heaven" or Faith Hill's ballad "There You'll Be" from the movie *Pearl Harbor.* Some families hired photographers for the funeral and inquired whether the church would allow a video camera to tape the service. With no body to bury, the date of the service became a personal choice; some widows chose to memorialize their husband on his birthday or on their wedding anniversary. Families made up increasingly expensive programs, thick as small books with multiple glossy pages, full-color picture collages, letters from children, even baby pictures of the deceased. The word "wake" was hardly ever used, becoming "visitation" or "a gathering of family and friends." A memorial service was called "a celebration of life." Collations became full-scale sit-down dinners and were often held in catering halls. Sometimes, it seemed death barely came into the ceremony at all.

More people came into the mix when planning a ceremony than ever before. Extended family, distant cousins, stepchildren, all wanted to be a part. Sometimes the various contingents bickered, and the firehouse liaison would find himself in the middle of a nasty tug-of-war. One firefighter had two memorial services—one organized by his ex-wife, another by his girlfriend. His remains were later identified, and he had a funeral. Just one. Another family memorialized their lost firefighter, then, on the advice of a family priest, held a second memorial service some weeks later, after which they buried a coffin filled with pictures and memorabilia so they could have a cemetery plot at which to grieve.

Some families asked that the honor company of firefighters be seated in front of the dignitaries inside the church, reasoning that the mayor and his cronies hadn't sacrificed nearly as much, so the firefighters should have the front-row seat.

The ceremonial unit tried to be flexible with the families' requests, while maintaining some kind of uniformity in the procedure. The chief officer in the ceremonial unit, Lt. Walter Dreyer, understood each family's desire to have a service as individual as their loved one was, but he was committed to the traditional aspect of the funerals. In his view, each man was a brother, each man died the same way, each man should be accorded the same honor. When he got uptight and snappish about it, the other officers ribbed him; his inflexibility was a symptom of his German blood, they said. The jokes only made him madder. At one funeral, they allowed a Jeep porting a surfboard to be part of the procession, because the dead firefighter had enjoyed surfing. At another service, the firehouse dog was allowed to stand in the lineup of firemen, because the deceased had been so affectionate toward the animal. Every time a request like that was granted, the officers in the ceremonial unit shrugged and muttered that they'd "given up the show."

In the future, Lt. Dreyer envisioned a ceremonial free-for-all and increasing pressure from family members demanding to know why they couldn't have the additions they wanted. Too many adjustments to the ceremony made control impossible. He was forced to draw up a new procedures manual, to finally put words to the idea of honor that he clung to in his mind. The nine-page document sometimes took a defensive tone, justifying the protocol in direct response to complaints and demands. For example, firefighters from a deceased member's former house, or from a volunteer company where he'd begun his career, sometimes wanted to add themselves to the honor guard, and their fire trucks to the procession, making it twice or three times as long as before. Lt. Dreyer's entry on escorts read:

> *Escort Apparatus*—Why Only One.
> Caisson or escort apparatus should be limited to one because:
>
> — Length of procession and logistics
> — Time—Delay getting to service
> — Turning and position in front of church may be limited
> — Diesel and smoke fumes at formation area
> — Limits the "Parade Thru Town" effect, as one apparatus gives as much status, impact, recognition to the Fire Department as we need
> — Dignity is maintained

If the honor company insists on marching behind the caisson or escort apparatus, the following should be considered

a. A maximum of 25 for a single house and 50 for a double house. Use of seniority, rank, relationship, prior assignments and other personal factors should be used to include members of prior assigned units into this maximum of 25 or 50.
b. This slows the procession if it begins too far from the church. Assemble at pipers' location.
c. Causes a problem with limited space in front of church and difficulty reassembling on the steps. "Where do we go from here" syndrome.

Honor company should line the steps to the service (church)

— Limit number in honor company—not to extend beyond inner sidewalk or at least not impede immediate family to enter. Large numbers are inappropriate.
— Impedes and has a negative or frightening effect on immediate family. They need an open area to file into and feel comfortable. This is a most difficult time and a large open area helps.
— The honor company is diluted if 40, 50 or 100 firefighters are involved.
— When family in crowd and extended family and friends see 100 to 150 honor company move toward the church, they become aggressive and difficult to control.

In contrast, the pipers' duties had not changed at all. They always played the same tunes in the same order. Very occasionally, a family requested a special tune, like "Danny Boy." But most of the time the band stuck to the same set. Over the past three months, playing at funerals and memorial services nearly every day of the week, the pipers had grown accustomed to the repetitious death ceremony. Being together all the time, they had formed a new culture and had solidified their own cliques. Certain men always went to lunch at a deli together. Others sought out the nearest pub, where they could drink away the two hours or more between the beginning and ending sets. Now the pipers were adept at a system of mental math—given the number of eulogies, they could quickly forecast how long they had to loiter over lunch. They followed a new set of unwritten rules, organized by residential location and individual dedication. When Tom McEnroe made the rounds with his clipboard to check off which pipers would play at the next day's services, the band members answered yes or no according to where they lived. If a man had a legitimate prior commitment, like having to take his mother to the hospital, he was let off. If the basis of his complaint was shaky, Tom, who seemed to be constantly sweating these days, made him repeat the reason until he was shamed into showing up anyway.

The pipers had long since discovered new sources of annoyance in each other, like who never had enough cash to contribute for lunch and which ones left their empty coffee cups in the van for the driver to clean out. They bickered over ceremonial details, whether they were supposed to march in front of the fire truck or behind. By now, they were eager for the end to come. One more day, December 15, and that would be the final memorial service scheduled for the year. The pipers hoped they would be given an unofficial two-week holiday until January 1, when they would finally return to their firehouses and achieve some semblance of normality once again.

An officer from the ceremonial unit emerged from the crowd and signaled to the pipers in the parking lot that the family had arrived. The funeral procession was about to begin. Liam glanced at the raindrops that blurred his view through the windshield and climbed out of the van. The band members headed to a spot two blocks from the church to tune their pipes and warm up. When the procession was ready, Liam led the march up the street, past the line of firefighters on one side and a class of young children from the nearby school on the other, holding Greek and American flags. The pipers blew the last notes of "Dawning of the Day" as they marched beneath the forty-by-twenty-five-foot American flag suspended from two fire-truck ladders that arched over their heads. The music subsided and the march was sustained by the choppy beat of a snare drum. The 7 train rumbled and rocked as it sped by on the aboveground tracks at the edge of the block, momentarily drowning out the drummers' dirge. Then the 348th bout of silence. The 348th solo of "Amazing Grace." The 348th salute to the air as family members followed a coffin into the church. Finally, the 348th break for lunch.

"Let's go somewhere nice today," Kippy said as the pipers made their way back to the parking lot. Since Kippy lived the furthest upstate, in Warwick, he drove one of the vans every day. He rose the earliest in the morning, sometimes at 5:00 A.M., in order to pick up six or seven pipers along the way and make it to the city in time for a 9:00 A.M. service. Sometimes he didn't get home until after 10:00 P.M. He ate every meal on the road, and in a hurry—greasy ham-and-egg sandwiches from fast-food joints for breakfast, hero sandwiches from a deli at lunch, a plate of pasta and a few plastic cups of stout at the collation. He had nearly constant indigestion as a result.

"How many eulogies?" one piper asked.

"Six, I think," another responded.

"Do Greek services run long?" The others shrugged. They figured they probably had two hours before they'd have to return for the final march, to play "Going Home" and "America the Beautiful."

Kippy knew an Italian restaurant in the neighborhood, a fancy joint where he and a group of firemen from his company had taken their wives for a Christmas party a couple of years ago. Some of the guys wanted to go to a nearby deli. Another group wasn't hungry—they wanted to stay in their vans and wait for the service to end. Liam stood by his van and shifted his weight awkwardly from foot to foot. He punched buttons on his cell phone. Kippy walked over to him.

"Will we go to the Park Side, buddy?"

Liam shook his head and answered in a low, raspy voice, "I don't know. I don't know if I feel like it."

Kippy conferred with the other pipers with whom he often ate lunch. Kevin O'Hagan would stay behind, but Tim Grant would go, and Bill Duffy, and Bill Duffy's son. Liam opened the back door of his van and slid his staff inside.

"Did you guys check out my pile hat?" he asked, pointing to the trunk. His smoke-blue construction hard hat was covered with stickers: the American flag; "9–11–01 We Will Never Forget"; logos from the ironworkers' and carpenters' unions. A couple of pipers approached and looked at it from a few feet away, mildly feigning interest.

"Come on, Liam," Kippy cajoled. "You'll feel better. I promise."

Liam shrugged his shoulders and nodded, barely. He climbed into the rearmost seat of Kippy's van. Liam phoned the restaurant on his cell, to see if they would need a reservation for lunch. They wouldn't. Liam sat silently as Kippy drove.

A few weeks earlier, the interview for which Liam had sat one night in October, when he was exhausted and had just finished working a lengthy shift at the site, had aired on *Nightline.* The piece began with footage from the Father's Day fire. Captain Brian Hickey, who had been interviewed shortly afterward, explained how the explosion had splintered the floors, blown some men into the air, and separated everyone inside. His words, though spoken months before September 11, had a surreal familiarity.

> We rode down on the truck that morning with six men and came back with four. That is something nobody wants to happen to them. Nobody. We don't go out the door thinking that. But now we came back and it's reality.

Then Donna, Brian's wife, explained how Brian had felt responsibility for the men who had died. The worst part for him had been the fact that he could not control what had happened. He could not have saved the men. But he'd worked through those feelings, she said, and he was going to back to work to rebuild the company.

Father John Delendick appeared on the screen.

> These guys consider themselves tough guys. You know, they sit around the kitchen table and they talk about how they can deal with this. And the reality is many of them can't.

Then Liam. His curly hair was mussed. Stubble poked out from his chin. His eyes were red and bleary.

> I haven't gone in for any counseling. I'm just—my counseling is kind of staying busy and, you know, keep working at the—you know, down at the Trade Center.

Father Delendick again.

> I believe that that in about three—you know, three weeks, four weeks, six weeks, all the memorial services will stop. They'll no longer be going to the piles to dig. And they're all going to look at each other, "What do we do now? How do we move on?" I do foresee that there will be problems creeping up.

Back to Liam.

> Maybe if I had a little more time to reflect and we weren't so busy, you know, maybe the emotions would start to come back.

Another firefighter from Rescue 4 appeared onscreen, talking about how their focus was on finding the men and returning them to their loved ones so that the families could have "closure." Then, immediately, Liam.

> Closure. That's a word I've been hearing a lot for the last few weeks. I don't know. That's what I'd have to say. Nobody has ever experienced anything like this. The best word I have to explain what we experienced down there was "biblical." You know, closure, I'm working on it.

And then Donna, Brian Hickey's wife, again.

> Definitely there will be no closure for me or my family unless they bring him home. And I know in my heart they will. They tell me every day, they call me. They're going to look for him until they are told they can't look anymore. Brian loved being a fireman. And he had said to me after the Father's Day fire that if he has to die, this is the way he would like to do it. That it's an honor to die that way. And I hold that in my heart.

Liam felt that the way the piece had been edited made him look like he was going nuts and didn't know it, or that he was somehow at odds with the other, more sane men in the firehouse. He no longer had any desire to talk to people who didn't know what he was all about. His words got misconstrued; his attempts at communication were badly interpreted. Many of the men working at the site felt this way—starkly disconnected from the outside world. Things that mattered to the recovery workers meant little to their families, friends, and others who didn't do the same work they did. To them, finding a body mostly intact brought a sense of glee. To others, the thought induced horror. Going to a funeral wasn't the grim event it once had been; indeed, the gatherings were often enjoyable social events to the firefighters who didn't go inside the church. But when yet another funeral was mentioned in conversation, outsiders voiced dread or offered misplaced sympathy and sometimes asked a question that could not be answered: "When will it be over?" People would tell the firefighters to let it go, and they absolutely would not, could not let anything go. Increasingly immured by his chosen duty, Liam kept more and more things to himself, including the secret he still had not told Donna: She did not know that they had found her husband's helmet in early October. No other sign of Brian Hickey had been uncovered. The helmet was perhaps all that was left.

Kippy pulled the van up outside the front door of the restaurant. An attendant immediately emerged and took the keys. The firefighters puffed their chests slightly as they strode in. Liam had often sat in the park across the street and eaten sandwiches during summertime lunch breaks with the crew from Rescue 4. But he'd never been inside this posh place.

Two Italian men with slicked-back hair and three-piece suits smiled at them from behind the host's stand. The elder Bill Duffy knew one of the men, and they chatted politely about the incredible number of funerals and what a great loss the Fire Department had suffered. The host gestured them inside with an open hand and told them to sit wherever they chose. Kippy picked a brightly lit table near the window, and the men relaxed into round wooden chairs with intricate wicker backs, next to a garden of bonsai trees and hanging plants. Liam disappeared to the restroom to wash his hands. When he came over to the table he stood for a moment, removing his sash. Kippy smiled up at him.

"Unbuckle, brother," he said.

Liam sniffed. He took off his belt and coat, revealing the navy blue Father's Day fire T-shirt that he wore underneath, and sat down.

Kippy told Liam to pick the wine, and the men delved into the basket of bread. Tim smeared butter on his bread and poured olive oil on his bread plate so he could cover each bite with both. Liam chose an extra-large bottle of the house cabernet. A waiter returned with it in seconds and poured generously into each glass. Two waiters swept in behind him with small bowls of fettuccini in red sauce, filled with tiny chunks of lobster. Kippy giggled and pointed at Tim. He had butter on his goatee. Tim wiped it away and smiled. They lifted their glasses, and Kippy toasted to better times.

The entrees arrived on abundant plates, the veal piccata for Liam, the whitefish for Kippy. Liam poured out more wine for everyone. Before the bottle had a chance to be emptied, a waiter arrived with another. He indicated that it was courtesy of the men seated at the corner table. The pipers looked up, and four Italian men nodded and waved. The pipers grinned at each other and raised their glasses to the men.

The wine loosened the tension in Liam's shoulders, and he began to talk. In the news, there had been stories of a group of a thousand firefighters who had just taken a vacation trip to California. The outing was sponsored by a security-camera company and described in the papers as an "uplifting memorial dedication." Meanwhile, there had been six funerals that week. Six! How could those guys go on a trip when there were still brothers whose bodies had not yet been recovered? The way it used to be in the department, before September 11, absolutely no one would have gone away on vacation if there was a firefighter being buried. Then there was the dwindling attendance at the funerals. There had to be plenty of guys who could have taken a couple hours off and come to the service. He'd heard that the medical office was advising some men not to go to funerals, out of concern for their mental health. Okay. But the burials weren't over yet. Liam's tone grew more rancorous. How could a person decide that one guy was more important than another? That one funeral was more worthy of attending than another? Weren't they supposed to be brothers? Off-duty guys would be sitting around in their firehouses with a funeral going on down the street and not go. There were more out-of-town firefighters at the funerals than there were New York City firefighters. It was an embarrassment. What about the guys who worked in firehouses that had lost men but didn't go dig at the site? What did they say to the families when they stopped by? How could those firefighters look the widows and children in the eye? The way Liam saw it, this whole disaster had been one big litmus test for the job, the job they'd all professed to sacrifice their lives for. Long before the dust ever settled on the towers' collapse, Liam had been able to see clearly enough who his friends really were, or weren't. Some guys he'd thought would step up, didn't, and a few he hadn't expected to, had. Overall, he was disappointed in a lot of guys he'd once trusted.

Now the guys in the pipe band were scheduled to go back on the chart on Sunday, but he'd heard them pining for a break, hoping that maybe headquarters would give them an impromptu two-week holiday for all the funerals and memorials they had played. For the first two months after the attacks, the band had played at services on fifty-four out of sixty-two days, with just eight days scattered throughout when there had been no funerals or memorials. Liam told the men at the table that the best thing they could do was just go back on duty Sunday as scheduled and not say a word about it. No one in the band should complain. Nor should they give up now. They should be the shining examples for the job.

The more Liam talked, the more silent the others became. His words did not invite response. They let Liam vent.

Tim chewed quietly, lowering his eyes to his plate and glancing up occasionally to show he was listening. He'd never explained to Liam why he hadn't followed him the night of September 11, when Liam thought he had a radio and called him toward the buried officer. Nor did he tell Liam about his thoughts of his one-year-old daughter, the wooziness that forced him to get off the pile and go home, or the residual guilt he felt for not being able to stay and search that night. He didn't think he had to say it. He didn't always talk to Liam much when he saw him these days, but then, Liam didn't talk much to anyone. Tim knew his friend was hurting, and he figured silence was the best way to cope with it. Leave him alone, and someday he'd go back to the way he was.

So Tim hadn't told Liam yet, but he had decided to stop being pipe major at the end of the year. Hundreds of orders for the band's CD piled up in a spare room at home, nagging to be sent out. He was exhausted and still plagued by nightmares of the towers collapsing. Going to funerals all the time was depressing, and he was tired of it. Most nights, before he came home, Tara riled up their daughter, Jessica. "Daddy's coming home!" she'd say over and over, clapping her only child's hands together, stretching her own mouth into a wide smile, then a round "Ooh!" of excitement, which the child would mimic. Soon Jessica would begin to bounce up and down on her rubbery legs, her straw-colored hair flapping with each motion. By the time Tim opened the door, Jessica was so giddy she'd tumble toward his legs, grip them and squeal in delight. The big event. Daddy's home.

Beyond the accumulated stress of all the funerals, for Tim the band was no longer the enjoyable, raucous distraction it had been. Teasing jabs that used to seem funny now turned nasty. He didn't want to lead them anymore. He'd enjoyed the status of being the pipe major and holding the responsibilities the chief role entailed, but he hated being the "bad guy," repeatedly giving orders that the others refused to follow. Being the band's webmaster was a time-consuming job in and of itself. He didn't have the time or energy to do both anymore. He'd stay on as a piper but relinquish the leadership to someone else. Public relations ideas spun through Tim's head. He could work more on the Web site. He could start making arrangements to have the band's CD in Irish stores across the country. He could arrange corporate sponsorships with national retailers. He could focus on being the voice of the band in the outside world.

The pipers lingered over the meal for more than an hour. When they were finished, they debated whether they had time for cappuccino. Tim called Tom McEnroe to see if the mourners were anywhere near the end of the service. Tom said it would be at least fifteen more minutes. Liam ordered a round of cappuccinos for everyone, except Kippy, who ordered an espresso with a shot of Sambuca liquor. When the men got up to leave, they felt warm and relaxed. The valet returned with the van, and Kippy told Liam to drive. Liam opened his palm to receive the keys. Liam was one of Rescue 4's chauffeurs and regularly drove the rig when he was on duty. He hated being driven around by other people. There was always a better route to follow, a quicker way to take off from a traffic light.

Kippy climbed into a back seat by the window. For the past several days, men had been coming up to Kippy at funerals and congratulating him on his upcoming promotion to lieutenant. He wasn't sure exactly when the promotion would occur. One more day and the funerals would be over for the year. The men would return to their firehouses. Kippy would, too, but only for a short time. As soon as the notification came though, he'd leave the firehouse where he had spent the last seven years, take a month-long lieutenant's training course, and then start his rolling assignments in different firehouses across the city. He hadn't fought a fire in months. He'd only been back to his firehouse a few times since September 11, since the day he decided not to go down to the World Trade Center. That terrible decision. He still regretted it. Sometimes he told himself he'd made the right choice. Going downtown without a mask was reckless. Besides, he'd been off duty, and that rig hadn't even been going to the Trade Center, so whether he'd jumped on or not didn't matter. But some of the guys who made it onto that rig had been able to go to the site to search that day. And Kippy knew there were men in the Fire Department who would say any firefighter in his situation should have gone. Many had gone, mask or not. Off duty or not. He secretly doubted if he still had what it took to be the kind of gutsy firefighter he'd once been. He was out of practice. The next time a call came in, would he be able to jump on the rig?

The van slowed to a crawl as Liam ran into a traffic jam. Kippy, who'd grown up in the nearby neighborhood of Woodside, called out directions. Liam, who worked in Woodside and drove the fire truck around the borough all the time, shook his head and bellowed back, "I am personally offended at your giving me directions, Kippy."

"I'm telling you, man," Kippy protested. "We'll never get back in time by going this way."

Liam jerked the wheel and careened through a maze of side streets until he once again had to cross the main strip where traffic had stalled.

He had to get through in order to get back to the funeral. Liam checked his mirrors, glanced around, and pulled the van up onto the sidewalk. He drove right past the traffic jam, shaving by storefronts and startled pedestrians. The others stared out the windows in silence.

Kippy caught a glance of his reflection in the window glass, his shorn white-gray hair and puffy eyes. He looked so different to himself now. Not at all like the guy in the picture taken five years ago, the one that was now enlarged and framed on the mantel at home, of Kippy talking with Father Mychal Judge. Kippy was squinting at Father Judge. The priest was facing him, holding his thumb and forefinger to his chin, and laughing. He looked as if he were solving a problem for Kippy, who looked much younger then, with a full head of wavy brown hair framing his frowning, questioning face.

"Hey, Liam," Kippy leaned forward in his seat. "Did I tell you what Bill Mackin in 80 Engine said to me one time?"

Liam shook his head.

"He goes, 'Hey Kippy, what the hell happened to you these past couple of years? All of a sudden, you look like a snow cone with all the flavor sucked out.'"

The van rocked with the pipers' laughter.

Liam smiled widely and chuckled for the first time that day. "That's a good one," he said, as he looked out at the road. "That's a real good one."

One day later was the memorial service for Battalion Chief Ray Downey of Special Operations Command (SOC), the last service scheduled for the year. The chief's superior knowledge of special operations led many firefighters to nickname him "God." His service was held in Deer Park, Long Island. The midweek rain had washed away all that remained of the warm autumn temperatures. Just the night before, a summer-like humidity had coated the city. Today, the sun shone from what seemed a long distance away. It was a bitter, blustery day.

A crew of eight firefighters fought against the whipping wind to restrain a colossal American flag and attach it to two ladders so it could be suspended over the procession. The flag popped and billowed with each gust. Each time the firefighters tried to grasp all four corners, one flew stubbornly awry. Finally, two men knelt on the bottom corners and pinned them down to the asphalt on the road while four men gained control of the sides so the top edges could be fastened with twine to the tip of each ladder.

A line of firefighters assembled atop a slim median across the street from the church and stood watching the ensuing struggle. There were rumors that President George W. Bush would attend the memorial service, and increased security demanded a thorough check of the nearby shopping mall, the cars in the parking lot, and the cubbies and corners inside the church. About three hundred of the firefighters had lined up early, at least an hour before the service was to begin. The icy wind numbed their toes and bit at their cheeks so ferociously it made their eyes water. They shivered and wiped the tears from the corners of their eyes.

In the front row of the lineup, about twenty feet away from the flag, one firefighter began to sway. His knees buckled, and suddenly he collapsed in a heap on the street. For a moment, panic rippled through the crowd. The man did not get up. He'd fainted. "That happens all the time," a newspaper photographer on the press bleachers grumbled aloud. "They just get overwhelmed." An FDNY ambulance arrived and escorted the firefighter away.

The procession began forty-five minutes later. First a police motorcade. Then the seventy pipers and drummers, grimacing as they tried to ignore the chill that numbed their hands and made it increasingly difficult to finger the notes. Liam extended his mace to the right and steered the band into the half-circle driveway outside the church. A Squad 1 fire truck idled in behind them. The firefighters stood to attention as a piper who worked in SOC played the solo of "Amazing Grace." The notes wended though the air, meek and thin with artful embellishments. A team of pallbearers removed a thin plank covered with red, white, and blue carnations from the back of the fire truck. Downey's body had not been recovered. In place of a casket, this flower-covered board was carried into the church.

When the detail was dismissed, most of the pipers rushed to shelter at a firehouse nearby. Six pipers made their way further to a tiny shack-like pub aptly named UNeeda Rest, which sat tucked around the corner from a massive overpass four blocks away. The pipers turned their faces down against the force of the wind, watching their shiny black toes crunch atop the dirt path leading to the green door. A jumbo American flag was draped over the left side of the brown shingle roof. Inside, men in dress blue already crowded the place to capacity, so many that they pressed against the wood-paneled walls, even though the service had begun just minutes before. A string of red lights hung over the bar in a nod to Christmas. The place was literally spilling over with firefighters, but they stepped aside for the pipers, who gently elbowed into a space far in the back.

Among themselves, the pipers spoke again of how they hoped that the families would decide to hold off on any more memorial services until after New Year's.

Tommy found his way to the bar to order a round of beers for the others. With the holidays approaching, his family looked toward festivities with trepidation. Kathy had no any desire to shop for presents. She claimed not to want a Christmas tree that year, but Tommy had gone out and bought one and hauled it into the house anyway.

"How many funerals have you all done?" a young firefighter asked. The pipers looked at each other and shrugged. There had been too many to count. None of them had kept track of his individual number. They could only offer a guess. Some had done about fifty, some might have done seventy . . .

Tommy turned his head, from the corner of the bar where he stood. "One hundred and fifteen," he said.

CHAPTER

10

HOLIDAY

This grief of the keen is no personal complaint for the death of one woman over eighty years, but it seems to contain the whole passionate rage that lurks somewhere in every native of the island. In this cry of pain the inner consciousness of the people seems to lay itself bare for an instant, and to reveal the mood of beings who feel their isolation in the face of a universe that wars on them with wind and seas. They are usually silent, but in the presence of death all outward show of indifference or patience is forgotten, and they shriek with pitiable despair before the horror of the fate to which they all are doomed.

—John Millington Synge, *The Aran Islands*

JEANNETTE Schardt climbed out of an ebony limousine at the corner of Hylan Boulevard and Penn Avenue in Staten Island on the icy morning of New Year's Eve. Surrounded by a formation made up of fewer than a hundred firefighters, she stepped slowly into the cruel wind and toward the church. A gray-mustached piper named Ed emerged briskly from the inside of the church, where he'd been waiting out of the furious wind. He stood on the sidewalk like a brightly colored statue and began blowing into the bag. A young, sallow-faced firefighter standing in the honor guard near the church door blew a sigh through his lips and lowered his eyes, filled with pain. The deep humming of Ed's drones made a gasping, raspy sound.

Jeannette walked by, being serenaded by "Amazing Grace" for the second time in as many months in honor of the death of John, her husband. She was followed by others dressed darkly like her, some tearful, some numb. A few gave a quick glance at Ed before averting their eyes. They could not bear to look at him for long. After two refrains, he swept his pipes up in a quick motion to bring on the end.

The dozens of relatives and friends and the small crowd of firefighters who came that day weren't enough to fill all the pale wood benches inside the tiny church. The coffin rested right in the center between the two halves of pews. Those who rose for Communion almost had to sidestep it. Mayor Giuliani spoke first. Today was his last day in office. He told the mourners that he had to run off to be at a ceremony swearing in a class of three hundred new probies. He did not apologize. He talked about the juxtaposition of sad and celebratory events and how he would have wanted nothing else than to be at a firefighter's funeral on his last day in office. September 11, he said, was still on everyone's mind. If he had any notes before him, he didn't appear to look at them once. He said, "John died a hero," several times.

About ten minutes into the service, as the priest was pontificating about the meaning of eternal life, an elderly lady seated with the family cried out and stood up. She held her hand up to her forehead and, pleadingly, shook her head. Her eyes squinted with pain. Men next to her grabbed her arms, and a fireman led them out to the vestibule.

Jeannette rose from her pew in the front. Her round belly showed slightly through her black sweater top. She walked up to the altar and gave a double pat to the coffin, as if tapping an old-time buddy's shoulder as she passed. She said that since they had already done the eulogies during the memorial service on November 12, she would be addressing John directly today. He was there now. She read the lyrics of Kansas's "Dust in the Wind" and a poem she wrote for John, its words woven in youthful simplicity, about two hearts broken because they are apart. She told of how she wished she had begged him not to go that day, how she wished that he were still there next to her. She spoke with tears in her voice but did not weep. He was her lover, she said. She would always love him.

During the funeral, the pipers sought shelter in a nearby coffee shop. They'd already played at this church several times, including a service just three days before, for fire patrolman Keith Roma, who was not counted officially among the Fire Department's 343 missing but who many agreed deserved a fireman's sendoff. None of the pipers knew Jeannette. Only one went into the church, darting in briefly to check on the progress and estimate for the others how much longer it would be.

As of December 15, the band members had thought only twenty-four services remained for men who had not yet been buried or memorialized. But the much-anticipated break after Chief Ray Downey's service never came. Recoveries were still being made at the site, and other remains were being identified through DNA from samples that had been retrieved weeks or months earlier. Those found after having been memorialized nearly always had a full funeral. New funerals or repeat services were scheduled for December 17 (FF Jonathan Ielpi, FF Robert Lane), December 19 (FF Lee Fehling), December 28 (FP Keith Roma), December 29 (Capt. Patrick Brown, FF Greg Buck), December 31 (FF Steve Coakley, FF Vincent Princiotta, FF John Schardt). A few had been recently recovered at the site.

Liam and a handful of pipers and drummers had showed for all, at least for one service each day when more than one was scheduled. The band again split to cover multiple services on three of those days, but their numbers were drastically lower than before. Many pipers, like Tim and Kippy, had simply decided to take a break and did. The firefighters who came to make up the formation dwindled, too. Out-of-towners no longer came en masse like they had before. Most were in their home states, preparing for the holiday with their families. The remaining New York City firefighters numbered about eighty most days. Often, the same faces could be seen at every service.

The two weeks between December 15 and the end of the year were lonely and cold for the funeral-goers. One day, one of the drummers shut himself in his car during the break and just sat there, resting his head against the window. No one in the band knocked on the window to see if he was okay. The others saw him, shot a cursory glance in his direction, and hurried on toward the closest coffee shop, in a strip mall across the street.

When John Schardt's funeral was over, the band members marched the caisson out onto the street, and stood to the side as the procession passed. The pipers trembled inwardly through "America the Beautiful" in the icy outdoors. They watched Jeannette being driven away. Liam saluted the pregnant widow, who reclined alone, inside the shelter of her black limousine.

The band's annual mass and Christmas party had been held two weeks earlier, on the night of Ray Downey's memorial service. Forty or so band members and their partners attended the Catholic service in circular chapel in Douglaston, Queens. Father Mychal Judge had said mass every year since he'd become the band's chaplain. This year, Father Brian Jordan presided. He had been a close friend of Father

Judge's for many years; in fact, Father Judge was the reason he had become a friar priest in the first place. He'd worked almost daily at the World Trade Center site since September 11 and had befriended many of the firefighters, construction workers, and police officers there. Father Jordan was terse when he spoke, laughed little, and had a stiff, dry manner. Certainly, he was exhausted and stressed. He also swore on occasion, and the firefighters appreciated his candor.

At one point during the mass, Father Jordan asked everyone to come to the center of the chapel and form a circle. Some mutters of reluctance at this unconventional suggestion were heard.

"Come on," Father Jordan urged. "I do things my own way here. Come on up. We're going to take Communion together."

Everyone did. They formed a double circle around the altar and, at Father Jordan's prompting, joined hands and lowered their heads in prayer. Father Jordan spoke of the difficult year that was now coming to an end. He asked that they all say aloud the name of a person they'd lost and would like to remember at this moment. Among the peppering of names spoken, the most audible was "Mychal."

Karen and many of the widows of other band members who'd passed away all came for the mass and the dinner afterward. Karen sat at a table with Liam's sister Denise. Liam sat nearby, at a half-empty table. Tim and Tara sat at a full table, where they chatted amiably, and later they worked the room together. In all, about half the band had come for the dinner, most with girlfriends or spouses. A few pipers' wives were notably absent.

After the meal, Jimmy Ginty rose and addressed the group. He spoke of the trying experience they had all been through but asked that they remember they'd been through it together and that their work had had great meaning to the families of the lost. Then Bill Duffy Sr. spoke. Bill was also an original member of the band and had taught more than a dozen of the newest members how to play the bagpipes. He praised the wives for their support. He and Jimmy called Jack Clarke to the front of the room, and the three charter members of the original seventeen stood modestly as those in the room applauded them. All were retired firefighters in their mid- to late sixties. These older men knew mostly fathers who had lost sons on September 11. They empathized with them, imagining the pain of losing their own child. The elders felt the pain differently than the younger ones, who'd never lived through war and who'd lost so many friends and brothers so unexpectedly that fateful day. But the experience of years gave them no power, only the understanding that things shouldn't happen this way—and that there was nothing they could do about it.

While many of the firefighters were doing their best to celebrate the holidays, Rescue 4's focus turned inward. On Tuesday, December 18, the members of Rescue 4 began keeping a journal at the firehouse. In a black-and-white-speckled composition book, with "World Trade Center Duty" on the front, they noted events and recoveries at the site for each other, to keep one another informed and to document the remaining story of a place that soon would exist no more. The detail schedule of twenty-four hours on, forty-eight hours off had come to an end, and the firefighters returned to their regular chart—two fifteen-hour night tours, followed by seventy-two hours off, then two nine-hour day tours, followed by forty-eight hours off on the usual twenty-five-day cycle. Most continued to arrange schedules with each other to work twenty-four-hour mutuals. Rescue 4 still maintained a daily presence at the site. One or two firefighters went every day shift and most night shifts. Rescue 4 was there as an unofficial SOC aide, present because they wanted to be, but also there to assist the chiefs in any perilous work, like investigating the subway tunnels or providing counsel on tricky voids. Mostly they patrolled the terrain, surveilled the deconstruction progress, and oversaw the new thirty-day task force details of firefighters who were assigned to the site. Many of the men on thirty-day details were there for the first time since September.

On Sunday, December 23, one Rescue 4 firefighter noted the day's developments in the book.

7:20 A.M.	Tower 2 Elevator Core area. Partial Bunker Pants and Boot Serial #00062748.
8:20 A.M.	Same area. Partial boot.
11:30 A.M.	Old style firefighter boot, Vista.
1:15	Gun scope and bone fragments, south side outside north tower.
1:30	Partial civilians male and female, south side north tower towards Vista.
2:45	Small piece of bunker gear and flesh, Vista.
3:00	Firefighter boot with foot, tower elevator core area. Serial #0007902112E.

6:15 South side Tower 2 in between tower and slurry wall. Fire fighter [name removed] pulled out by grappler. Two halves, nearly full body.
* No Task Force Christmas Day*
3 and 2 plus 2 chiefs rotated throughout day. SOC unit as assigned. 6 grapplers will operate at site.

The next day, another firefighter who'd worked the night shift made a detailed entry, including GPS coordinates from a grid map of the site to indicate the precise location of the recoveries.

0037 K_{11} L_{12} Civilian Parts north corner of Vista South Side of north tower.
0345 N_{10} Full civilian Body courtyard north of south tower.
0900 L_{12} Ladder 7 Roof Rope Northeast Side of Vista.
0945 MN_{10} Civilians Intact. 7 Civilians were found intact. Found in the area of northwest corner of the courtyard. Civilians were found on top of each other, 2 at a time. Plenty of identification, wallets, pocketbooks, watches, wedding rings.
1155 L_{13} Civilian Arm. Bottom of South Road heading to Vista, Turn Right. Found on Left Side of Road.

The firefighter had inked a nickel-size black star next to 0945 and traced over the number 7 several times. Christmas Eve had been what the firefighters considered a good day at the site. Multiple recoveries, with ample identifying evidence that could give numerous families some solace with the holidays approaching. Still, the recoveries had been all civilians, no brother firefighters. The firefighter had pressed his pen against the page with a force that could have been motivated as much by joy for the civilians' closure as by anger at his own absence of it.

One of the many unwritten codes in firehouse life is the Christmas rule. Married firefighters arrange to work Christmas Eve, and single firefighters work Christmas Day. That way, the singles can attend Christmas Eve parties, and those with families can be home to exchange gifts on Christmas morning.

Liam's own family had seen little of him since September 11. He occasionally visited the Fowlers—his sister Denise, her husband, John, and their three young boys. When he was at their house on Long Island, he wrestled and clowned around with his nephews like he always had, but he hastily turned his head to watch September 11 documentaries or news of the site whenever it came on the television. He had hardly seen his mother and father in four months, though they called him almost daily on his cell for a brief chat. His parents didn't ask him about his work at the site. They knew how devoted he was to his brothers and how hard he was working. His mother grew weepy at the mere mention of funerals. His father wondered if Liam wasn't spending a bit too much time there, but he didn't bring it up. Usually they waited to see what Liam would say first. Liam didn't talk about it.

Liam scheduled himself to work the day tour on Christmas Eve at the firehouse. At 6:00 P.M., he left to work the night shift at the site. Rescue workers found the remains of a fire patrolman around 10:00 P.M. The man's father had been at the site all day, and many days before, searching for his son. He'd just gone home for the night when his son was discovered. Firefighters reached him by phone and he returned immediately to help carry his son's body out.

Not many machines were operating that night. Many New Yorkers showed up around the periphery to leave flowers for the lost and to wish happiness to the workers who were there. The band's instructor, Brian Meagher, came and played his bagpipes on the pile, a few holiday tunes and "Amazing Grace." About fifty people, almost everyone working that night, gathered for midnight mass under the iron cross. Father Jordan gave the service. Communion wafers were passed around so that all the workers could take them into their mouths at the same time. Someone handed Liam a chalice of wine. When he sipped, the drink had a sharp, burning taste: some Irish whiskey had been poured into it to warm them against the freezing night. He passed it on. A fire chief came up behind Liam, gripped his shoulder, and told him he knew he'd see him there this night. Liam laughed, and said, "I'm not crazy, Chief. I swear!"

Liam went back to the site again on Christmas Day. From his cozy house on Long Island, Tim called Liam's cell phone and wished him a merry Christmas. Liam sounded happy to hear from him, Tim thought.

Tim made his move to step down as pipe major official two weeks after Downey's memorial service, at the start of the new year. He took a brief vacation and returned to his South Bronx firehouse for the first time. After four months of constantly rushing to funerals and memorial services and playing the same tunes on the pipes over and over, he was eager to cook a beef stew with his brothers in the firehouse. Eager to lounge on the couch again and talk to the guys about normal things. Not death. Not funerals. Not 9/11. He longed for the day when September 11 would not come up in conversation. As he pulled his truck into the parking lot behind the firehouse, he felt a twinge of excitement. When he walked in, the others greeted him with smiles and asked silly questions—like if his lips were tired, or if his lungs were shot from blowing on the pipes so much. Tim shook his head and laughed. He jogged up the stairs to his locker to get out his bunker gear and hang it up next to the rig downstairs, as he always did at the start of a shift. But when he opened his locker, his gear wasn't there. Tim stared inside. He tried to think of where it could be.

He walked back downstairs and looked around. Then he saw his bulky coat and pants, resting over a bench in the corner. On the September nights when the firefighters had returned from Ground Zero, they'd hosed down their gear downstairs so as not to track the soot and dust upstairs near the kitchen and eating areas. His gear was still there in the corner, right where he'd left it the last night he'd worked at the firehouse, before he'd been taken off the chart and assigned to ceremonial duty. No one had moved it in all that time. He grabbed his gear and hung it next to the rig.

Tim started back upstairs, through a hallway to the kitchen. Hundreds of crayon-colored cards from schoolchildren were fastened to every available space on the walls, carrying messages like "We Love You FDNY" and "Sorry Our Firefighters Died." As he passed the large framed collages of old photographs that had hung there for the past year, his eyes fell on the pictures of Dennis Devlin, who had been Tim's captain for several years when he worked in 75 Engine. Dennis, smiling widely, so full of life in the photos. Dennis, who was now dead. Like his hunting buddy Tommy Foley. And Billy McGinn, who'd helped Tim pass the lieutenant's test. And Bronko. Tim hurried the rest of the way down the hall. The cards fluttered in the air behind him.

Kippy returned to his firehouse around the same time, knowing he would soon be promoted and would have to say farewell to his friends there of the past seven years. He wondered how he would react when the next voice alarm came over the intercom. Three months had passed since he'd heard those sounds.

On his first night back, an alarm came through at 4:30 in the morning for a 10–75, a fire in a six-story tenement on 147th Street and Amsterdam, just ten blocks away. A probie named Mike had joined the firehouse since Kippy had been gone, and he had anxiously awaited his first chance at a fire. The first fire is a probie's chance to prove to the others he can really do it.

The bells sounded and the call came over the intercom. Mike let out a yelp. "Yea!" A smile grew on Kippy's face.

Kippy grabbed the irons, the tools used to pry open doors, and jumped on the rig. He was a member of the inside team that night, along with the officer on duty and the probie, who held the can, a kind of fire extinguisher. Together they would go straight toward the source of the fire. The can contained two and a half gallons of water and pressurized air, which was not much but often enough to keep the fire at bay until the engine company arrived with the large hoses. This fire was a small one, confined to a couch in an apartment on the second floor. Kippy and the probie made their way in. The probie pulled on his mask. "Hit it!" Kippy told him, and the probie blasted the fire with the can. In seconds, the flames were gone.

The fire was routine. Everything went according to plan. As he left the building with the probie, Kippy punched at the kid's arm and grinned. "I didn't know you were a buff," he said.

Around the holidays, Kippy called Liam to ask if he would consider taking a break from the site. Kippy recognized a depth of pain in Liam that most others did not see. Liam had been a rock of support for Karen, Bronko's family, Michael Cawley's family, and dozens of others who were related to the missing members of Rescue 4. But he often said the work at the pile was "punishing," and Kippy knew firsthand that this was true, physically and mentally. Liam would not allow himself to be sad. To waver emotionally would cause his focus to falter. He needed absolute concentration to shoulder the burden he carried. Kippy understood this, too. He'd often thought that simply not having time to absorb the enormity of the events while rushing from funeral to funeral had helped him get through the most difficult days. But Kippy saw Liam acting as if he were expendable, submitting himself to the toxic air without wearing a mask, devoting himself to a grisly duty that would someday be finished. Liam didn't have children of his own, or a wife to go home to. Liam's sole reason for living was centered on the dead.

Every time Kippy suggested leaving the recovery work for a while,

Liam deflected him. Three men from his firehouse were still missing, and Liam admitted that he felt guilty whenever he was away from the site. One of them was Lt. Kevin Dowdell, and his teenage sons often stopped by the Rescue 4 firehouse. Sometimes Patrick and James went to the site with Liam to dig for their father, and they played with the pipe band at funerals when they could. Sometimes they asked Liam if he thought they'd be able to find their dad. Liam couldn't imagine the boys asking him what was going on at the site and his answering that he didn't know because he wasn't down there. Because he'd taken a break? Because he was off playing with the band? Impossible. When Liam mentioned the Dowdell kids, Kippy backed off.

Sunday, December 30, 2001

> Lots of digging, no bodies or parts recovered all day. South side of south road, lots of virgin territory dug, nothing found. Some digging just north of where our guys were found. Nothing. Lots of activity in north tower. Nothing. Better luck tomorrow I hope. It can't get any worse than today.

On January 3, Billy Murphy wrote in the journal a mock entry, supposedly penned by a firefighter from another company who had just spent his first day at the site since September. The fake firefighter had arrived at around 9:00 A.M. and marveled, "What a difference in three months! I don't recognize anything at all. It used to be a pile. All of a sudden they're calling it a pit." Then, "Two hours for lunch!" At the end of his day, at around 5:00 P.M., he wrote, "Exhausted! Don't know if I can take another day like this one!"

On January 7, Liam wrote his first entry. He wrote in capital letters, and each letter took up the entire space between the top and bottom lines.

> LOTS OF MACHINES WORKING, MINIMAL RECOVERY. GOT A NICE COMPLIMENT FROM CHIEF RASWEILER ABOUT THE COMPANY AND OUR VIGILANCE. WANTS US TO KEEP UP THE GOOD WORK. WAY TO GO BOYS.

The firefighters waited anxiously for excavation to begin on the South Road at the site, a makeshift path that had been carved over a section of the rubble pile that used to be the south tower. Many workers called it the Tully Road, because Tully Construction had initially overseen that area. The road had been used as a ramp since the early stages of the cleanup operation, so construction vehicles could travel from the upper end of the site to the lower depths of the debris pile. Hundreds of feet away, toward the western end of the site, a steel ramp was being built perpendicular to the original road. The new ramp would serve as an alternate route, so that the remaining debris could be searched. Rumors circulated among firefighters and their families of the potential finds—at least fifty men, or eighty, maybe even hundreds of firefighters and civilians could have been clustered in this area, because it was so near the command post that was in the south tower.

Bronko, Terry Farrell, Pete Nelson, Al Tarasiewicz, Billy Mahoney, and Michael Cawley had been found within a hundred feet of the road area. Liam and the others in Rescue 4 were optimistic that Pete Brennan, Kevin Dowdell, and Brian Hickey might now be found. Officers might have been clustered in that area, near the command post, giving or awaiting directions on how to proceed. Through bits and pieces of information he'd heard over the months, Liam knew that Rescue 4's men had reported to that command post just before heading into the lobby area of the south tower. A firefighter from Squad 18 had told Liam he'd seen Bronko that morning, walking toward the building. Bronko wore a serious frown and had nodded a quick acknowledgment at the firefighter as he passed. Moments later, the tower had collapsed on them. It stood to reason that Lt. Dowdell might have remained near the command. Perhaps Pete Brennan was with him. Capt. Hickey might also have been nearby, since he was the officer on duty in Rescue 3 that day. Perhaps their remains would be uncovered together.

On January 17, 2002, Liam made another entry.

FOUND LOTS OF SMALL BODY PARTS AS THEY DUG UP THE ROAD FROM WEST STREET INTO THE PIT. UNFORTUNATELY, MOST OF THE BODY PARTS WERE PILED INTO ONLY 2 RED BAGS. SPEAK UP IF YOU SEE SOMETHING LIKE THIS.

AS CREWS ROTATE AFTER 30 DAYS, THE NEW CREWS HAVE TO BE COMPLETELY RETRAINED.

IT LOOKS LIKE IT IS GOING TO BE A LONG TIME BEFORE THEY DIG UP THAT SOUTH TOWER RAMP.

IT IS GOING TO BE THE MAIN ACCESS ROAD INTO THE PIT UNTIL THEY COMPLETE "THE BRIDGE."

NO BROTHERS FOUND SINCE [SUNDAY, JANUARY 13]. ATTENDING

THE 8:30 AM AND 5:30 P.M. MEETING IS AN EXCELLENT WAY TO KEEP UP ON WHAT IS BEING PLANNED FOR THE SITE. THE MEETINGS ARE INTERESTING AS WELL AS INFORMATIVE.

STEEL I-BEAM TRUSS TO SUPPORT SLURRY WALL WAS COMPLETED TODAY AND THEY WILL RETURN TO DIGGING IN THAT AREA ONCE AGAIN.

MANY BROTHERS' BODIES HAVE BEEN RETRIEVED FROM THIS AREA, WHICH WAS PART OF THE MARRIOTT HOTEL.

I HEARD IT MAY BE 6 WEEKS UNTIL THEY DIG UP THE SOUTH TOWER RAMP, WHICH IS WHERE WE BELIEVE THE BROTHERS FROM OUR HOUSE ARE.

Liam was fixated on the politics of how the site was being handled. He surveyed the new administration carefully and kept track of every funeral that city dignitaries missed during their first weeks in office. He kept an eye out for slackers in the Fire Department, too, and dealt verbal blows to the ones who didn't follow his own rigorous code.

As a result of sitting in on the daily meetings at Ground Zero, Liam became a firsthand source of information. His popularity and status rose higher and higher. Firefighters in dress blue flocked around him at funerals. Those who couldn't get into the tight circle of men around Liam stretched out their hands to him for a shake and offered a quick joke or a congratulatory word as they passed by. In these circles of conversation, Liam repeated the same political rhetoric over and over. The firefighters lapped it up.

Even as his reputation rose to new heights, Liam's inner circle was shrinking. The more he was around the band, the more his eye fell on those who weren't stepping up as he'd expected they would. He'd kept track of which ones had not come to the funerals at the end of the year, when barely eighty firefighters and fewer than a dozen of the pipers had showed up. "You'd think when you died, your friends would light a candle in the window for you," he said. But when it came to confrontation, he could not find the words to articulate his anger.

One day at the end of January, Liam drove a group of pipers to a coffee shop during the break between the start and end of a funeral. A firefighter friend sat in the front seat next to Liam, while Tommy and another piper, Frank, climbed into the back. Liam overhead Frank saying he was planning a ski trip in February. Tommy told him it was well overdue, he deserved a break. Liam flashed a fiery glare in the rearview mirror and held up his fingers: three-four-three, in sequence. Frank glanced at him and turned his chin back to the conversation, shaking his head slightly.

Liam snapped at Kippy one afternoon, telling him that the donated van he'd been driving had to go back to its owner. He didn't explain why, just walked over to him, said it was time, and walked away. Another day, Liam reprimanded Tim for not taking part in a ninety-day assignment designed for soon-to-be lieutenants who were needed to fill in at companies that had lost firemen. Tim had explained that he wasn't skipping his duty; he'd already completed one such assignment before September 11, and besides, he had qualified out of it because he'd been in the band and their work covering funerals was considered the equivalent.

A new task force had recently started at the site, and Liam noticed some men weren't watching the machines as closely as he'd have liked. "New task force has some lapses," he penned in the journal in early February. "Need to be vigilant." Bits of bone and flesh continued to be found in the north pit. The work on the bridge was moving faster than expected. Liam had hopes, but he also had doubts. It had been so long since any sign of the Rescue 4 men was recovered. The road was everyone's last hope.

On Wednesday, February 6, Liam took members of Michael Cawley's family to tour the site. Michael's mother, Margaret, hoped Liam would take them right past the fences and down on the ground where the firefighters walked and the grapplers trekked. But Liam told her they couldn't do that; they should stand near a fence on the street level and look in from there. Margaret wanted to know everything about Michael's death and pressed Liam for details. Where was he found? What his body like? What position was he in? Was he hurt? How did he die? As his mother, Margaret felt she had a right to know, and she felt she could take the harsh realities—she was, after all, a nurse who dealt with late-stage cancer patients. Liam tried to answer as delicately as he could. He could talk freely to firefighters and ironworkers and others who worked at the site about the details, but saying those same things to a person who did not work at the site every day, a woman the same age as his own mother, no less, made Liam unsure of how to express things, afraid he'd say the wrong thing and upset her.

Her persistent questions stirred another unease deep within. He hoped she wouldn't ask why her son had been on the rig that day. Of course, Margaret knew how dedicated her son had been to the job. And she understood the logistics. Rescue trucks are built differently than engine or ladder trucks, which have a certain number of seats inside. Rescue vehicles have two seats in the front cab, four in the middle, and long hallways inside, so more than an entire shift of firefighters could fit inside if they wanted to. What she might not know, and what Liam didn't want to say, was that one reason Michael jumped on might have been to show he could be a part of Rescue 4. And why? Because Liam had wanted him there.

On Saturday, February 9, Tim stood on the sidewalk outside the church in Middle Village, Queens, watching Liam from afar. Today's funeral service, for Lt. Kevin Pfeifer, was another repeat. Pfeifer had been memorialized in October, but his body had just been uncovered the previous week. By now, the pipers had played at more than sixty-five of these second services. Tim looked over at Liam, who stood twenty feet away in the street, surrounded by five lieutenants in crisp white hats. He and Liam had spoken little in the past several weeks. Tim wondered if Liam's sweet-sounding response to his holiday phone call had been sarcastic. He thought he might have a talk with Liam to try to clear the tension between them. Maybe later. Not today.

When the pipers lined up in rows to play the ending set, Liam walked around, flicking his fingers to signal one to take a tiny step left, another to move two inches right. He arranged them in perfectly straight lines, then took his place at the front and turned to watch for the casket coming out of the church.

The crowd outside fell silent as the firefighters stood to attention. Out walked the priest and altar boys. The coffin would follow, but it was not yet in view. Suddenly, Liam screamed, "Going Home!" The onlookers whipped their heads around, startled. His voice was frightening—angry and desperate and full of raw edges. He'd called the tune too early. The coffin wasn't out of the church yet. Liam stared straight ahead and met none of the eyes that fell upon him. The silence hung heavily in the air for what seemed an eternity as the pipers waited. Finally, the coffin emerged and was loaded onto the fire truck. The pipers began to play "Going Home," then "America the Beautiful."

The funeral procession disappeared into the cemetery across the street, and the line of firefighters relaxed. The pipers were hustling off to a wedding right after the funeral, and they began exchanging directions. Liam knew where it was. Tim did not. Tim paused at his truck to get something out of the front seat, and when he looked up, the other pipers had already followed Liam halfway up the block. Tim had to run to catch up. Liam was gone.

A few days later, Tuesday, February 12, 2002, Liam made one of his last entries in the Rescue 4 journal.

> SLOWEST DAY I HAVE SEEN. GPS HAD NO RUNS UNTIL 7:30 P.M. WHEN A CIVILIAN WAS FOUND NEAR THE WEST SLURRY WALL IN THE HOTEL AREA.
>
> NEW TASK FORCE BEING BROKEN IN.
>
> POSSIBLE NEW OT DETAIL IN THE WORKS TO MONITOR A 24/7 CONFINED SPACE OPERATION. CHIEF NORMAN WILL RUN IT BY THE HIGHER UPS.
>
> FIRST SECTOR OF BRIDGE LAID.
>
> SITE IS CONSIDERABLY SHRINKING.
>
> THE NORTH TOWER PIT IS COMPLETELY DUG OUT.
>
> LOTS OF GRAPPLER OPERATORS LAID OFF TODAY. SOME GREAT GUYS THAT HAVE BEEN THERE FROM THE BEGINNING.
>
> BRIDGE CONSTRUCTION SLOWED BY OSHA WHO CONDEMNED THE SLINGS BEING USED TO LAY THE SECTIONS. NEW TASK FORCE SEEMS VERY GUNG HO. DID A GREAT JOB SIFTING THROUGH THE DEBRIS ALMOST THREE TIMES.
>
> IT WON'T BE LONG NOW.

CHAPTER

11

HOME TURF

The only good is knowledge and the only evil is ignorance.

—Socrates

On a cloudy afternoon in early February, Kathy sat at her dining room table, flanked by her brother-in-law Mike and her best friend, Maureen. Kathy wore a white soft-knit sweater. Her fine hair was neatly trimmed. An auburn glass ashtray the size of a Frisbee rested a few inches in front of her. When the bottom grew cluttered with crushed cigarette butts, someone would pick it up and dump the contents in the trash. Then it would begin to fill anew. The freezer in the kitchen was full of frozen glasses, not food. Maureen always made sure there was a twelve-pack of Coors Light in the fridge for Kathy, and a couple of bottles of chilled pinot grigio for herself.

Some weeks earlier, the body of a firefighter who'd lived in the same neighborhood as Kathy and Vinny had been recovered, and a funeral was held for him on January 5, 2002. His remains were mostly intact. Kathy had gone to the widow's house and hugged her graciously. Now she could finally have some peace, Kathy told her. That woman was able to touch her husband's body. She could feel the curve of his shoulder bones beneath the body bag. Kathy mimed the movements as she spoke, the way Kathy herself would gingerly pat Vinny all over if she had him back. Kathy'd told her she was happy for her. But inside she seethed with jealousy. She just wanted it to be her turn.

Around the house, reminders of Vinny were scattered everywhere. The mantel across from the couch displayed the triangular folded flag, carefully tucked in a wood-and-glass case, the one Kathy was handed after Vinny's memorial service was held on December 13. A sixteen-by-twenty-inch Fire Department portrait of Vinny, smiling in his captain's uniform, hung on the wall at the foot of the stairs. Smaller photographs lined the shelf below the flag. One, of a missile headed for Afghanistan, bore the inscription "For Captain Vincent Brunton, FDNY 9–11–2001." A pile of unread newspapers, dating from September 11 to the end of that month, had accumulated at the bottom of a closet. Kathy intended to have a look at them someday, just not yet. She pulled open a drawer from a cabinet beside the dining room table. Inside, it was neatly stacked with envelopes and bills from before September 11 — all paid, all handled by Vinny. Across the table and out of her reach sat a cluttered shoebox, containing the important pieces of mail Kathy had been meaning to get to. The first month after the attacks, she had to relearn how to write a check. She forgot to sign the first batch, and they were all returned.

Sometimes mail would still come addressed to Mr. Vincent Brunton. Even the fire officers' union was sending duplicate mailings for a while, one addressed to Kathy and another addressed to Vinny. It was a telemarketer who forced her to finally say the words she couldn't even whisper to herself.

"Is Vincent Brunton there, please?"

"No," Kathy told the voice on the phone.

"Will he be back any time soon?"

"No," Kathy snapped. "He's deceased."

She slammed down the phone and wept. After that, she tried not to answer the phone anymore unless she knew who was calling.

Kathy thought of asking a friend who liked quilting to make her up a quilt of Vinny's old running T-shirts. Maybe then, if she could wrap that around her, she could go back to the bed. She could still hardly bear to be in that bedroom. When she finally collapsed from exhaustion late at night, she curled up on the couch by the front door. It had been almost five months since Vinny went missing. She still wanted to be close by, in case he walked through the door.

She was no longer comfortable being in the world outside, where she felt vulnerable and alone. Most of the time, she was too afraid to leave the house, so she didn't. Afraid she was hearing whispers behind her back, afraid people were talking about how good she had it now, how much money she had to spend. She had not returned to work since the attack and didn't plan to until the next school year.

A few weeks earlier, Kathy had ventured out to go to a Fire Department function, where she ran into an acquaintance who had also lost her husband in the attack.

"Well, so you're a WW now," she said to Kathy.

"What's that?" Kathy asked.

"A Wealthy Widow," the woman answered, laughing. Kathy walked away in disgust.

"I never wanted it," she said, referring to the victim's compensation money without saying the word, pointing to the cabinet that held the bills. "I opened another account and put it all in there. I don't know what to do with it. Vinny took care of us while he was alive, and he made sure we were taken care of after he died. I keep thinking Vinny's going to come home and say 'Give it all back. That's blood money.'

"I don't want it," Kathy said again. "I would give it all back just to have ten more minutes with him."

She gestured briefly to the door and then glanced away.

"I'll never forget that night when you came in the door," she said to Mike. "All covered in dust."

Mike bowed his head and choked quietly, trying to hide his rage and shame, but his tears spilled anyway. He pressed at them with a tautly folded tissue.

Mike told the women that they couldn't fathom how horrible it was down there. He talked of digging through rubble with his bare hands and seeing bloody masses of flesh strewn all over. At one point, he glimpsed a row of tiny white bones, like a spine. Someone's torso. He dug and dug all around to try and turn the head toward him so he could see the face. He motioned with his hands, as if holding a person's cheeks between them.

"It was like turning over a Halloween mask," he said.

Kathy turned her head away, shielding her eyes with her hand.

"Mike, don't," Maureen said softly.

"It's just . . . you can't imagine trying to find one person in all of that," he said. He shook his head determinedly as he gathered his next words.

"We'll get him, Kathy," he said with a lifted chin. "We'll bring him home."

Later that night, Tommy sat beside his brother at the table. Two lieutenants, both sporting bristly gray crew cuts and dressed in their immaculate navy blue uniforms—they had both been at a firefighter's memorial service earlier that afternoon. They twiddled with the sweaty bottles of Bud before them.

Soon, a couple of friends from the neighborhood stopped by. Kathy's sister and Mike's wife had joined the conversation, too. The table was crowded again.

Tommy told immodest stories about when they were kids, and Mike grew quiet. One of Tommy's first memories in that house was how their mother used to shove the three of them in the bathtub together. One night, little Vinny pooped in the tub. Tommy saw it and screamed, dragging Mikey with him as he scrambled out of the tub and ran dripping out into the hallway. Everyone giggled at Tommy's tales.

Later, as Tommy got ready to leave, he paused at the mantel by the door, picking up the pictures of Vinny one by one.

"Mike ain't handling this well at all," he said. "He's really angry. He always felt like he had to do something for them all."

Tommy paused. "He shouldn'ta done it," he said. "You can't promise the girl something like that. We might never find him."

Kathy had purchased a cemetery plot that awaited Vinny. His resting place would be in a sunny spot, away from the shade of the trees. She thought he would like it there, because Vinny was fair-skinned and always liked to work on his tan. His chaise longue was still out on the roof in back, with the striped towel still on it, despite the lashing of rain and snow that the change of seasons brought. Kathy hadn't been able to touch that, either. Some day, at the cemetery, they'd have a place to be together. As she talked of it, she leaned back in her chair and pressed her hands between her knees.

"We'll sit there in the sun, and we can talk and reminisce just like we used to." She nodded. "When he comes back."

Kathy had been battling a fear that the family might go away now that Vinny was gone. It was an absurd notion, she knew. Sometimes she got angry with Vinny. He'd decided to save other people for a living.

What about her? Wasn't she the most important one? There were days when she wished she could be left alone for a while, free from the support of her friends and family, away from the unrelenting company. If she could just go away somewhere quiet for four or five months, maybe she could get a handle on all this. Then, when she came back, she'd be on top of it. She sometimes thought about moving on with life, maybe marrying again someday. After all, she'd only just turned forty-four. It was not something she would consider now, of course, but life is long. She was only thinking.

A few nights earlier, Kathy had a dream that she was in a Manhattan nightclub that played hip-hop music, dancing with two men. Although it was a kind of dancing she'd never done before, she was getting the moves down pretty well, she remembered, and was feeling pleased with herself. Afterward, she ran into Vinny outside the club. He was there waiting for her. "What the hell were you doing in there?" he asked. Then she woke up.

She pulled out Vinny's mass cards and the program from the day of his memorial service. The picture on the back was a black-and-white shot of Vinny taken outside a fire. He was grimy with soot, looking upward with an expression of awe. Beneath was a caption:

> *The bravest are surely those who have the clearest vision of what is before them . . . and yet . . . go out to meet it.*
>
> —Thucydides

She ran her thumbs in circles over the picture as she studied it, then pressed it down hard on the table. She rubbed it up and down with both hands. Up and down, over and over.

"It's the not finding him that's killing me so bad," she said. "Just give me a boot and tell me it's his. Anything. I don't care. I don't want him down there anymore."

CHAPTER

12

LOST CELEBRATIONS

I never saw a man who looked
With such a wistful eye
Upon that little tent of blue
Which prisoners call the sky.

—Oscar Wilde, "The Ballad of Reading Gaol"

THE month of March brought a rush of activity for the band. Every weekend they were scheduled to march in one St. Patrick's Day parade, sometimes two or three, which would take place all over the five boroughs. Now, the band members would take their first steps back toward a pattern of celebration, and they wondered what the change would be like. In January, they had begun Monday night practice sessions again to refine their marching and polish new tunes. Tom McEnroe, who'd resumed the pipe major slot he'd ceded to Tim a couple of years earlier, led the practices. For the first hour, every time the band started a tune, Tom hollered at the members to stop. He tapped his foot and counted to a faster beat. Then the band would start again. Everything they played was too slow.

Tim took his vacation during the month of March so that he could be part of all the festivities. No longer the leader, he anticipated he could fall in with the rest and enjoy performing for the crowds. But in spite of his youthful vigor, nature played a cruel trick on him. In late February, his toe became infected with gout, a painful inflammation due to a build up of uric acid that normally afflicts men over age forty. His foot swelled like a soufflé and sent excruciating stabs throughout his body when he tried to walk. He followed his doctor's advice, changed his diet, avoided alcohol and rich foods like beef, and hoped the pain would subside by the time the parades began. Still, he knew that stress and extended marching would only aggravate the gout.

Kippy's day onstage came on February 28. After four years of waiting, he was finally promoted to lieutenant. Rumors of his approaching change in rank persisted through the holidays and into January, and only four days before the ceremony was he notified that it was actually going to happen. That morning, Kippy dressed in his firefighter's Class-A uniform for the final time. The ceremony would be held in a college auditorium near Fire Department headquarters. Afterward he'd receive his new gear—a round, flat-topped white hat, a glinting new badge, a differently styled navy jacket with one silver bar on the wrist. The auditorium was packed with family members. Congratulatory banners lined the side walls. A rustle of activity persisted even as the mayor, fire chiefs, and union officials spoke at the podium. Kippy stood among the new lieutenants in the audience and raised his hand and spoke the oath in unison with the others as they were sworn in together.

> I, Christopher Walsh, having been promoted to the rank of lieutenant in the Fire Department of the City of New York, do solemnly swear that I will support the Constitution of the United States, and the Constitution of the State of New York, and that I will faithfully discharge the duties of such rank, according to the laws, regulations, and orders governing the Department, and will obey the orders and directions of my superiors to the best of my ability, so help me God.

When his number approached, he walked onto the stage, sandwiched in line between two of his closest friends, Jerry and Bob. All three had gone through probie school together, all three had worked in the Harlem firehouse known as "Vinegar Hill," and all three were now being promoted at the same time. Coincidentally, their scores had earned them three sequential spots on the promotion list—622, 623, and 624. They stood across the stage from Dan Nigro, the new chief of the Fire Department. The officer at the podium announced his name: "Lieutenant Christopher Walsh." Kippy took one step forward and snapped his fingers to his brow in salute. He strode over to the chief and shook his hand, then paused between the chief and the mayor for a quick snapshot. Nigro looked at them and said, "Three guys in a row from Vinegar Hill? What'd you do, sit together during the test?" The men laughed. After he stopped seeing spots from all the flashbulbs, Kippy looked out into the audience and saw Mary and Danny, grinning up at him. A couple of months earlier, Mary had given him a scrapbook with clippings of all the funerals and memorial services at which he had played. He'd been taken aback by the gift. He hadn't realized she'd been following that part of his life so closely.

A few days later, Kippy began a month-long course in officer training, called FLPS, or "Flips," for First Line Supervisors Program. After that, he would be assigned to a battalion and would spend a couple of weeks in one firehouse, a short stint in another, to cover for officers on medical leave or on vacation. He would be the boss, giving orders to other men, responsible for their lives and actions in fires, in neighborhoods he might not know much about. The training courses kept him busy enough. He still didn't take too well to being applauded by strangers. He didn't march in many parades.

Mike Brunton began marching with the band's color guard at funerals shortly after the New Year. Most of the services in January and February were repeat services for firefighters who'd already been memorialized. He and Tommy were together more than ever before. The brothers turned out for most of the parades, needing to do something that at least used to be fun for a change. Tommy took his usual spot in the formation, somewhere in the middle toward the back, and marched, but his face had taken on an ashen tone. He dressed the part but looked as if he weren't there.

The first parade of the year was on Saturday, March 2, in Rockaway. The parade's starting point was just a block away from the crash site of American Airlines Flight 587, which had careened into the residential neighborhood on November 12, 2001, minutes after taking off from JFK Airport, killing all 255 people aboard. Five people on the ground died in the impact, and several houses were destroyed. Hundreds of firefighters had responded to the disaster scene, including many members of the pipe band. Some were playing at a funeral that morning and rushed to help put out the fires. Liam and others from Rescue 4 had climbed into the wreckage of the burned-out houses to assist in removing the bodies. One hundred and sixty-one people were removed by nightfall. When the firefighters talked about it later, they remarked that it hadn't affected them at all.

The pipers packed into a side room at the Harbor Light, a tenebrous pub located diagonally across the street from the crash site. The owner of the bar had lost a son at the World Trade Center. Patrick and James Dowdell lived nearby, and they had come to march. Some pipers talked of the large number of losses the area residents had endured. They looked around at the living, who stood closely together in the crowded bar, many laughing, pressing their beer bottles against their chests. A momentary silence fell over their little circle. "Coulda been worse," one piper then joked to another. "The plane coulda hit the pub."

Out in the street, several bagpipe bands began to warm up their instruments, lining up between floats and fire trucks. Residents in Aran sweaters converged on the sidewalks for a prime view. Mayor Mike Bloomberg arrived sporting a kelly green jacket. Children shot luminous streams of gooey plastic from spray cans at each other, and adults scolded them when it tangled in messy clumps on their own clothes. Young boys with toy machine guns and green-painted faces dodged in and out of the crowd, making shooting noises with their mouths. One boy trolled the edge of the thin wood wall, reaching his gun high and pretending to shoot into the window holes. When the parade began and the bagpipers passed, people clapped and cheered from the street's edge and hollered out from keg parties on balconies. The route was long, and when it was over the pipers were exhausted. The next day, there was a parade in Bethpage, Long Island. On Sunday, March 10, the band split in order to play at parades in the Bronx and Mahopac.

Liam missed all the early parades. He spent his days at the site, his nights working in the firehouse, sleeping over sometimes at his sister's house in Long Island. He never stayed in the same place for very long. On the first day of March, he noted a brief entry.

> SLOW DAY. CIVILIAN REMAINS FOUND AT ABOUT 4 P.M. BRIDGE IS ALMOST READY.

Tully Road demolition was scheduled to begin on March 5. That day, a firefighter noted in the journal, "07:15. Chief Rasweiler informed us that two recoveries were made during the night under the Tully Road. Possibly members." On March 6, they recovered a firefighter's boot with a foot still in it and gave it the entire honor guard. However, it was several days before a firefighter at Rescue 4 wrote of the recoveries all had anticipated.

Tuesday, March 12

Finally the towers are starting to give up the dead. Bodies of three firemen uncovered but unable to identify. A little later, two more firemen. [Three firefighters from] Ladder 4. Throughout the day, the road yielded more members. [A lieutenant from] Ladder 3 and several more but no ID.

Also found officer's tool from Squad 41—the first thing found from this company. A total of 10 firemen and two civilians while I was there.

The reports of officer recoveries renewed Kathy Brunton's hope. She began volunteering as a food server and all-around helper at the giant white tent across from the site on West Street, just to be nearby.

Patrick and James Dowdell went to the site on weekends or nights they had free in order to help the men from Rescue 4 dig. Rosellen Dowdell had been hesitant to allow it at first, unsure how the site would affect her sons, but she soon recognized that Liam was a positive influence on Patrick and James. Being at the site made both of her sons feel like they were doing something important. The teenage boys wanted to be around other men. And Liam, Billy Murphy, and the other firefighters from Rescue 4 were among the only ones who could tell the boys stories about their father. Patrick was the same age Liam had been when he got on the job as a carpenter with his dad. Like Liam then, Patrick was learning how to act by watching someone older. He grew to regard Liam as part friend, part father figure.

By March 11, the six-month anniversary, 755 people had been identified in the wreckage of the World Trade Center, among 15,794 remains and 276 whole bodies. One hundred eighty members of uniformed services had been recovered—147 firefighters, 10 New York City police officers, and 17 Port Authority employees.[1] No funerals or memorials were advance-scheduled for the entire month. Still, the idea that men were not yet buried made the act of celebrating a troubling notion. At most of the early March parades, the band numbered only twenty or thirty men.

But on the morning of March 16, every member of the band who was well enough to stand showed up at St. Ignatius School on 84th Street on Manhattan's Upper East Side. This was the one day of the year every band member looked forward to. The opportunity to march in New York's St. Patrick's Day parade was one reason why most of the men had become interested in joining up in the first place. Thousands of firefighters turned out for the parade every year, either to march or to spectate. The bagpipe band was the FDNY's crown jewel.

The men started arriving as early as 8:00 A.M., even though the parade wouldn't start until early afternoon. Most came wearing FDNY T-shirts of some variety and either a pair of shorts or a kilt, toting their bagpipe cases or drums inside with a smile on their faces. Some brought their wives and kids, and the handful of men outside greeted and kissed the women, offering a full greeting to each. "Happy St. Patrick's Day, Mary. Happy St. Patrick's Day, Kay. Happy St. Patrick's Day . . ." No matter how many times they had to say it, each time they delivered it in full, with the same enthusiasm.

Inside, the pipers meandered around the school gym, depositing their coats and cases, blowing into their bagpipes, and chatting animatedly with each other. Family members filed into seats at the picnic tables along one side of the room. A line formed near the back by the stage, where pastries and coffee were being served. Several framed pictures lay on the edge of the stage, among them a portrait of Father Mychal Judge and a snapshot of Liam and Bronko with their bulging biceps wrapped around the Ford and Fahey boys, taken on a sunny day the previous August at Jets training camp. Near the front entrance, another line soon formed, where pipers lined up to collect a rectangular white pin with an oval picture of Bronko on the front and to purchase blaring red mock turtleneck shirts embellished with the names "Mychal and Bronko" in small Celtic print.

The air outside was moist, and so were the streets. The sky hung low and gray. One piper peered skyward and, over the squeaking and trolling of bagpipes warming up just beyond the open door, wondered aloud whether the rain would arrive. "Bronko and Mychal will look out for us," a sturdy piper named Tom answered. "Just like they have all season."

Away from the rest of the crowd, Liam slid his thick arms into the sleeves of his tunic and buttoned each of the five silver buttons down the front. Then he slung the black leather shoulder belt over his right shoulder, through and under the shoulder tab, and looped it under his left arm, fastening the buckle near the front of his chest. Then he buckled his black leather waist belt. He ducked his head under the five-inch-wide green-and-gold sash, which would fall in the opposing direction, over his left shoulder and under his right arm. Finally, the drape. He had to find someone to help him pin it under the flap on one shoulder. His stomach pressed against his red wool tunic, causing it to ride up and buckle. The seams on the shoulders tugged at his arms, and his embroidered cuffs fell two inches short of his wrists. He took no notice of it. Fully suited up, Liam headed outside, where a reporter and TV cameraman stood a short distance away on the sidewalk, waiting to interview him. Liam had agreed to speak to ABC that morning. The reporter asked a few questions and Liam responded, looking him straight in the eye. "This year, it's—I—I wouldn't call it a celebration. It's not a celebration for me this year," Liam said, as he told the reporter about Bronko. "As well as being a member of my company, Rescue Company 4, he was also a member of the pipe band. And he was my best friend."

Eventually, the entire band was outfitted and draped, their instruments tuned to satisfaction, and they trickled out the doors of the school and walked toward the nearest subway stop. They sauntered up the street in groups of two, three, or four, their shawls flapping in the wind behind them. Taking the subway to Grand Central Station was a tradition among the men in the band. They'd hobnob with the riders for six or seven stops, then get off a few blocks from where they would circle up again and tune their instruments in preparation for the parade.

Liam jogged down the steps into the subway station, with James Dowdell at his side. As a crowd of pipers assembled at the platform edge, Liam and James stood together at the back, absorbed in their own low-toned discourse. Liam grew impatient with waiting. He heard the low rumble of an approaching train on the level beneath, grabbed James's arm, and turned and darted down the stairs to the express train.

The dozen or so pipers who remained on the platform wound up on a crowded local train. There was no room to sit, so they stood in the aisle, gripping the bars overhead. Conversation lagged. They stared blankly out the windows at the black and graffitied tunnel walls the train pounded past.

The subway pulled to a halt in Grand Central Station, and the pipers got out. As they walked through the dimly lit station, chatting and laughing with each other, heads turned and fingers pointed. "Happy St. Patrick's Day," some people called. "Look, it's the bagpipers!" Others just followed them with their eyes and stared. One piper puffed air into his pipes and began playing an Irish tune. The squeal of his pipes echoed off the marble floors and carried throughout the station.

Once on the street, near 44th Street and Fifth Avenue, the pipers circled up and began to tune again. They warmed up as photographers surrounded them. Sometimes a lens would get so close to a piper's face that he'd have to shoo the photographer away, but generally the men were accommodating. This was their day to be stars. When a photographer was directly in front of a man's face, he would wait, with his lips loosely around his mouthpiece, so the photographer could take the shot and the piper could avoid being captured with cheeks strained and double chins protruding. Liam stood for photographs with his arm around James's shoulder, smiling appropriately for the camera. James smiled widely and innocently, but Liam's eyes, tilted by a hint of a scowl, betrayed a certain weariness.

Finally, around noon, the parade began. Liam clutched his mace in his left hand. He wrapped his forefinger around it one-quarter of the way down. The staff rested on his second knuckle, tilted at a forty-five-degree angle, silver cap at the top. First, out marched the color guard—six men dressed in their navy blue Class-A uniforms, the inner four holding flags, the poles rising in front of their faces, the fabric whipping in the wind behind them. Then, ten feet behind, five more members of the color guard proceeded out in a sweeping curve, shoulder to shoulder, clutching the "Emerald Society Pipes and Drums" banner in their white-gloved hands.

To the tune of "Garryowen," Liam led the band out onto Fifth Avenue. He advanced several paces ahead of the rest of the band, reaching out with his right arm and contracting his left elbow, pulling the mace up and down, up and down. Six rows of pipers strode behind their drum major, each line at least ten deep. The front row was composed of members who led in seniority and rank—the pipe major, Tom McEnroe, at the front right from the band's perspective, marching forward; then band founder Jimmy Ginty to his left; band chairman Joe Murphy to his left; and so on. Tim took a spot on one edge, a few rows back from the front. Kippy marched several rows behind him. At the back, two tenor drummers flipped and twirled their white padded sticks, pounding on drumheads painted with large green shamrocks, though the outsides were still draped in the black and purple mourning. Every drummer had fastened the pin with Bronko's picture to the front of his drum. Liam wore the pin attached to his plaid drape, just over his heart.

All along the street, women and men and children wore cream-colored Aran sweaters or kelly green jackets and tops. Some waved Irish flags. Some wore navy blue FDNY baseball caps. Others held up signs: "E-280, Dad, You're My Hero." "FDNY We Love You." "Thank

You." Capt. Brian Hickey's teenage daughter, Jackie, stood on the sidelines wearing plastic shamrock antlers. She'd brought a handful of her friends and a large white sign on which she'd painted "We Love You Brian Hickey" in green sparkly paint. She held it up proudly to anyone who would look.

Nearly every parade-goer, it seemed, cheered and whistled at the pipers. The lengths of clapping and smiling people seemed to have no end. The fanfare was so loud at times that the pipers in front couldn't hear the drumbeats coming from six or seven men back. But always, as the troupe in red and green marched closer, some faces in the crowd would darken. Some tears would spill as men with plaid cloaks and flag passed by. Their pipes wailing in sorrow, they were colorful grim reapers.

The band passed St. Patrick's Cathedral, where Bronko's funeral had been held just four months before. A few blocks later, the parade came to a halt. The pipers and drummers marched in place for a moment, then stopped. Liam shouted, "About, face!" Each band member swiveled 180 degrees for a moment of silence. With their chests facing downtown, toward the empty space in the air where the towers once stood, they bowed their heads. Staunch faces, lowered eyes, Liam's jaw set, Tommy looking blank and gray. The wind gusted at their backs. The spectators fell silent. After a few moments, a roar of cheering could be heard from blocks away to the south. The sounds rippled north, through the lines of parade-goers, and the band turned back around to a full chorus of clapping, whistles, and cheers. Today was the first time the band had ever turned around in the middle of the parade. Later, the band members talked about this small act of ceremony, which seemed significant in and of itself: Never before had they paused and turned around without the intent of moving forward.

Tangled between grief and joy, they marched up Fifth Avenue. The crowds had never been so large. The pipers spotted familiar faces in the crowd, and occasionally nodded at the people on the sides who cheered them. In previous years, toward the end of the parade route, the band had often marched alone past the bare trees. This time, the crowds sometimes thinned for a block or two, but for all forty blocks people lined the sidewalks, pressing against the steel barricades, as the pipers marched.

Liam, who never looked his age and rarely seemed tired, even when he'd pushed himself to the limit, today did appear older than his thirty-six years. Crow's feet were visible around his eyes. He looked uncomfortable, sweaty, as if he couldn't breathe very well. Heavy. Even as he stood tall, barking out names of tunes and pausing to chat with band members during moments when the parade came to a halt, his eyes remained distant, dreary. His smile was strained. The invisible wall that shielded was firmly in place.

When the band finally reached the end of the parade route, the members fell out and lined up along the east side of Fifth Avenue and 86th Street. They continued to play as they watched the other contingents pass.

Three hundred and forty three probies marched by, each carrying an American flag for one of the firefighters killed on September 11—before most of them had joined the department. The waving fabric enveloped the young firefighters in a sea of red and white, and prevented them from seeing very far in front of them. Their young faces peered out, displaying pride and innocence.

An honor guard of about fifty fire officers passed by. Then came a troupe of firefighters carrying portraits of their deceased friends and brothers; Eddie Zeilman had several mass cards stuck onto his hat, one of which was for Bronko.

The Emerald Society Green Berets followed, wearing their navy Class-A suits and electric-green knit berets with a puffball on top.

One group of firefighters was led by six men holding a banner that showed a picture of the bagpipe band kneeling in prayer at Ground Zero in early October, bordered by the Fire Department shield and the Maltese Cross with the shamrock in the center. The sign was like a memorial to the band, and the band stood to attention as it passed. The pipers followed this unexpected depiction of them with their eyes. The banner read: "Lest We Forget."

Once all the Fire Department groups had gone, the band retreated to the school gym where the members had warmed up earlier that morning. Inside, kids played basketball on climbed on a jungle gym in the back, near the beer station. Stout and lager flowed freely from a series of taps behind a table. Corned beef and cabbage was served from large metal trays

Later that afternoon, Liam stepped out on the sidewalk with Kippy for a breath of fresh air. While Kippy chatted with others outside, Liam pulled his cell phone from his satchel and dialed Eddie Morrison. Eddie was a firefighter in Rescue 4, the nephew of the band's founder, Jimmy Ginty, and was working at the site that day. "Your family's all here," Liam told him, then asked what was going on there. Eddie told him that there had been no recoveries and the work was slow. Liam hung up and looked at Kippy. "Nothing," he told him. "Nothing today."

The festivities ended, as they did every year, with a speech by the band chairman and the official induction of new members. The new members each brought a bottle of Red Breast Irish whiskey, which they opened and passed around.

Around 7:00 P.M., the crowd began to disperse. Liam made rounds to see who could play at the two extra gigs he had booked for the night—a St. Patrick's Day party at a restaurant in midtown, and another one later at the Manhattan Center ballroom. Most were well into their cups, and Liam had a hard time pinning them down. He asked more men than would be needed, just in case. Kippy told Liam he'd see what he could do, but then took Mary home. She was four months pregnant and growing tired and itchy at the end of a long day. Tommy agreed to play at the later gig.

Liam climbed into the passenger side of a Fire Department van, Tim took the wheel, and two musicians from the Dublin Fire Brigade piled in the back: John Daly and Pete Hedderman, whom everyone called Hedder. John was affable and witty. A couple of years older than Liam, he was a snare drummer, as Bronko had been. Hedder was tall and gangly, with pale blond hair and translucent skin. John and Hedder shared a history with Bronko and Liam. In 1995, Liam and Bronko and several other members of the band had gone to Glasgow to compete in the World Pipe Band Championships for the first time. The FDNY placed ninth among sixty-five bands in Grade IV competition, which all considered a more than reasonable success. Afterward, they flew to Ireland and met the Dublin Fire Brigade band at the Rose of Tralee Festival, where the Dublin band played each year. One night, a crew of the boys went out drinking together. The American guys ran out of steam around 5:30 A.M., and while the Irish guys kept drinking, Bronko and Liam decided to crash. However, they hadn't arranged for a hotel, so they went to the sports complex where the Dublin firefighters had planned to sleep on mattresses on the floor. John had left two sleeping bags there for himself and Hedder. Bronko spotted one and snuggled inside, and soon was fast asleep. John and Hedder finally left the pub and went to a restaurant for breakfast. When they returned to the sports complex, Hedder spotted Bronko in his sleeping bag. Now Hedder had no place to sleep. He switched on all the lights and began roaring at the top of his voice, "Wakey, wakey! One up! All up!" His screams were shrill and piercing and incredibly annoying. Bronko soon awoke, climbed out of the bag, grabbed Hedder and hoisted him up on a coat hook, where he left him hang by the seat of his pants. John had to get up and take him down. Bronko grabbed a blanket from somewhere, and everyone fell asleep again. A couple of hours later, some of the Americans, including Bronko, awoke and decided to take their revenge. They circled around Hedder, tucked snugly in his sleeping bag. In unison, the men began to holler, "Wakey, wakey! Eggs and bake-y!" Bronko and Liam had laughed hysterically about it later on, and whenever they saw John and Hedder, they always called out, "Wakey, wakey!" Tonight, the Irishmen mentioned it again in the van, but Liam didn't laugh.

Tim didn't know the way to the restaurant where they would be playing. Liam, who hated being driven by others but probably felt he'd had too many pints of Guinness to drive himself, gave him orders. Tim drove jerkily as he tried to maneuver through the heavy traffic, stopping and starting when he shouldn't, and once nearly clipping a stopped cab with the van's nose. The second a light turned from red to green, Liam would shout, "Go!" Tim would gun the engine. Liam warned Tim that he was going to leave pinstripes on the car to his right. He didn't. Finally, they reached their destination. Liam jumped out of the van, opened the back door and grabbed his pipes. "We gotta tune up!" he barked. But the rest of the band was already walking toward the restaurant to scope out the bar.

From inside the restaurant, John looked back at Liam. He had never seen him so wound up—pacing around, struggling with his drape, trying to tune up his bagpipes in the howling wind. John and Hedder had thought they might play a set or two with the New Yorkers, but now they slipped over to the bar without bringing it up.

A dozen or so pipers and drummers circled up at the front of the restaurant and played a handful of tunes for the patrons, many of whom came to the front to stand near the musicians as they played. They laughed and clapped loudly. When it was over Liam and the others rushed back to their van and headed for the concert hall at Manhattan Center to play their last gig of the night. There, they met up with Tommy and others from the pipe band who had come straight from the school. Liam's sisters, Maureen and Denise, were there, too, with Karen. They stayed close to Karen's side and tried never to leave her quiet or alone. She'd cut her long blond hair so it fell just below her ears, and she looked even thinner than before. When asked how she was, Karen just murmured, "Mmmm." The laugh lines under her eyes now cut deep diagonal creases. She could squinch up her cheeks in an effort to appear merry, but she rarely laughed anymore. Today was Bronko's holiday. He would have loved to be there. She would have loved to be with him. They'd be engaged, possibly planning a wedding, looking at houses, thinking of a baby. Earlier in the day, Mike, the friend who'd driven her to the hospital the day they'd heard Bronko was alive, had given her one of the pins with Bronko's smiling face that all the band members wore. Karen had pinned it on her jean jacket. When she looked down later, it was gone. She fretted over misplacing it. "I can't believe I lost it," she said to Maureen and Denise.

The Bay Ridge parade, the final St. Patrick's Day parade of the season, took place in Liam's neighborhood in Brooklyn on Sunday, March 24. At one time, Bay Ridge had been one of Brooklyn's predominantly Irish communities, along with Gerritsen Beach, Park Slope, Windsor Terrace, and Breezy Point. Since the 1920s, Syrians, Lebanese, and other Arab immigrants began moving into the neighborhood, and over time, their numbers increased. A string of Irish pubs still lined the main strips of Third and Fifth avenues, wedged in alongside Middle Eastern bakeries, Italian restaurants, French bistros, and Greek- or Chinese-owned bodegas. These days, Irish accents were heard much less frequently among people walking the sidewalks, and signs in grocery store windows advertising Irish candy and sausages had faded. Still, many cops and firemen of Irish or Italian lineage made their homes in Bay Ridge, alongside the newer immigrants. After September 11, most windows in Bay Ridge displayed American flags. More flags were installed on the curbs, several on every block. If you were walking down the sidewalk, you sometimes had to duck them to avoid being smacked in the face.

Little more than a single row of spectators lined the sidewalks through most of the parade, and it finished to the total absence of a crowd. Afterward, the band gathered at Liam's apartment, a few short blocks from the end of the parade route, as they had the year before. Last year, Bronko had been there, and Michael Cawley had come by, too. Bronko had led the group in singing "The Streets of New York," a song about an Irishman who moves to Brooklyn to meet up with his brother, only to discover his brother has been murdered, so he eventually becomes a cop. Liam had brought out his guitar to accompany the singing. The celebration had gone deep into the night. The uproarious event had been a fitting cap to the month of St. Patrick's Day.

As the pipers slung off their busbies and traipsed up the street toward the front of Liam's building, they looked up and saw a massive American flag, which Liam had suspended from his balcony on the eleventh floor. Liam opened the door to his compact apartment, and twenty or so members of the pipe band filed in. They reached into ice-filled coolers for beers and dropped their gear on the white carpet. Those who were early enough slid into the few available spaces on the white couch.

Tommy dodged his way through the living room, past the sliding glass doors and out to the balcony with his brother, Mike, and the handful of smokers. As they looked out, they could see a full view of lower Manhattan and the gaping hole in the cityscape where the towers had once stood. The smoke that had risen from the site for months after the towers fell was now gone. The sky was clear and gray. Each person who came outside to the balcony paused for a moment, rested his hands on the rail as he took in the view, then turned his back on the city to face the others and the party inside. Tommy sucked on cigarettes and entertained everyone with vividly detailed stories of firefighters who'd sustained gruesome injuries in this fire or that fire. One poor fellow with a broken femur had to have a metal bar inserted that ran from his buttocks to his knee. Tommy held up his hands to show the length of the rod, as if demonstrating the length of a fish he'd just caught. "Can you imagine? A fucking rod!" He bent over and made a jerking motion with his hands, as if shoving the rod upward. He screwed up his nose and opened his eyes wide. "Up his ass." The others spewed smoke through their lips and swung their heads away in mock disgust.

Inside, Tim set a photo of Bronko on top of a table in the living room and propped it against the wall. Bronko was grinning widely in the photo, and his engaging eyes looked right at the camera. The shot had been taken at Danny McEnroe's wedding on September 8. Liam disappeared down the hall and into the bedroom, then returned with a small black duffel bag. He pulled out a black shoe and rotated it in the air before him. The shoe was shiny, perfect, a medium-sized man's dress loafer with three crisscross laces. The shoes were Father Judge's; along with his band shirt and kilt, they had been given to Liam earlier that week by a friend of Judge's family. The room fell quiet as Liam told how he'd come to have them. Then Liam zipped the shoe back into the bag and took it back down the hall.

Liam had a tall stack of pizzas delivered. The room soon grew more crowded. A few pipers had brought their wives or girlfriends, and one brought his three small children. The men weaved in and out from the balcony to the living room to the coolers in the kitchen. The chatter rose to a convivial level.

Tim slid a video into the VCR, a recording of last year's St. Patrick's Day parade. He adjusted the volume so some of the sound could be heard, but not enough to drown out the conversations that were going on. Heads turned as the skirl of bagpipes became audible, and the group from the balcony came back inside. The camera panned up and down over the band as the members marched up Fifth Avenue. Onscreen, Liam marched proudly at the front, swinging his mace. Someone in the room shouted, "Throw it!" As if on cue, the videotape showed Liam spinning the mace in a full circle, then hurling it ten feet into the air like a baton twirler, catching it gracefully without a moment's break in stride. Liam watched the images before him, gave a quick laugh, then turned away. He never performed tricks like that anymore.

Tommy stood at the back of the room and peered over the shoulders of the men in front of him, continuing to watch the tape even though most of the others had turned their attention back to their conversations. The Emerald Society Green Berets were passing by a close-up camera held by a network cameraman on the street. They smiled and waved and shouted greetings. Vinny had been marching with them last year. Tommy quietly searched the screen for a sign of his brother, but the camera switched back to the long shot taken from above. The tape went by too fast. Tommy didn't recognize Vinny in the crowd.

The beer coolers emptied, and no one offered to go get more. Some of the pipers began gathering their things and saying good-bye. Liam piled the used paper plates and cups into plastic bags and shuttled them down the hall to the garbage chute. The party had gone on for just over an hour. It wasn't even dark out yet. One firefighter who'd been memorialized in September had received his funeral a day earlier. Another man's was scheduled for the next. The night before, Liam had responded to a house fire that raged deep into the night. His apartment empty and silent, Liam collapsed into bed and fell asleep.

The next week, Liam began his first vacation since the terrorist attacks. He was due five weeks. When the officer on duty in Rescue 4 wrote on the board in the kitchen, "Flaherty to vacation," others in the house scribbled next to it, "Wow!" and "Thank God." He had accumulated so much overtime, others were relieved to see him take a break. But true to form, Liam spent the extra time down at the site. Entries in the Rescue 4 journal had tapered off. Even on days of many recoveries, the firefighters no longer diligently kept track. Gallows humor crept in, as it did so many places.

> March 30, 2002. Good Saturday.
>
> ABSOLUTELY NOTHING going on. Tully Road almost gone! Some digging in north tower—nothing recovered. Iron workers cutting down Building 5. Back to business Monday. Billy Murphy sucks.

In late March, Kippy was assigned to his first tour at Ladder 58, in the 18th Division in the Bronx. The tour began on a Monday morning, and Kippy made sure to arrive early. He knocked on the firehouse door at 7:00 A.M., carrying a sack of bagels and a newspaper, expecting a sit-down with the captain, who would tell him about the firefighters at the house and prep him on the types of calls to anticipate in the neighborhood.

No sooner had he stepped in the door than Kippy heard the alarm sound. The captain came sliding down the pole at the back of the apparatus floor. He saw Kippy and threw a radio at him. "You ready to ride?" he called out. Kippy blinked at him, dropped the bagels and paper, and threw on his bunker gear. The captain handed the riding list over to Kippy. Kippy climbed into the passenger's seat of the rig, and the truck pulled out the door. He heard the dispatcher's voice talking about multiple calls and a fire on the top floor. It sounded serious. Kippy didn't know any of the men on the rig. He didn't know where they were headed, or how he would lead these men and be responsible for their safety, much less keep track of who was who. They were following him, and he didn't know where the hell he was going.

After a few minutes on the road, the dispatcher sent the men back to the firehouse. As it turned out, the fire was a false alarm. Kippy exhaled.

The next time Kippy saw the captain, it was weeks later. He told the captain of his panic and ensuing relief. The captain laughed and said he should have spoken up. He'd thought Kippy had filled in there before and knew his way around. He would never have sent him out raw like that if he'd known it was his first tour as a lieutenant. The gaffe made for a pleasant icebreaker.

Years ago, Mary Walsh had quit smoking and started exercising regularly, trying to get in shape for her next attempt at conception. Getting healthy took time, but she eventually lost some weight and began to feel and look stronger and more fit. This time, her morning sickness had not endured very long. She didn't gain as much weight in her first five months as she had before. Though she stopped riding her horses at three months, she continued to groom them and clean their stalls, which was vigorous exercise in itself.

Before Danny was born, Kippy and Mary had decided not to find out the child's gender before the birth. This time, they just wanted to know. Boy or girl. As soon as possible.

Mary sorted through the old baby things she'd saved from Danny's first years—blue sleeper suits and boy-colored blankets and other toys—deciding what to throw out or keep. She knew this was probably the last time she'd ever feel an infant moving inside of her.

At a five-month sonogram, she and Kippy found out. Danny was going to have a little brother. That would be fine with them.

CHAPTER

13

CLOSING GROUND ZERO

One of the ways a priest gets through a lot of things is through ritual. You know? We all get through stress through ritual. You get out of bed in the morning, you have a ritual. We all do. When a ritual gets interrupted it ruins the rest of the day. We get through difficult times through ritual. Like a funeral mass is a ritual. It's done the same way. So we have that to fall back on. The rituals that we've created for ourselves.

—Father John Delendick, FDNY chaplain

GLOAMING had just begun to seep into the warm night air on May 28, 2002, when Liam stared out over the site from a momentarily isolated spot on Liberty Street. Police barricades cordoned the site off from the public on the east and north sides. The West Side Highway had reopened. Traffic again sped by one edge of the near-empty pit. The healing cross still stood tall atop a concrete median on the eastern edge. Liam spread his fingers wide and inserted them through the diamond-shaped links of the tall wire fence that separated him from the pit. Through the wires, two hundred feet or so ahead of him and about three hundred feet below, he could see the final obstacle—a rusted, spray-paint-decorated fifty-eight-ton pillar of steel, the last column to be removed from the Trade Center site. The girder, more than thirty feet tall, had remained stubbornly erect throughout the recovery effort, planted deep into the ground where it was originally anchored when the south tower was built nearly three decades before. It had sustained the crushing impact of more than a million tons of debris. Now, coated in crumbling rust, the column was painted at the top in blue with the numbers of the dead, "PAPD 37," and below that "NYPD 23," and below that, in orange, "FDNY 343." The identifiers continued down the beam. Many firehouses had spray-painted their company numbers in various bold colors. Some pictures were fastened onto the lower reaches. Nowhere on the column was anything from Rescue 4. Liam had despised the competitive way the Port Authority had drawn its number of the dead on the very top. Some companies that hadn't even lost men had scrawled their company numbers there. To Liam, there was something cheap about writing on the column, like leaving a souvenir to say, "I was there." He and some other firefighters joked about the girder, calling it "the Totem Pole" or "the Beam of Shame," because it displayed a pecking order that did not reflect their experience. Those who had really been there and really suffered losses had no need and no desire to sign and didn't want to see their company number alongside the impostors. To see it underneath would have been worse. Liam tightened his knuckles around the wire, lowered his head, and leaned back. The force of his weight tugged the fence backward.

This was the day of which all those at the site had warned themselves and each other—the day when the work would officially be over. Tonight would bring the first of two official ceremonies signifying the end; this one was just for the recovery workers. But the recovery effort had long been over, and the workers at the site had known it for several weeks. Throughout the month of March, twenty-nine firefighters, five police officers, and four Port Authority officers were identified; forty-four whole bodies were found, 3,216 body parts taken to the morgue. Lt. Kevin Dowdell was not among them. Liam had been with the two boys the night they'd filled a coffin with their father's spare set of bunker gear, letters from Patrick and James, a few snapshots, a piece of oak wood to represent the flooring work he had loved to do so much, and a small box filled with randomly collected soil and dust from Ground Zero. All that was left. They'd held a memorial service and buried the coffin on April 20.

Around that same time, the last of the active debris piles in the north tower near West Street was searched and sifted. Liam had assisted in the last firefighter recovery. He'd looked inside the bunker coat and read the man's name, Denis Germain, a thirty-three-year-old firefighter from Ladder 2. His brother, Brian, was a firefighter from Kippy's firehouse, Ladder 23. Since then, the firefighters had been raking through the dirt that remained on the ground in search of the tiniest bits of bone. One thousand more pieces of remains were turned in to the medical examiner's office between March 31 and the end of May, a small number when compared with the almost four thousand that were found in the single month of October. During the last two months, only four "whole bodies" had been found. The kind of recovery that could result in a rush of elation had become a dim memory.

In a couple of days, the site would be closing to most recovery workers, with more than 1,695 bodies yet to be found or identified. All the lost had burned up or been crushed to the dust. People on the outside seemed to think that a funeral was enough to set an end point to grief. Liam knew the act of finding a body wasn't enough to put an end to suffering. Not knowing where Bronko was had been draining, anxious, all-consuming. Liam could think of little else but bringing him home. After he was found, people had asked Liam, "How do you feel?" Liam had responded, "I feel happy." But finding Bronko didn't bring him back to life, and soon enough, the old feelings of numbness and coldness resurfaced. It was the day after the funeral, and the day after, and the day after that, and the specter of the endless line of days to come that weighed the heaviest.

Suddenly, someone whistled from the pit below. Liam slipped through a hole in the fence and, wearing his firefighter's helmet, yellow construction vest, and navy pants, soon blended with the hundreds of other workers who swarmed around the site. Tonight would mark another milestone, another step, an inch further away from the events of September 11.

At around 7:45 P.M., the workers' ceremony to cut down the final column was about to begin. A cluster of firefighters from Rescue 4 and relatives of the dead walked out of the firehouse of Ladder 10 and Engine 10, which opened right onto the street at the south end of the site. Many relatives of those killed from Rescue 4 also attended. Lt. Tim Kelly handed each of the family members a blue carnation. They walked through the gap in the fence, down to the family viewing area a couple of levels below Liberty Street.

Down at the floor of the pit, a giant red-and-gray crane stood poised to remove the column. Heavy steel wires stretched down in an upside-down V from the top of the crane to the top of the beam. At the upper end of the wires hung a green wreath. A large American flag waved in the slight breeze from top of the girder. A group of pipers and drummers from the carpenters' union, Local 608, were present to play. The

FDNY band was not. The procession began with three men carrying American flags down a long ramp to the sound of the drummers' dirge beat. Then a crowd of about a hundred construction workers marched toward the beam, carrying a banner that read "We Will Never Forget." Police helicopters flew overhead. There was a gap in the crowd, then more marchers followed, most of whom looked to be firefighters wearing yellow vests and fire helmets. The firefighters walked in a distinctly separate group, slightly more orderly than the rest. A priest sprinkled holy water on the column. A man-basket carrying three men was lifted to the top of the beam. One of the men carried a welding torch. He cut the flagpole from the top of the beam and raised it high in the air. Someone called out, "Hats off!" and the men removed their hard hats and fire helmets. Cheers of "USA! USA!" momentarily drowned out a trumpeter playing "Taps." When the song finished, the men in the basket hugged each other, and they were lowered to the ground to the sounds of more applause.

Someone shone a spotlight on the letters "PAPD 37." Then the light jutted down to the other pronouncements, "NYPD 23," "FDNY 343," and so on. Four workers approached the base, and a welder cut away at each corner. Cheers broke out again as the crane lifted the girder a foot off the ground. Then each man gingerly laid his hand on the edge of the beam and escorted it over to a large flatbed truck that waited nearby. The crane ever so slowly set the base on a wooden plank and lowered the column to lie flat on the ground. The motion of the crane was so gradual, it took several minutes. When the column touched the ground, there was more applause. A wreath of flowers was placed on top. Men gathered to sign the column, or touch it for the last time. The crane lifted it again, maintaining its horizontal position, and cradled it onto the flatbed. The men wrapped the metal in a black shroud. They worked intently, their heads down, running their hands over it to smooth every inch of the fabric.

Night had fallen. At the edge of the site, on Liberty Street, the members of Rescue 4 circled up and said a prayer. The family members handed their flowers to Liam, who gathered them into a bouquet and carried it down to the pit. He hopped up on the truck bed, knelt down, and laid the flowers on the covered beam, in the center of the wreath.

The crowd below began to disperse. Some construction workers, firefighters, and police officers lingered in the pit; others began to stream out. Liam jumped down from the truck and paused for a moment. Then he turned and walked away. He climbed over a short barricade that separated the path back to the ramp from the rest of the site. He walked alone, as he wanted to be.

Two days later, on the morning of May 30, 2002, Tommy and Mike stood next to each other near the upper end of the ramp that stretched for more than five hundred feet down into the pit. At the bottom, Patrick Dowdell stood behind Liam. James waited with a group of FDNY pipers at the top, near the exit onto West Street.

Today, New York City would mark the official end to the recovery effort at the World Trade Center site.

As firefighters and family members of a lost fire captain, Tommy and Mike wore their lieutenants' Class-A uniforms and stood side by side, part of the honor guard that lined the edges of the ramp, instead of marching with the band that day. Firemen in bunker gear or coveralls or navy uniforms lined the west side of the ramp. Each wore a purple lei. Opposite the firefighters stood the politicians—Governor George Pataki, Mayor Michael Bloomberg, former mayor Rudolph Giuliani—and other city and state officials, as well as construction workers.

Three rows of bagpipers, each eight men deep, waited at the bottom of the pit. Liam stood in the center. To his left were the Port Authority pipers and drummers; to his right were members of the NYPD pipes and drums band. The drum majors to either side of Liam were much older men, decked out in long-sleeved coats and elaborate drapes. Liam wore a short-sleeved white shirt and his kilt. His pink cheeks defied the frown lines on his forehead. Behind him stood pipe major Tom McEnroe, band chairman Joe Murphy, pipers Frank McCutchen and Patrick Dowdell, then drummers Brian Grogan, Al Schwartz, and Teddy Carstensen. All the FDNY band members in the lineup below had been affected by the loss of someone close and had been heavily involved in the recovery effort and the funeral and memorial detail. They'd each paid a heavy price for their presence there. They would be the ones to lead the final march out.

At 10:29 A.M., the ceremony began. Jimmy Sorokac rang an FDNY fire bell in the four-fives sequence, to signify the death of a firefighter. The procession began with an empty stretcher. The men in the honor guard drew their hands up in salute as a crew of twelve men, who represented every agency involved, from the FDNY to the FBI to the Department of Design and Construction, trudged up the ramp with it. An American flag lay folded atop it, to symbolize the nearly 1,700 who, like Vinny Brunton and Kevin Dowdell and Brian Hickey, had never been recovered. An ambulance waited midway up the ramp. The men placed the stretcher inside and gently closed the door.

Liam called out the order to march, and the bands began to step forward, up the long, artificial slope. The drummers began a funeral dirge beat, three slow taps and a roll. The echo of the drums rebounded from large speakers placed nearby, making it difficult for Liam to discern which set of drumbeats was coming from the men behind him and which was being picked up by microphones and retransmitted. Instead of marching off on the left in a sure stride, he misstepped, shuffled his feet, and struggled to regain control of the march.

Behind the pipers and drummers, the large flatbed truck that held the final column began groaning and spitting smoke as it lurched up the ramp. The column was still covered with the black shroud, and the top quarter, like a giant coffin, was covered with an American flag, stars at the head. Just a few feet below the end of the flag lay the wreath of red roses and white carnations; in its center was the cluster of blue carnations that Liam had placed there two nights before. The men along the sides saluted the column as it passed.

When the three bands reached the top of the pit, they turned and slipped through their ranks in a countermarch, so they all ended up facing the front of the truck. Liam called out, "America! Quick march!" and the bands began to play "America the Beautiful," not at the slow, mournful pace that they used at funerals but as a cheery anthem. The FDNY pipers at the top joined the men who had marched up from the pit. Together, they marched out onto West Street to the waterfall trills of "Garryowen" and walked northward just over a dozen blocks. Other than Liam's marching orders, no words were officially spoken at the ceremony that final day.

Afterward, the band members gathered at Chumley's, an old writers' club and former speakeasy at 86 Bedford Street in Greenwich Village that, because of its side-courtyard escape route and indiscernible front entrance, gave rise to the term "86 it." Now the trendy hideaway with the easy way out was a bar and restaurant. A handful of firefighters from the nearby firehouse of Engine 24 and Ladder 5 worked part-time as bartenders there, including the pipe band's Frank McCutchen. The owner, Steve, nurtured an affinity for firefighters. He had befriended a fire captain named John Drennan in the early 1990s; in 1994, after Drennan died as a result of burns he'd sustained in a fire over a month earlier, Steve had put up an enlarged portrait of him over the bar. As other firefighter friends were killed over the years, Steve hung their photos along a wall in the back room, over a square table next to, of all things, a wooden throne. Now Father Mychal Judge and Fire Captain Patrick "Paddy" Brown each graced an upper corner over the bar, and the back room was covered with eighteen more pictures, including eleven who had been killed from Engine 24 and Ladder 5 on September 11. There were other decorative elements, too: a near life-size plastic bulldog on the bar; three live bulldogs who roamed freely about the premises; four-foot-high black-and-white portraits of Eugene O'Neill, John Steinbeck, F. Scott Fitzgerald, and other writers; and bric-a-brac lining the walls in the restaurant section.

When the pipers stepped inside, the air was hot and close and the restaurant was dark, a sharp contrast to the bright noontime sun outside. The place would be theirs alone for some time.

Tommy and Mike hustled around behind the bar in their blue shirts, filling glasses and taking orders. Mike barely broke his rhythm of turning, filling, wiping glasses to release the long ash from the cigarette hanging out of his mouth. The taps weren't cold, so the brothers sent for ice. James Dowdell emerged from the basement with a large barrel. Frank soon followed, hauling another, his brow dripping wet near the fresh edges of his summer haircut, sweat dampening his white T-shirt. A pile of twenties grew taller and taller on the bar.

The pipers filled every stool at the bar, every seat and nook in the two rooms. Someone turned on the air-conditioning. Conversations burgeoned. Tim had been promoted to lieutenant two days before and had also just found out that Tara was newly pregnant with their second child. Jimmy Ginty rolled on the floor with two of the bulldogs, who jumped on top of him and licked his face. Liam sat in the seat between two tables in the middle of the room right by the bar, and pipers filled in the seats all around him.

Kippy wasn't there. For the past week, Mary, now seven months along, had been experiencing early contractions. That morning, the intensifying pains seized and ebbed just a few minutes apart. Kippy had rushed her to the hospital and stayed at her side.

Attention turned to the television sets placed in corners over the bar. CNN was showing highlights of the march out that morning. The volume was muted, but for a moment an image of Liam marching up the ramp flashed on the screen, and the men shouted and cheered. Liam smiled and told the others how he'd stepped off on the wrong foot. He'd been sure that would be on TV. It wasn't. The piper next to him asked to borrow his *sgian dubh* so he could carve his name into the wooden table. Liam reached down into his sock, pulled out the knife, and handed it to him. "This is Bronko's *sgian dubh,*" Liam told him. He had kept it with him since October.

A couple of the pipers at the table nudged the conversation toward the site. One mentioned he'd heard that the medical examiner might be identifying body parts for years to come. The pipers had long planned some kind of celebration to mark the last burial, whenever that might be. After a regular line-of-duty funeral, they'd often play a quick march tune, like "Garryowen" or "The Wearing of the Green," to bring an end to the somber remembrance and a beginning to the celebration of the brother's life. The men had refused to invoke this tradition during the September 11 burials, wanting to hold out until the final funeral out of respect for all the men. A few had even decided never to play the bagpipes at any occasion other than a funeral or memorial—no weddings, no impromptu jigs in a bar, nothing—until the mourning was finished.

"Yeah, you know how we were talking about the last funeral?" Liam asked Brian Meagher, the band's instructor, who sat across from him at the table. Meagher leaned forward and nodded. "We'll never know when that will be," said Liam.

The medical examiner's office was already storing remains it could not identify, in the hope that someday improved DNA technology would allow more effective analysis. They'd all thought there would be a final day to all of this, a set date in time when it would truly be over. Soon they would begin to mark the one-year anniversary of all the firefighters' deaths with the traditional plaque dedication ceremonies, when square bronze plaques inscribed with the name and circumstances of death would be unveiled at the city firehouses and the bagpipers would play. Then, in October, there would be the annual memorial service for all firefighters who died in the past year; it would be longer than ever since the October 2001 service had been postponed while the city recovered from the attacks. But now they could see further into the future. The last funeral could be years away.

Irish music began pouring from the jukebox, a soupy, mellow chorus you could imagine people swaying to, lined up with their arms strung around each other's shoulders. The song was "Four Green Fields."

> "What did I have?" said the fine old woman.
> "What did I have?" this proud old woman did say.

"I had four green fields, each one was a jewel,
But strangers came and tried to take them from me.
I had fine strong sons, they fought to save my jewels,
They fought and died, and that was my grief," said she.

"Long time ago," said the fine old woman,
"Long time ago," this proud old woman did say,
"There was war and death, plundering and pillage,
My children starved by mountain valley and sea.
And their wailing cries, they shook the very heavens.
My four green fields ran red with their blood," said she.

"What have I now?" said the fine old woman.
"What have I now?" this proud old woman did say.
"I have four green fields, one of them's in bondage
In stranger's hands, that tried to take it from me.
But my sons have sons, as brave as were their fathers.
My fourth green field will bloom once again," said she.

"Where's Bronko when you need him?" Frank called out from behind the bar, a finger pointing skyward. Liam acknowledged Frank with a slight nod. It was a gesture of reconciliation, an inching away from the anger that had consumed Liam, as it had nearly all of them to different degrees at different times, and caused them to say and do things they didn't mean.

Patrick Dowdell sat on the king's throne in the back room and chatted with the pipers around him. He would be leaving for West Point in a few weeks to begin basic training. James hovered around at the other end of the room and talked quietly with another piper, one-on-one. He had just gone to his senior prom and would be attending Iona College in the fall. Liam had begun to think of the Dowdells as his boys. He would miss them when they went away.

As the conversation continued all around him, Liam grew silent for a moment. He flashed a quick nod, tipped his glass gently, and drank. A toast to the air. To a friend who was no longer there.

The terror attacks of September 11 ceased to monopolize the news. Americans had other stories to follow. Winona Ryder was arrested for shoplifting. Britain's Prince William turned twenty. Mobster John Gotti died in prison, of cancer. Barry Bonds reached 587 career home runs, for fourth place on the all-time list. Martha Stewart faced allegations of improper conduct in an insider-trading scandal.

More firefighters' funerals and memorials took place during the spring and summer. June brought seven memorials and five repeat services for men who'd been memorialized and were now identified.

On June 11, Rescue 4 held its ninth and last memorial service for the men the company counted among its lost. Brian Hickey's life was remembered on what would have been his forty-eighth birthday. Several hundred firefighters and mourners braved the oppressive temperatures and turned out for the service, which took place at his parish church, St. Martin of Tours Catholic Church in Bethpage, Long Island. Hickey was posthumously promoted to the rank of battalion chief. Around the time the site closed, the men at Rescue 4 had finally told Donna Hickey that her husband's helmet was all they had been able to recover. That was what she had placed in the coffin to bury.

Liam sat next to Patrick and James Dowdell. They listened as Christine Ebersole sang "Amazing Grace" and Pat McGuire played acoustic guitar and sang "These Hands," just as they had at Kevin Dowdell's memorial service. When it was over and the band played "Going Home," Liam held his staff in the air to signal the final notes. He kept his arm extended, the mace rising high, in an effort to prolong the last note. The bagpipers did not sustain the music to match Liam's direction. Liam let the top of the staff slide back down into his hand and grimaced slightly but said nothing.

Liam was struggling for control of himself, trying not to let these things bother him anymore. In March, he had called Karen to check up on her, and she'd turned some of his questions back to him. They talked about his anger. He said he was trying to stay positive. Karen had told him, "Not everyone can be like you." Her words remained with him. He knew he could not reconcile with some of the people he'd felt had let him down, but reminding himself that he could not hold everyone to his same standard, seemed to assuage his fury

That year was a slow summer for fires in Rescue 4. The house held a plaque dedication ceremony near the first anniversary of the Father's Day fire. The men made up new construction projects to keep themselves busy. They completely revamped the TV room and painted the kitchen walls. Liam helped with building projects on the widows' houses. That summer, death moved a little further from his life.

On June 27, Kippy played at his last service for a close friend from 21 Truck, Gerry Atwood. Years ago, he'd played bagpipes at Gerry's wedding. Kippy was the only one in the band who knew Gerry well and the only one from the band who went inside the church for the service.

At the end, Kippy stood once again in the front line of the pipers, fingering his chanter, blinking back tears. The rest of the men in the band stared ahead with dull eyes

Kippy hadn't been coming to the funerals for a while. When Mary had gone to the hospital, she'd been given a shot to halt the contractions and put on an IV for rehydration. Her doctor had prescribed restricted activity and as much bed rest as possible from then on. She took a leave from work and stopped cleaning the horses' stalls. Still, the contractions had not entirely ceased, and she crouched with pain every time she rose to her feet. Now, in her eighth month, she suffered from excruciating backaches. From the beginning, Mary's physician had told her to plan for a C-section since she'd had one before. She had hoped she could somehow deliver naturally, but eventually she decided to take her doctor's advice. They set a date in mid-July, two weeks prior to her due date. For Kippy, preparing for the new life while commemorating the dead made for too harsh a contrast. After Gerry's memorial service, he didn't come again.

Through the summer, services continued to interrupt the band members' efforts to settle back into some sort of normalcy. The final service for a member of Ladder 105 was held on June 28, for the young firefighter Dennis O'Berg Jr., whose father had dug at the site nearly every day for his son and had never given up hope that he would be found; a squadron of firefighters who had lost sons marched in the procession toward the church. Other families scheduled services for the summer months to coincide with special occasions like anniversaries or the deceased's birthday. One memorial service was held in July, and there were four services in August.

One summer day, a woman approached Liam on the street. "Is there a parade today?" she asked.

"No," he answered. "A funeral. For a firefighter killed on 9/11."

"Oh," said the woman as she stepped away. "I thought you were all done with that."

Another day, Liam told an inquirer that the funeral was for someone who died in the World Trade Center. "Wasn't that like, a long time ago?" the person asked. Liam did not answer.

The culture that firefighters had known as "the Job" had forever changed. The phrase that so many firefighters had used as parting banter—"See you at the Big One"—no one ever said anymore. Late in May, after the site closed, the band had scheduled a fortieth anniversary party, but hardly any of them felt like celebrating their existence, so the party was canceled. A few members of the band had retired, including the band's only Jewish piper, Al Schwartz. He made his part-time job, working as a stagehand, his full-time occupation, and his girlfriend said she'd never seen him happier. For firefighters throughout the department, being a firefighter just wasn't fun anymore. More and more were abandoning their jobs. Because their pension was based on earnings in the last year of service, and so many firefighters had worked overtime in the aftermath of the attacks, it made fiscal sense for many who had accumulated twenty or more years to leave. Lt. Freddy Scholl, who had been Liam's partner at the site for months, was promoted to captain and soon after began planning to retire before the one-year anniversary of the attack. Another lieutenant in Rescue 4 also got set to leave. The men who stayed on the job came up with their own ways to keep the realities at bay. "You don't have to accept it," Liam would often repeat. "You just have to get used to it."

Kippy and Mary arrived at the hospital at 6:00 A.M. on July 18. With Danny, she'd planned for a natural birth, but after twenty-one hours of labor, the doctor had performed a C-section. This time, without labor, she expected the procedure to go quickly.

Mary changed into a hospital dressing gown and winced as a nurse administered a local anesthetic to her lower back. She bent over, sitting at the edge of the bed, and held on to her feet, positioning herself so the doctor could insert the catheter for the epidural. Her bulbous belly pushed against her lungs, making it hard to breathe. She began to feel nauseous. The doctor had some difficulty with the procedure, and she had to remain curled over, struggling for air, for nearly twenty minutes. Finally, the catheter went in. Within seconds, it seemed, her legs numbed and she couldn't feel anything from the chest down. The nurses eased her back down in the bed and rolled her along the hall to surgery.

Even reclining, Mary's nausea persisted. The morphine they'd given her made her head spin. She gagged and felt she was going to vomit. She could barely move because of the anesthetic, and she struggled to turn her face to the side so she could throw up. Finally, she reached the room where the surgery would be performed. The medical staff stretched a blue cloth drape over Mary's chest so it formed a wall in front of her face. Kippy came in, wearing a sterile cover over his chest and arms.

Mary didn't feel the slice of the incision, just pressure and a tugging sensation as the doctors pulled her open. Her diaphragm seemed to be pressing against her chest. "I can't breathe!" she shouted, gasping for air. She heard someone reply, "It's okay! It's normal!"

The doctor pulled, and the baby slipped upward through the opening in Mary's abdomen. He made a couple of gurgling sounds. "You got a nice, big boy," Mary heard a voice say. A member of the medical staff held the infant up in the air, very briefly, and Mary caught a quick glimpse over the edge of the drape. His blood-coated skin was bluish-purple. He wasn't crying or making any noise. When Danny had been born, the nurses had cleaned him up, wrapped him in a blanket and angled him right up close to Mary's face and against her neck so she could see him and kiss him. Now she heard someone saying, "Okay, let's go. Chris, let's go." The baby was in respiratory distress. He'd swallowed some fluid in the birth canal, which was preventing him from getting enough oxygen. Before Mary had a chance to get a good look at him, Aidan was whisked to the fetal intensive care unit.

On September 9, 2002, an army of locusts buzzed angrily as an empty coffin was removed from the caisson outside a church in Williston Park, Long Island. Small children peered out of windows in the school across the street from the church. The summer heat was oppressive. The coffin was lifted from the truck and handled with delicate care, even though it did not contain the remains of firefighter Thomas Kuveikis, who was being memorialized that day. The New York tabloids touted it as the last of the 343 firemen's services. But everyone in the pipe band knew this not to be true. The family of Michael Ragusa from Engine 279 was steadfast in its intent to wait until some remains were identified as his.

More people turned out for the Kuveikis memorial service than usual, probably because the anniversary of September 11 was on the public mind again. On television the shots of the planes crashing into the towers were shown again and again. The firefighters had been more or less left alone since the six-month anniversary and the closing of the site. Now, abruptly, the press hounds were back, asking how things had changed in a year, and had they been able to move on? As if an appropriate period of time had passed, and the Fire Department should be recovered by now. As if suddenly the world cared again.

On the night of September 10, the pipers would embark on the longest march of their lives. City Hall had decided to mark the first anniversary of September 11 by arranging bagpipe processionals to march in to Ground Zero from the far reaches of every borough of New York. The FDNY band would depart from the upper tip of Manhattan, at Broadway and 220th Street. The NYPD would march in from Brooklyn, the Sanitation Department band from Staten Island, the Corrections Department band from the Bronx, and the Port Authority Police band from Queens. For all the bands, this meant more than twelve miles of marching. Of course, there was plenty of griping that the NYPD had it easiest, with only thirteen miles to walk from southeast Brooklyn, while the Port Authority and Corrections bands would have to hump it for nineteen miles each. The FDNY pipers and drummers would march 16.2 miles in all, from the top to the bottom of Manhattan. The journey would be almost seven times as long as the band's longest parade, the New York City St. Patrick's Day parade. They would march all night and arrive at the site when the sun was coming up.

Kippy thought the whole idea was ridiculous and inappropriate, too much like a parade to be a fitting commemoration for the lives lost on September 11. Besides, the band had been through enough, playing at funerals and memorials, doing parades and fund-raisers and street dedications on top of it. He was sure that no one was going to be out in the middle of the night to see them go by. And he was exhausted. Baby Aidan had spent his first two weeks of life in the hospital. He had pneumonia and was hooked up to what seemed like a dozen machines. Just when he was ready to be released, the doctors discovered he'd had a brief period of apnea. So they sent him home with a breathing monitor—a belt that strapped around his tiny chest and electrodes that connected to a pocketbook-size machine. Every time Kippy and Mary put the infant down for a nap, they were nearly paralyzed with fear. Whenever he shifted in his sleep or took a deep breath, the electrodes and the monitoring belt slipped, and a frighteningly loud alarm sounded. Kippy and Mary would race for the crib to see if he was breathing. He always was.

And who knew what would await them when they arrived downtown? A Code Orange, an elevated but nonspecific terror alert for the nation, was issued around the time of the anniversary. The site could be bombed again, a nuclear attack could strike, a deadly gas could be released among the mourners. Liam began calling it "the death march," a phrase that quickly spread among the pipers and brought rueful smiles to everyone's faces.

The night began with more than its share of the usual bickering and griping. The men had finished the funeral for Peter Bielfeld at around 2:00 P.M. Some had gone back to their firehouses or homes for a nap; others had gone to their firehouses and found it impossible to sleep; still others had started drinking in the afternoon and had not stopped. They'd arranged to meet at 12:30 A.M. at a Sanitation Department parking lot near Canal Street, where they would wait for two buses to arrive to shuttle them up to Inwood. This way, they could park their cars near downtown and have them close by when the march ended the next morning. But the busses were more than an hour late. Exhausted and bitter, the men complained to each other, "Hurry up and wait." One bus finally arrived and took half the band up to Inwood. The remaining half had to wait another forty-five minutes for the second bus to come. The longer they had to wait, the more what they were about to do seemed absurd. Honestly, who was going to be up in the middle of the night? Nobody! The mayor should be awake with them, marching with them, if this was all his bright idea. What were they going to sound like as the night wore on? Bagpipes weren't meant to be played for such long periods. They'd resemble a pack of ailing hyenas by the time they finished.

Tim was one of the few who looked forward to the night of marching. He imagined it as a sort of pilgrimage, an honor to the men and women who'd died. He was excited to be a part of it, and he planned to march the entire route even as others decided to take breaks along the way.

Liam, Kippy, and Tim climbed off the bus at 220th Street and Broadway and were taken aback by what they saw. Lights flashed on fire trucks and police cars, and an enthusiastic gaggle of about fifty people cheered them as they descended the steps into the street. African American teenagers and Hispanic kids clapped their hands and hollered for them. Firemen from local companies waved hello and came over to chat. A robust ironworker carrying a ten-foot long American flag stood poised to follow them into the city. Such a buzz of activity was a giant boost.

Once the band members were suitably tuned, Liam lined them up and took his place at the front. He called the starting set. Tonight, they would pipe almost their entire repertoire of upbeat tunes, jigs, and reels, including the ones they'd mostly played only as warm-ups in the past year, like "Scotland the Brave," "Give My Regards to Broadway," and "Twenty Men from Dublin Town."

The band marched in a relay. One group marched for twenty blocks or so while another group rode in a bus, resting until it was their turn again. At a designated spot, they jumped out and relieved the others, who clambered onto the bus, out of breath and sweaty. The second bus eventually came to pick up the pipers who'd been stuck waiting downtown; when they caught up with the rest of the band around 180th Street, they eagerly joined in the rotation.

All along the streets, people had gathered to cheer on the pipers. Not many people. A handful on each block, some who'd just emerged from the closing bars. For a few blocks, a crew of inebriated teenagers marched and clapped alongside Liam, kicking their legs straight out in front of them. Their antics solicited a brief grin from Liam. Farther on, the crowds swelled. People brought out candles and American flags to wave in the swampy night air. A crowd of about twenty, led by the ironworker with the flag, had marched behind the band ever since the procession started. New additions fell in behind the band for a few blocks, then fell away. Fire trucks from each consecutive neighborhood joined the cortege of pipers and drummers for the length of their primary response area, driving in front or behind the band, then turned back to their firehouses, roaring their horns with pride. Dew mingled with sweat on the pipers' faces. Their shirts grew slack and damp; their shoes pounded against the pavement of the streets. They looked up at the buildings and saw that most of the apartment lights were switched on.

Liam allowed another man to lead just once, for a dozen blocks in upper Manhattan. Otherwise, he didn't give up the drum major position at all. After a few hours, his voice grew hoarse from shouting the names of jolly tunes and sets. "Irish One!" "Irish Three!" "Garryowen!" At one point, he belted, "Rakes of Mallow!" with decided exhaustion.

Tim smiled and said back to him, in a subdued tone, "Is it 'Rakes of Mallow' or"—he raised his voice enthusiastically—'RAKES OF MALLOW!'" Liam allowed himself a short chuckle, and repeated the tune's name with similar gusto.

Suddenly, what they'd thought would be an endless night began hurtling forward. Different crews took breaks on the bus, grabbed beers and bottled water, pounded on the doors of the lavatory in the back. They collapsed with exhaustion into the empty seats. During one of his breaks, Tommy sat quietly and gazed out the window at the dark buildings going past. Mike was marching in the color guard that night, stoically hoisting a flag with the others, and resting little.

Swarms of people converged on the streets as the procession reached midtown. Times Square was near. Everyone in the band leapt off the bus for this stretch. The neon lights and bold electric signs flickered and buzzed overhead. The band members lined up in eight rows and spanned the entire width of Broadway. The night sky and the pavement were pitch black. Cheers and whistles grew louder. The nighttime moisture cooled but did not chill them. Liam advanced at a faster pace. Photographers bobbed and weaved through the crowds to get a shot of the men, elbowing each other out of the way and getting into each other's shots. Marching through Times Square as a unit in the middle of the night was truly a once-in-a-lifetime experience. The pipers' music filled every molecule of the air with proud, thick notes. They played the same tunes again and again, fifteen, thirty, sixty times that night. They did not tire.

One moment, night's veil was brown and gray. The next, the firmament shone in lucid blues, pale yellows, and whites. The band was approaching lower Manhattan. The crowds along the streets were consistent now. People packed the sidewalk, stood on raised concrete walks, and climbed over the grass and bramble by the edges of the water. A group of women lined up signs for the men to read as they passed. "We Will Never Forget You FDNY." "You Are the Best." A man with a pious, pained frown had begun following the band. In his hands he clutched an open newspaper with hundreds of headshots of the dead. Soon the mass of followers, which numbered in the hundreds by now, was cut off by security guards and police officers. The site was now in view. They would not be allowed to march any farther.

As the band marched closer, their faces grew apprehensive. At the head of the band, Mike gripped the flagpole with his gloved hand, thumb facing down so that the back of his hand lined up with his nose.

He set his chin and shoulders back, his chest out. His expression was one of defiance.

Tommy stood toward the back of the band. His searching eyes and tilted brow told of dread. Three hundred more people, including twelve firefighters, had been identified by the medical examiner's office since the last time he'd come to the site, at the end of May. Vinny was not among them. A couple of days earlier, Tommy had gone to the Great Irish Fair. Only a dozen or so FDNY pipers and drummers attended the event this year. Liam had stayed away. Tommy and several friends from the neighborhood drank plastic cups of beer inside the Buckley's tent and hollered above the din of the music. As the sun began to set on the lazy afternoon, talk turned to Vinny, as it often did. Tommy became suddenly motionless, frozen in place, his head leaning down to one side, much as he looked at this moment, approaching the site. At the fair, he'd shaken his head, quiet, while the others around fell silent, waiting for him to speak. Finally he'd said softly, "God, I miss him."

Tim looked over to his left, at the vast airspace that had not existed a year before. After the first few miles, he'd realized he hadn't the strength to march and blow into the pipes the whole way, and he'd paused for stretches with the rest. Seen from so close, the new skyline was just a cluster of short skyscrapers around a gaping hole in the ground. He tried to picture what it would look like if the buildings were still there.

Kippy held on to his spot in the front line, where he'd marched since Times Square. He didn't complain anymore. He felt tired but exhilarated, beaten up but deserving. The march had been worthwhile. Now he could see the importance the band brought to the day. The crowds around proved that they hadn't walked alone all these months.

On West Street, just to the northwest of the site, the band came to a stop. Before them, a colorful mural decorated by a heart-shaped flag hung the entire length of one of the buildings. It read, "The human spirit is measured not by the size of the act, but by the size of the heart." But what about the size of the act when the act was mourning the dead? So many dead that the services lasted twelve months? Or when the act was marching all night to recall the innumerable marches of the months before? Were these acts not a significant measure of heart? In the hazy white light of day, the faded Maltese Cross patches on the men's sleeves proved answer enough, bleached nearly blank by the sun of 445 services.

The band began marching again. The men veered right and came to a halt off West Street at the southern edge of the site, where the firefighters would wait for the other bands to arrive. Kippy sat on an elevated curb with a line of other pipers and took off his shoes. Tommy walked up the street alone, heading for a cup of coffee. Men filed in and out of the portable toilets. The man with the newspaper continued to hover near the pipers, holding it open as if inviting them to look. He stood next to Bobby, the piper who'd circled the faces of men he'd known on a newspaper many months before. Bobby squinted and turned his head away.

Liam was flooded with revulsion at the prospect of marching back into the pit. He hadn't been back, save for once over the summer, to show Tim and Tara. Now he was repelled by the emptiness of the pit. He felt no remnant of the presence of the dead that he had felt there in the months during the recovery effort. At that moment, the ground no longer felt sacred to him. He couldn't stand to be down there.

Finally, the other pipe bands arrived and formed a thick line in the street. The procession began again. One after another, they marched into the site and formed a circle, surrounded by the hundreds of family members in the pit. At 8:46 A.M., the wind kicked up fiercely, rousing brown dust into a whipping smoke. The pipers closed their eyes to the onslaught. Their eyes were stung anyway. They played a brief tune and marched back out.

Grateful to be done with the march, most of the pipers and drummers headed to Frank's, a nearby restaurant where they'd arranged to meet for the afters. The group that had arrived late for the march had trouble tracking down the bus that had driven them, which still held much of their gear. After zigzagging around in the traffic, searching for the bus, calling the bus driver on cell phones only to get no response, some of the pipers folded themselves down on a concrete barricade to rest. Several photographers swung by and snapped pictures of the line of worn-out men. The pipers' feet were heavy. They thought about getting up to move but for the moment were too weary. They weighed the possibilities of losing the goods they'd left on the bus—bagpipe cases, jackets, spare clothes. Eventually someone tracked it down, and they climbed aboard. At Frank's, a subdued celebration was already under way, as the band gathered around an immense, curved wooden bar for Bloody Marys and settled in for brunch at white-cloth-covered tables. Some changed out of their sweaty shirts and kilts into FDNY T-shirts and jeans; others hadn't thought that far ahead and remained in their uniforms.

The sound of alternating voices reading the names resonated off the walls inside the restaurant. Liam's friend from the site, Jimmy Miller, who'd donated his rainmaking trucks and so much else to the recovery efforts, was there—he'd followed the band for a significant portion of the march. So was the Rev. Everett Wabst, who had led the prayer service on the pile on October 7 and had provided much spiritual support to Liam over the months. The minister circled the room, pausing to pray with each man. With him he carried a special small bottle of holy water that Father Judge had blessed. The water was muddy brown, mingled with ash and debris that someone had removed from Father Judge's coat after the towers fell. Wabst dipped his finger in the water, traced a cross on each man's forehead, and prayed. Kippy stayed around, and so did Tim. Liam listened for Bronko's name to be read, his eyes cast to one side as if waiting for a slap in the face. The entire bar fell silent as the end of the *O*'s approached, and the beginning of the *P*'s. Finally, "Durrell V. Pearsall." The room crackled with a cheer, and the men raised their glasses, drank, and shook their heads.

Liam brought out a chalice and a bottle of clear poteen, a grain alcohol that his relatives in Galway had produced. He'd brought it back with him after a late August visit there. Men came up to a center table and took a sip. The drink looked like water but tasted like distilled fruit, warm and piercing as it traveled down the throat, mellow and fuzzy in the belly.

Someone hollered that they needed a photo. The men assembled at one end of the room and handed out cameras to a few of the wives and girlfriends who'd arrived. As the women shot pictures of the smiling crowd, the men began to sing in rough, merry voices.

> Well I've been a wild rover for many a year
> And I spent all my money on whiskey and beer . . .

Tommy didn't join the party with the rest. When it was over, he walked back down into the pit, where family members clustered on the dirt floor around a circle bordered by short wood panels. Many wore dark sunglasses, had pictures of loved ones on their chests, and carried bouquets of flowers in their arms. He meandered through the crowd and found his sister, Maryann. Her cheeks were wet with tears. Maryann bent and laid down a photo of Vinny, and a purple rose. When she stood up, she noticed Tommy was sniffing, wiping at his nose with his shoulder.

"Do you want a tissue?" she asked.

Tommy shook his head. "I don't need one."

Maryann pulled him into a tight hug. "I love you, Tommy," she said.

"I love you, too." He paused. The Brunton siblings had rarely said those words in the past. Meant them, but not said them. One full year had passed since Vinny was killed. Tommy had dug for other people's body parts, played at other people's memorials, worked to keep his family together, and used his work to blur his own pain. He'd heard people harp on the tired cliché "Time heals all wounds," but in his experience, it didn't. He had grown used to having Mike at his side. Sometimes, late in the night and after many pints of beer, Mike's lower lip would stiffen and quaver. Overcome by guilt, he'd bow his head, press his fingers to his eyes, and weep with shame and sadness. Mike was inconsolable at these moments. Whenever Mike broke down, Tommy always stayed at his brother's shoulder, hanging on to his arm, telling him in a soft voice that there was nothing else he could have done. They didn't fight as much anymore. They both tried to take the best of Vinny's life and make it a part of their own—the joy he'd taken out of the smallest pleasures, the way he'd tell them they were both being jerks when they bickered. They both joked that Vinny delivered them a kick in the ass whenever they got to feeling too sorry for themselves. In death, Vinny maintained the peace between them, just as he had in life. Yet there were times when nothing Tommy did could fill the aching void that Vinny's passing had left in him. No 365 days could change the fact that he could still not bear to see his baby sister cry. His grief was so personal, he'd been unable to share his pain. Now, enveloped in swirling dust at the final ceremony, Tommy let go.

"Everybody's hurting so much," he said, his words muffled against his sister's shoulder. "And I can't make it better."

On September 26, a firefighter named Gary Celentani sat in his basement apartment in Queens. He arranged a selection of pictures and mass cards before him. Some were of his friends John and Joseph Vigiano, a firefighter and a police officer who'd both been killed on September 11. He added pictures of other deceased men from his company, Squad 288 and Hazmat 1, the company that had lost the most men in the attacks, nineteen in all. He added photos of his two brothers, both firefighters, both alive. He penned a note, writing of the breakup with a girlfriend. Then he lifted a rifle to his chest and squeezed the trigger.

A lieutenant from Rescue 3, who was also a piper in the band, called Liam to tell him the news. Liam was teaching at the rescue school that day. He was sure this was some sort of black humor. A sick joke. It wasn't.

Liam mused over drawing a 345 on his own forehead and sticking a gun in his own mouth. He said to other firefighters, "Hey, if any of you guys are gonna shoot yourselves, just let me know in advance so I can apologize for anything mean I mighta said to you." But again, his drab eyes betrayed his attempts at humor. Times had been placid since the site closed. The rescue workers had walked into and out of supposedly treacherous anniversaries and the dreaded downtime in between. But so far nothing bad—nothing worse than medical leave due to lung and breathing problems, anyway—had happened to the men who'd stood up to the task of the recovery work, and it was beginning to seem as though nothing ever would. In Liam's new world order, there was "them," the ones who crumpled at this ultimate test, and "us," the brothers who'd put their lives aside to bring the bodies home. Celentani was like Liam, he'd lost his two closest friends on September 11, and he'd dug at the Trade Center and probably attended dozens of funerals for men he knew and men he didn't. He was with "us." When Celentani yanked the trigger, he shattered that delicately constructed barrier that Liam had placed between himself and the rest of the world. By focusing on the dead, committing his life to honor and respect the traditions he had known, Liam had been sure he was doing the right thing. His belief that men like him were invincible was now exposed in the harsh light of truth.

The Fire Department counseling unit dispatched extra personnel to talk with firefighters at their firehouses. No suicide could be attributed to a single event, they told them. Celentani was not the first. An EMS worker who'd worked at the site had taken his life some months before. In both cases, a number of psychological stresses, disappointments, and life events had come together to form the lethal combination that led the person to suicide.

Celentani's two brothers petitioned the Fire Department to have their brother's name added to the list of the Trade Center dead, making him 344. The Fire Department refused. The department accorded him the same ceremonial aspects it would a firefighter who'd died of natural causes outside the line of duty. The code was a 6–52. The Fire Department caisson was not made available for the service, so Celentani's brothers arranged for a different caisson to be part of the procession. Only six pipers were commissioned to attend. A few extra showed up anyway.

Liam was among them. After what had felt like a million ceremonies, he thought he didn't care anymore, couldn't care anymore. But suddenly, he did. The ceremony was impuissant, the skirl of the pipes ironic. Instead of according honor, now the sounds conveyed a brotherhood broken, reminding Liam of all that he had been powerless to control. The ritual could not make the pain go away.

EPILOGUE

We can draw lessons from the past, but we cannot live in it.

—Lyndon B. Johnson

On the evening of November 4, 2002, the second floor of the Elks Lodge was dusty and dank. The air was smoky from burning cigarettes and thick with the aroma of fried fish and chips. A flood of new faces filled the rehearsal room. Circles of strangers sprang up across the floor, each anchored by one bagpiper or drummer dressed in jeans and a sweatshirt. Eventually, Tom McEnroe hollered at everyone to grab a chair and go into the back room.

Mike Brunton was among the first to obey. He set up his chair in back and folded his arms across his chest as he listened to Tom outline the challenges ahead for the new class of pipers. "This is the most frustrating, most rewarding thing you'll do with your lives," Tom called out to the circle. "The first thing to do is buy a chanter. Don't worry about the bagpipes yet. We'll tell you when you need to get them. Anyone been in a band before?"

Earlier in the evening, Mike had filled out the same form as all the other new guys, writing down his name and address and checking off "pipes" or "drums" in ink on the photocopied sheet. "Do you have to say why you want to be in the band?" he said wryly to another member of the color guard who stood near him. The man shook his head and gave a quick exhale through his nose, a snort to show his understanding.

Tommy Brunton wasn't there that night. Preferring to play on his own time, he didn't much come to practices anyway, even before September 11, 2001. Maryann continued to struggle with her grief, amazed at the depth of pain she felt. She'd never imagined her sorrow would be so sharp or last as long as it did. The most unexpected things would bring it washing over her—like one day when someone mentioned the "three of you," referring to Maryann and her two brothers. They were no longer four. Kathy returned to her two jobs. Even the site closing hadn't taken away her hope that someday remains of Vinny would be identified.

Tim Grant, too, stayed away. He worked mostly behind the scenes with the band these days. He revamped the Web site and started planning a CD-ROM that would teach new pipers to learn on their own. He'd been working overtime in the firehouse and had started renovating a room in his home. Tara, now five months pregnant, wanted him around more. He continued to hope that someday he and Liam would return to being the friends they'd been before. They spoke occasionally, but not about anything serious, and usually not about September 11.

Kippy loitered with a crowd of pipers in the main hall while the recruits listened to the speakers in the back. Aidan had just come off his breathing monitor that week and seemed to be fine. Sometimes, Kippy and Mary held the baby between them in bed and marveled at how his smallest smile made every sadness go away. The band chairman, Joe Murphy, was stepping down, and Kippy had decided to run for the post.

In the back room, Tom's speech was meant to discourage. He gave the men plenty of reasons to back out. Up-front costs were significant, at least a couple of hundred dollars, not to mention the thousands that would come in when it was time to buy the instruments. The time it would take to learn and practice would be hefty. Near 100 percent attendance was required, especially in the beginning, when they would practice every Monday night. And now, every piper was expected to compete in annual contests. Many had tried, he told them, and many had failed. Tom knew he didn't have to dissuade the men. He'd seen large turnouts before, when fifteen in a class produced three or four new band members. He figured plenty would give up regardless of what he said. But when he finished his speech, few faces had fallen.

The band instructor, Brian Meagher, rose to address the circle. He told them how his grandfather had been the first instructor of the band. This could be the best thing they'd do with their free time; a feeling of pride would come out of it that no one could ever take away. The other pipe sergeants would teach, but he would always be there to help, he said. "You can do it," he told them. "You just have to really want it."

Over the course of the night, the veteran band members who rose to speak asked over and over, "Are there any questions?" Not a man in the room had one.

After the October 12, 2002, annual Fire Department memorial service for all fire personnel who had died since October 1, 2000, and then the October 26 plaque dedication for the nine men of Rescue 4, Liam's period of mourning finally came to an end. He'd demonstrated the depth of his love through the length of his grief. Now he decided to break away from the rituals. A week and a half earlier, he'd begun his first true vacation—away from the firehouse, the funerals, and the site. Tonight, he dressed in civilian clothes, a windbreaker and jeans. In a few days, he'd fly to California. He was relaxed in his time off, and being away made him relish his contact with old friends, like Kippy.

Before practice, Liam stopped by the Rescue 4 firehouse to find that the list of soon-to-be lieutenants had just been released. His number was 214. Out of approximately seven hundred, that was a positive result, especially since he'd done a minimal amount of studying. But the list was evaporating fast. Some said that 137 men had already been promoted from the top of the list, which meant Liam's number was soon to follow. He'd have to leave Rescue 4, and, like Kippy, he dreaded it. So instead of coming in to see the fresh faces and hear the opening spiel, he preferred to banter with Kippy and some of the others. To these men, Liam voiced some possibilities aloud for the first time. What if he got into a new house where there were guys who hadn't dug at the site, how would he control himself? The others shrugged, in a manner that said, "Let it go." Maybe it would be good to work somewhere else for a while, maybe Brooklyn. Or maybe he'd try for an assignment in midtown Manhattan, where there were fewer fires, to be sure, but he'd be closer to his sister's eyeglasses shop, and surely there'd be a plethora of single women around, just waiting for him. At this, the others laughed enviously.

In all, there had been 445 Fire Department funerals and memorial services for the 343 men who were killed. Ninety-one had had funerals only, 148 had memorials, and 103 had both. The band had played at them all, except on the rare occasions when a family had requested otherwise.

All the band members knew, and took as part of their duty, that funeral rituals exist more for the living than for the dead. Ceremonial honors serve to convey the importance of a life. Under most circumstances, funerals contribute to healing. But the year following September 11, 2001, taught the band members truths they wished they could unlearn. Like when living for the dead became their life. Or like what happened to firefighter Gary Celentani, who'd ended his own life. Like the skewed celebrity, suddenly having hundreds of "friends" and being the most-photographed men in the Fire Department. For many of the men in the band, getting a perspective on what they'd been through was impossible.

Some would not remember what they'd bought their children for the holidays in 2001, or precisely how they had been able to sustain the endless tide of grief. The year of 2002 would be largely effaced from memory, and some would be consistently surprised when the calendar showed 2003.

By being present throughout the mourning, the bagpipers had played a crucial role in the nation's healing. Their duty had forced them to cling to the past while others moved forward. They'd talked of how it would never be over, but that autumn, the services did cease, and the pipers were thrown back to a reality in which they were once again relatively obscure and their ordeal was an outdated remnant of a terrible time that most yearned to erase. Over the past thirteen months, death had been a constant companion. They were lonely in its company, and alone again without it. But there were other companions. Each other. Old friends would stay, and new ones would come. Each moment of life would be differently cherished than before. The recollections would be shared in the lives they led, though spoken of less and less. In years to come, the pain would ebb, the memories smooth over. But they would never forget.

NOTES

INTRODUCTION

1. The instructors were Thomas Meagher, who was in the NYPD band, Tom McSwiggan of the County Tyrone Pipe Band, and John Doris of the County Armagh Pipe Band.
2. Original band members: Bob Abernathy, Ladder 176; Charlie Brennan, Ladder 49; Jack Clarke, Ladder 49; Jim Corcoran, Ladder 19; Bill Duffy, Ladder 17; Jimmy Ginty, Squad 2; Frank Griffin, Engine 73; Timmy Hart, Squad 2; Edward Keating, Ladder 17; Jack Kelly, Squad 2; Mickey Killarney, Engine 26; Paddy McAndrews, Engine 60; Ed McLoughlin, Ladder 17; Frank O'Rourke, Squad 2; Tom Reilly, Squad 2; Pete Sheridan, Ladder 37; Matty Smith, Engine 45.

   Edward McLoughlin's "History of the New York City Fire Department Bagpipe Band" (typescript in author's possession) was a valuable source.
3. Roderick D. Cannon, *The Highland Bagpipe and Its Music* (Edinburgh: John Donald Publishers, 1990), p. 4.
4. Henry George Farmer, *Military Music* (New York: Chanticleer Press, 1950), p. 10.
5. Raoul F. Camus, *Military Music of the American Revolution* (Chapel Hill: University of North Carolina Press, 1976), p. 25.
6. New York City Fire Department, "Origin of the Maltese Cross," http://www.nyc.gov/html/fdny/html/general/history.html.

7. R. Sutherland, quoted in Cannon, *Highland Bagpipe,* p. 7.
8. Information here and in the following three paragraphs is drawn from Sean Donnelly, *The Early History of Piping in Ireland* (Dublin: Na Piobairi Uilleann Teoranto and Royal Scottish Pipe Band Association [N. I. Branch], 2001). While Donnelly believes that the festival described occurred in 1079, he does not regard the poem as proof that bagpipes existed in Ireland before the rest of Europe or indeed before the Crusades began, since it is quite possible that additions or embellishments were made to the work between the time it was initially penned and the time when it was added to the Book of Leinster, where it appears. The Book of Leinster was begun in 1152.
9. Cannon, *Highland Bagpipe*, p. 8.
10. Immigration and Naturalization Service (INS) Statistical Yearbook.
11. Terry Golway, *So Others Might Live: A History of New York's Bravest from 1700 to the Present* (New York: Basic Books, 2002), p. 86.
12. New York City Fire Museum.
13. Alan T. Cohen, "Strike Up the Band," *The Housewatch Newsletter*, Fire Bell Club, March/April 1994.
14. Claire Morris, "History of the 69th of New York," http://www.69thnewyork.co.uk/history69/htm.
15. Cohen, "Strike Up the Band."
16. INS Statistical Yearbook.
17. Fintan Vallely, ed., *The Companion to Irish Traditional Music* (New York: New York University Press, 1999), p. 414.
18. Frank O'Rourke, interview with the author, New York City, December 1, 2001.
19. County Tipperary Historical Society, http://www.iol.ie/~tipplibs/Long.htm.
20. O'Rourke interview, February 2, 2003.
21. Golway, *So Others Might Live,* p. 214.
22. Frederick Melahn Jr. and Michael Boucher, eds., "Line of Duty Death Stories: 1731–Present." New York City Fire Department Mand Library, 2003.
23. Ibid.
24. Ibid.
25. New York City Fire Department List of LOD Deaths. New York City Fire Department Mand Library, 2003.

CHAPTER 3. SEPTEMBER 11

1. Anthony Fusco, "Report from Chief of Department," *The World Trade Center Bombing: Report and Analysis,* p. 2. Major Fires Investigation Project 076, conducted by Tri Data Corp. under contract to United States Fire Administration and Federal Emergency Management Agency, 1993.

CHAPTER 5. THE FUNERALS

1. Fire Department, City of New York, Fire M.A.R.C. (Managerial, Appraisals, Reviews, Comparisons), Citywide Performance Indicators, 1993–2000.
2. Ron Spadafora, interview with the author, New York City, February 5, 2003.
3. Edward Wyatt, "Department Promotes 168 to Rebuild Officer Ranks," *New York Times*, September 17, 2001, sec. A, p. 7.
4. New York City Medical Examiner's log of World Trade Center recoveries.

CHAPTER 6. DISCOVERY

1. Eric Lipton, "Struggle to Tally All 9/11 Dead by Anniversary," *New York Times*, September 1, 2002, sec. A, p. 1.
2. New York City Medical Examiner's log of World Trade Center recoveries.
3. Ibid.
4. Frank Lombardi and Michele McPhee, "Bravest vs. Finest in Melee at WTC," *New York Daily News*, November 3, 2001, p. 3.
5. Ibid.
6. Sean Gardiner, William Murphy, and Curtis L. Taylor, "Anger at Ground Zero: Firefighters Arrested after Clashing with Cops in Protest," *Newsday*, November 3, 2001, sec. A, p. 2.

CHAPTER 9. END OF THE LINE

1. Charlie LeDuff, "After a Mistake, a Funeral under the Right Name," *New York Times*, December 2, 2001, sec. B, p. 7.

CHAPTER 12. LOST CELEBRATIONS

1. New York City Medical Examiner's log of World Trade Center recoveries.

About the Author

Kerry Sheridan was born and raised in an Irish-American family in upstate New York. She has written for the *San Francisco Chronicle* and Irish-American newspapers in New York and California. She has a master's degree in journalism from Columbia University and lives in Brooklyn, New York.